Treblinka

JEAN-FRANÇOIS STEINER

PREFACE BY SIMONE DE BEAUVOIR
TRANSLATED FROM THE FRENCH BY HELEN WEAVER

SIMON AND SCHUSTER · NEW YORK

THE EVENTS DESCRIBED IN THIS BOOK ARE SO EXTRAOR-
DINARY IN THEIR NATURE THAT THE AUTHOR HAS
CHOSEN TO CHANGE THE NAMES OF THE SURVIVORS IN
ORDER TO PROTECT THE PRIVACY OF THESE HEROES
AND MARTYRS.

*To the memory of Kadmi Cohen, who gave me life,
and to Ozias Steiner, who taught me to love it.*

PREFACE

"Why did the Jews allow themselves to be led to the slaughter-house like sheep?" the young *sabras* of Israel asked each other indignantly at the time of the Eichmann trial. In Europe too, many Jews of the younger generation who had not known Nazism asked the same question. The fact is that in the world of concentration camps all peoples behaved identically: a conditioning process carefully worked out by the S.S. assured the submission of the condemned. In 1947, in *Les Jours de notre mort*, Rousset wrote: "The triumph of the S.S. required that the tortured victim allow himself to be led to the gallows without protesting, that he repudiate and abandon himself to the point where he ceased to affirm his identity. . . . There is nothing more terrible than these processions of human beings going to their death like dummies." Among the Russian prisoners, Communists and political commissars were separated from the rest and consigned to a rapid extermination: in spite of their ideological and military preparation, they put their courage into dying, but no resistance was possible.

This kind of explanation did not satisfy Jean-François Steiner. As a Jew, he felt uneasy. All the accounts he had read presented

7

the millions of Jews who died in the camps—among them his father and most of his family—as pitiful victims; should they not have refused this role? The constraint with which certain facts were recalled, the oblivion with which an effort was made to cover them implied that nothing could excuse them. Were they really inexcusable? Steiner decided to confront the past. This courage will undoubtedly cause him to be accused of anti-Semitism by the very ones whose silence, caution and evasiveness have aroused suspicion. And yet he was right to have confidence in the truth, for he has won. The story of Treblinka, pieced together from written testimony and conversations with survivors of the camp, restored his self-respect.

At Treblinka there was a *Sonderkommando* which was originally composed of Jews from Warsaw, many of whom were put to death and replaced by new arrivals. Numbering about a thousand, supervised by the Germans and surrounded by Ukrainian guards, they carried out the work of extermination and recovery for which the camp had been set up. A large number preferred to die, either by refusing to try their luck during selection sessions, or by suicide. But how could the others agree to pay this price in order to survive? The collusion with the Germans of Jewish notables forming the *Judenrat* is a known fact which is easily understood. In all times and all countries, with rare exceptions, eminent persons have collaborated with the victors: a matter of class. But at Treblinka, although certain Jews were less maltreated than others, the class distinction did not apply, either among the men of the work commando or those who landed on the station platform to be conducted to the gas chambers. What then? Must we, as in certain textbooks distributed to Israeli children, evoke a "ghetto mentality," an atavism of resignation, the mystery of the Jewish soul, or other nonsense? Steiner's book puts this cheap psychology in its place by accurately describing how things happened.

In the curious world we live in, aggregates of individuals who share a common way of life in a dispersed state—Sartre calls these aggregates *series*—show behavior in which they become enemies to one another and therefore enemies to themselves. In a panic, for example. the people trample, suffocate and kill one another, compounding or even creating a disaster which a reasonable evacuation of the premises would have controlled or avoided. The same is true of speculations or bottlenecks. As long as the workers remained isolated within their class, the employers had every opportunity to exploit them. Each worker saw the next one as a competitor who was ready to accept slave wages to get hired, and tried to sell his labor power at an even lower price. For the demands of labor to become possible, groups had to be formed in which, on the contrary, each individual regarded the next one as the same as himself. The skill of the Germans was to *serialize* the Jews and to prevent these series from becoming groups. In the ghetto of Vilna—and they used the same tactic everywhere— the S.S. divided the population into pariahs and privileged persons. Only the first group was raided, but the second category was divided again, up to the final liquidation. Even so, there was an attempt at resistance, but it was easily put down. It nourished no hopes; even if it had won over the whole ghetto, the Germans had the means to put a stop to it; and this also explains why it rallied only a small number of people.

It was also serial behavior that the Technicians elicited when they proceeded to make the first selections. All the men who wanted to survive, considering how many there were like themselves, thought: If I refuse, there will be others to do this work in my place, and so I will die for no reason. And indeed, the enormous human resources which the Germans had at their disposal could not consist exclusively of heroes. Foreseeing the submission of the others, each man resigned himself to submit too. This trap could have been foiled only if instructions to resist had

9

been given in advance, and if each person had been convinced that everyone else would follow him. This was not the case for a number of reasons, the first of which was that the situation was of such terrifying novelty that for a long time nobody wanted to believe in its reality. When brutally confronted by it, the Jews were plunged into a confusion similar to the one that causes panics, and had no way to coordinate their behavior. They did try, at first. The Technicians organized eliminatory ordeals: races on the belly, or on all fours. The first three quarters of the candidates would be spared; the last quarter would be destroyed. For a moment nobody moved; the whips landed everywhere; the candidates realized that if they refused to move, they would all be slaughtered; a few decided to start, and immediately the rest followed.

What the young *sabras* of Israel did not understand is that heroism is not inherent in human nature. Their whole education tends to inculcate it in them from infancy, in the form of military courage. The men of Treblinka were civilians, and nothing had prepared them to face a violent and usually atrocious death. Since during the first months the work commandos were liquidated and replaced at a very rapid rate, they did not have time to devise forms of resistance. The miracle is that certain men arrived at them anyway and that they succeeded in rallying all the prisoners. After the tragic descent which, without slurring over anything, Steiner relates in the first part of the book, he allows us to witness an extraordinary ascent.

The process of this ascent is the precise opposite of the process of abdication. If it takes only a few cowards to make the entire series become cowardly, it takes only a few heroes to make people recover confidence in each other and begin to dare. The solidarity was first marked by the effort of a few to prevent suicides, and later by the organization, under terribly dangerous conditions, of an escape network whose purpose was not so much to save

lives as to reveal to the world the dreadful truth of Treblinka.
A Committee of Resistance was created and, although success
seemed impossible, formed a plan for an armed revolt. After this
beginning the prisoners outdid each other in devotion and courage. The *Hofjuden,* although they enjoyed certain privileges,
joined with their more deprived brothers and took considerable
risks in order to help them. Two men from Camp Number One
chose to go down into the inferno of Camp Number Two to enlist
the two hundred pariahs who were imprisoned there in the revolt.
To do this they deliberately made a mistake in their work, which
could just as well have been punished by torture and death as by
transfer. The impossibility of procuring weapons was overcome
only at the cost of much bloodshed and suffering. In spite of the
failures and the temptations to despair, the Committee held out.
Its extraordinary courage cannot be attributed to the imminence
of the camp's liquidation. The first attempt at insurrection, which
miscarried without the Germans' finding out about it, took place
well before the visit from Himmler which condemned Treblinka
to disappear in a short space of time. Moreover, the members of
the Committee had already decided to sacrifice their own lives:
their role would be to hold back the Germans while the prisoners
fled toward the forest. What they passionately desired by mas-
sacring the German "masters" was to overcome their condition
as slaves and to demonstrate to the world that the Jewish people
had not allowed themselves to be led to the slaughterhouse like
a flock of sheep.

Having myself collected so many firsthand accounts of the
camps in 1945, I was dumfounded when I heard this reproach.
The story of the hours when the insurrection broke out and raged
should be read closely. Not only the Committee, but a large
number of prisoners behaved with an abnegation so complete,
a heroism so serene, that it seems monstrous that fatalistic resignation could ever have been imputed to the Jews. That they were

11

capable of such an uprising shows that their helplessness in the face of their executioners was not the expression of some secret blemish, some mysterious malediction. This book demonstrates brilliantly that it was due to the circumstances. It is not their initial helplessness that must astonish us, but the way they finally overcame it.

The author has not attempted to do the work of a historian. Each detail is substantiated by the written or oral testimony he has collected and compared. But he has not denied himself a certain directorial freedom. In particular, he has reconstructed conversations of which he obviously did not know the words but only the content. Although he may be accused of lack of rigor, he would have been less faithful to the truth if he had not presented this story to us in its living movement.

The tone of the book is altogether unusual: neither pathos nor indignation, but a calculated coldness and sometimes even a dark humor. The horror is evoked in its day-to-day banality and almost as if it were natural. In a voice that rejects any overly human inflection, the author describes a dehumanized world. And yet it is men he is writing about; the reader does not forget this, and this contrast causes in him an intellectual shock which is deeper and more permanent than any emotion. However, shock is only a technique. Above all, Steiner has tried to understand and to make us understand. He has fully achieved his purpose.

SIMONE DE BEAUVOIR

I also want to speak very frankly about an extremely important subject. Among ourselves we will discuss it openly; in public, however, we must never mention it. . . .

I mean the evacuation of the Jews, the extermination of the Jewish people. This is something that is easy to talk about. "The Jewish people will be exterminated," says every member of the party, "this is clear, this is in our program: the elimination, the extermination of the Jews: we will do this." And then they come to you—eighty million good Germans—and each one has his "decent" Jew. Naturally, all the rest are pigs, but this particular Jew is first-rate. Not one of those who talk this way has seen the bodies, not one has been on the spot. Most of you know what it is to see a pile of one hundred or five hundred or one thousand bodies. To have stuck it out and at the same time, barring exceptions caused by human weakness, to have remained decent: this is what has made us tough. . . .

This is a glorious page in our history which never has and never will be written.
> —Speech by S.S. Reichsführer Heinrich Himmler to a meeting of S.S. generals in Posen on October 4, 1943

A man must descend very low to find the force to rise again.
> —Hasidic poem

Treblinka

1

SINCE THEY HAD NOT succeeded in deporting all the Jews of whom they wanted to rid their empire, the builders of the Thousand Year Reich decided to exterminate them.

The invasion of the U.S.S.R. in June 1941 aggravated the problem. In the territory occupied by the Wehrmacht—Poland, the Ukraine, White Russia and the Baltic states—there lived a Jewish population of several million people. Accordingly, S.S. Reichsführer Heinrich Himmler gave the order to "treat" the new lands conquered by the Third Reich in its eastward expansion.

The operation was to proceed in two phases. The first stage was the relocation of the Jews in a certain number of ghettos. The second stage was the gradual liquidation of the ghettos thus created. According to the "Technicians," the Jews, being an inferior race, would let themselves be massacred without resistance. The perfection of the Nazi system excluded the slightest possibility of a revolt.

This is how the time of the ghetto, first phase of the Final Solution, began.

The resettlement of the Jews raised no practical problem. The anti-Semitism of the local populations was such that often the Jews even accepted this operation with relief.

To the Lithuanians, Vilna was their capital. To the Jews it was the "Jerusalem of Lithuania," the Jerusalem of exile. It was famous for its editions of the Talmud of Babylon; people came from France and America to study with its rabbis. A great spiritual center, Vilna was renowned throughout the whole Jewish world. But although its fame crossed the seas, it still did not cross the boundaries of the Jewish quarter. To the Poles and Lithuanians who lived in Vilna, the bearded scholars were only dirty Jews, who were burned, beaten and lynched at the whim of the pogroms.

With the exception of some personal communication, over the centuries the seasonal pogroms had become the sole contact between the two communities. The small pogroms lasted a day, the large ones a week. The Jews never defended themselves, never revolted. The most pious saw them as a punishment from God, the others as a natural phenomenon comparable to hail in vineyard country or grasshoppers in Morocco. They had learned one thing: the Gentile is stronger, to resist only fans his anger. "If a goy hits you," mothers told their children, "bow your head and he will spare your life."

This right to lynch was a kind of unwritten law which nobody dreamed of contesting—a fact that was accepted, admitted and taught from generation to generation in both communities.

So it was that in spring 1941, when the Russian troops left the city under the formidable onslaught of the German offensive, the Jews shut themselves in their houses in expectation of the pogrom with which the Gentiles would inevitably celebrate the event. It was the rule of the game.

There had been much discussion about what influence the German presence would have, and few had seen it as a special reason to fear the future. Old Dr. Jacob Wigodski, one of the

leaders of the community, was one of these few. But when, speaking to the students one day, he had said, "Storm clouds are gathering, difficult times are coming, will you be able to remember
the spirit of our teaching?" many had thought that the mind of
the holy man had been affected by age. He was eighty-six at the
time. The great argument of the optimists was the famous declaration of 1917 which General Ludendorff had addressed in Yiddish to "my dear Jews in Poland." There had been much discussion, but no conclusions.

The German troops had marched through the city for days and
nights, and nothing had happened. Terrorized and fascinated by
this extraordinary deployment of force, the Gentiles, like the
Jews, had shut themselves in their houses, waiting to see the intentions of their new masters. They were to exceed their wildest
dreams. This day in June 1941 marked the beginning of a fruitful
collaboration between passion and technology, good will and
know-how, tradition and organization, irrational hatred and cold
deliberation.

The Technicians of the Final Solution arrived in Vilna in the
trucks of the Wehrmacht.

Without wasting an instant they attacked the first point on the
program: transfer to the ghetto. So that it would take place without disorder they conceived the idea of obtaining the agreement
of the Jews themselves, and to do this they undertook a psychological conditioning.

Until then the pogroms had been the result of a certain popular
whim and had proceeded in the greatest disorder and the most
total anarchy. Of course the locals went about it with spirit—they
burned a few houses and hanged a few "Yids"—but the procedure had become so routine that the Jews were hardly afraid of it
any more. They met this unleashing of hatred with boundless
contempt and waited for it to pass.

This well-meant anarchy did not satisfy the Technicians. To them, the pogrom was not an end in itself, but the means of making the Jews want to hide behind the walls of a ghetto. It was necessary, therefore, to channel and organize the natural inclinations of the inhabitants.

The first measure was the creation of special pogrom units. They were given an impressive name—the *Ipatingas* (the elect) —and their members were clad in military uniforms. Attention to detail was even carried to the point of making them attend accelerated courses in anti-Semitism, which resulted in the ridiculous situation of young Lithuanians, whose anti-Semitism was perhaps more ancient than the Jewish race, learning why they must hate the Jews.

This preparatory phase lasted several days, time for the Jews to be reassured and for the optimists to say, "You see! Just as I told you! A great people like the Germans, there you are!"

The optimists were still laughing on the morning of July 4, when the Germans issued the first ordinances requiring Jews to wear over their left shoulder blades a white square in whose center the letter *J* had to be sewn in black on a yellow circle, and forbidding them to communicate with non-Jews, to sell their belongings, to take trains or any means of public transportation, to go to the market, or to be on the street after six o'clock.

The first pogrom took place the next day in Chnipichok, a suburb of the city. The synagogue was burned and the Jews were gathered together and forced to dance around it. They danced for a long time. Then, bewildered and breathless, they were led off to an unknown destination. The following days were calm. The pogrom of Chnipichok caused the ordinances to be forgotten. Life resumed.

Hope was gradually returning when the general pogrom broke out on July 17. Arriving by surprise just when hope was being restored, it took the Jews off balance. Panic ensued. And yet, when they thought about it afterward, this pogrom was not without cause. In the morning a Jew had been hit and had run away. You must not run away when you are beaten, the Jews concluded. The Jewish quarter had been combed all night. In the morning seven hundred men were gathered on the square at the edge of the quarter. Rabbi Novgorod was among them. They were made to kneel, then to crawl, then to hop like frogs. Finally they were led in a gymnastic step, their arms raised, toward the Lukichki prison. Suffering was their business, and when they filed by the Gentiles, who watched them contemptuously, their faces were impenetrable. They never returned, and a secret anxiety overtook the Jews, who began building hiding places under stairways, in attics, cellars and cupboards, and even by putting up walls in the middle of rooms. At night the Jewish quarter stirred like a hive, furtive noises and murmurs that ceased with daylight.

A lull followed the storm; the hiding places gave a false sense of security. The Jews recovered their confidence. When the Technicians ordered them to appoint a Judenrat (Jewish Council), many believed that life was going to resume its course, that the pogroms had merely been concessions which the occupying forces had made to the Lithuanians. When the Judenrat received the order to register all the Jews, they presented themselves without difficulty.

Then the raids resumed, led by the *Ipaingas,* but they no longer had the violent quality of the first pogroms. They were the last remaining element that prevented life from resuming an almost normal course. So, when the rumor of the creation of a ghetto began to spread, many thought: Inside the ghetto we will be poor and cramped, but we will be left in peace; there will be no more disappearances.

The conditioning had lasted two months. It had proceeded without a gesture of revolt, without a moment of unnecessary violence.

The Technicians prepared "Operation Ghetto" with care. Seventeen streets of five hundred houses, or ten thousand rooms, were chosen for the sixty thousand Jews of the city. With six persons to a room, given the fact that in the general confusion the families would be forced to live wherever they could, the emotional strain would be great. The names of these seventeen streets and the date of the operation were, of course, kept secret, although a certain number of false rumors were circulated in order to make the waiting more difficult. Finally—and this was the great originality of the operation—the Technicians decided at the time of the transfer to set the Jews their first "brain buster."

The technique of the brain buster, which was later used so abundantly, is based on a rather shrewd understanding of the Jewish intelligence, which is more speculative than practical. It consists of raising an insoluble problem in the form of two alternatives. When confronted by a complicated problem, the average man, like Alexander before the Gordian knot, is inclined to take his sword and slice it in two, which is a way of solving the problem by denying its existence. The Jewish intelligence, and more especially the intelligence brought up on the Talmud, tends rather toward the opposite defect. "It is not the answers that interest me," as the saying goes, "I know them all. What I want to know is to which question a given answer corresponds." A speculative intelligence which sometimes loses contact with reality, the Jewish intelligence is inclined to attach more importance to the manner of stating a problem and the manner of solving it than to the solution as such.

The brain buster thought up by the Technicians was simple. On the way toward the ghetto, they would divide the column in two at a certain crossroads. One branch would go toward the ghetto whose location the Jews did not yet know, and the other . . . The crossroads had been chosen at a place where the road began to rise after a long descent so that the Jews, seeing the

22

crowd divide from a distance, would have plenty of time to ask themselves: To the left? To the right? Toward the ghetto? Or toward the unknown?

On September 2, a few days before the transfer to the ghetto, this unknown was given a name. On that day sixteen members of the Judenrat were taken away. For the first time the Jews learned the destination: Ponar. This was the name of a locality on the edge of the forest four miles from Vilna. They remembered that peasants had mentioned hearing shots from there. At the time it had been thought to be a rifle range.

As if chance were on the side of the Technicians, the mystery deepened still further in a completely fortuitous way. Ruth Barstein, daughter of one of the sixteen deported members of the Judenrat, after waiting all day to try to find out what had become of her father, had burst into tears as she walked out of the Judenrat building. A soldier of the Wehrmacht had come over and had learned the story: Ponar. Moved, he had promised to go and see Mr. Barstein in Ponar and to come back the next day. News of the incident spread rapidly through the Jewish quarter, and the next day when the soldier returned, the square in front of the Judenrat was full of people. The soldier was embarrassed. He said that he had not been allowed into Ponar, that even senior officers could not get in. So Ponar became a mystery full of terror.

As the Technicians had anticipated, the transfer to the ghetto had been made amid very great disorder. One third had been shunted off to Ponar via a little transitional ghetto, and the others had thought: That was a narrow escape! Without giving it a name yet, they had already become habituated to death. Imperceptibly, the Technicians had brought them to conceive of the idea without thought of rebellion. Of course, death seemed ineluctable, but the apparent anarchy of the proceedings allowed each person to think that he could escape, that it was up to him.

When they had seen the crowd dividing into two columns before their eyes, each had asked himself which was the right direction and, relying on a vague rationale that was closer to intuition than to logic, had chosen. Those who had chosen the left had won, the others had lost. Those who had won told themselves, "I was right," and concluded that all they had to do was keep thinking carefully to reach the final destination. Their lives became a game of double or nothing, but one whose tragic reality they refused to recognize, for life in the certainty of death is unbearable.

A few days after he had moved into the ghetto, Dr. Ginsberg was awakened one morning by a furtive scratching at the door of the room which he occupied with his family. Dawn had just broken and the whole house was still asleep. Worried, he was wondering whether to go and open the door, when he heard a woman's voice call him by name. The voice was supplicating:

"Doctor, open the door! It's me, Pessia Aranovich, I have escaped from Ponar."

When he opened the door he saw a woman dressed like a Lithuanian peasant and carrying a bouquet of flowers. He was about to close the door upon the stranger when he noticed her face, which was distorted by fear.

"Who are you, what do you want?" he asked her with hostility.

He knew Pessia Aranovich well. He had watched her grow up and marry. She was a beautiful young woman who laughed all the time. This dirty peasant woman who seemed demented was not Pessia.

"I am wounded," she told him.

So he let her in and asked her to sit down. Then he went to heat up some water on the little alcohol burner which he had managed to bring to the ghetto.

"How do you know Pessia's name?" he asked her.

"But Doctor, I am Pessia Aranovich! I escaped from Ponar,

24

and a peasant woman gave me these clothes and this bouquet of
flowers so I could disguise myself and return to Vilna. The *Ipatingas* took me for a local peasant and let me enter the ghetto, and
someone told me that you lived here. I have come to be treated
and to tell you that Ponar is not a work camp! They kill all the
Jews there!"

"All the Jews? Oh, that's not possible. Why would they kill all
the Jews?" Dr. Ginsberg asked her gently, trying to bring her to
reason.

She waved her hand, and her face took on a childlike expression. The doctor looked at her with growing astonishment; now
he recognized her.

"Tell me what you have seen," he asked, sensing that she
needed to talk.

"When we saw the stream of people divide into two branches
everyone asked, 'What is happening? What does it mean?' My
husband told me that some people would not be sleeping in their
beds that night. At first I did not understand; then he added that
it was no time to make a mistake. He wanted me to go to the left
with our little daughter and himself to go to the right. I did not
want this. I told him that if we were going to be deported, it
would be better to be together. 'Let us hope that those who
choose the wrong road will risk nothing worse than deportation,'
he answered. I did not know what he meant, but I began to be
afraid. We looked for a sign which would tell us the right direction. We kept moving forward and the crossroads came nearer.

"The crowd had become silent. Everyone felt that his future
would be decided at that crossroads. Imperceptibly we let ourselves be carried toward the left. We could already make out the
few Germans and policemen who stood there, their bodies motionless, their faces impenetrable. They were like the prow of a
ship on which the wave of people broke. The first soldier, who
formed the point of this wedge, was a real German: tall, blond,

25

handsome. He was watching us amiably with a faint smile, a distant expression. His glance did not rest on anyone . . ."

Pessia's voice had become calmer. She was no longer afraid. She was telling something that had happened in another world, in another life. Mrs. Ginsberg had gotten up and made tea. Pessia had not touched the cup she had placed beside her.

"This German fascinated me: so handsome, so remote, so different from us. I watched him intently, trying to decipher from his face which road was the right one. My husband murmured something which I did not understand. He repeated in a dull and urgent voice, 'To the right, to the right, quickly,' and I felt myself being pushed before I had understood. When I realized what had happened the German was already behind us. My husband explained that when he had seen him smile pityingly at the stream that was passing to the left, he had understood that we had to go to the right.

"The street got narrower and we walked faster. Now we heard shouting behind us. Someone said, 'They are taking us to the Lukichki prison.' We had all heard it, but no one said anything. My husband's face was somber. 'As long as I wasn't wrong,' he said. When we reached the prison, we slowed down, uncertain, breathless. 'Well, this is it,' I thought. 'We were wrong. What will happen now?' A voice murmured, 'Let's run away.' But other voices answered, 'Where to? Wait and see! There will always be time later.' Nobody wanted to revolt. You don't revolt against the unknown. Suddenly a ripple went through the crowd. The word spread: 'We're going on.' The column resumed its normal pace. My husband squeezed my arm and smiled at me. 'We're too nervous, we're telling each other stories,' he said.

"Finally we arrived at what we thought was the ghetto. I was so exhausted I didn't care. My little girl had gone to sleep in my arms. My husband dragged me to a house. We went into a room. It was already occupied, but we were too tired to walk further.

The window was broken and there wasn't a stick of furniture, not even a chair. I sat down on the floor and fell asleep.

"In the middle of the night, I was awakened by whispering. My husband was by the window with a group of men. Although they were talking in low voices, they were arguing excitedly.

" 'We must run away,' said one.

" 'What about the women?' answered another.

" 'The men will force the barricade and the women will follow.'

" 'We will all be killed.'

" 'We will be killed anyway. They have surrounded the ghetto. We will all be taken away.'

" 'But do you have proof that they kill the Jews at Ponar?'

" 'Why else would they take them into the forest?'

"The one who wanted to revolt had a very low voice and spoke Yiddish with a Ukrainian accent. All I could see was his short, stocky silhouette. He inspired my confidence.

" 'Why would they kill the Jews?' asked another voice.

" 'Why do the Lithuanians kill them?'

" 'They don't kill us, they beat us. They only kill the Jews who fight back.'

"The discussion degenerated. The men obviously did not want to revolt.

" 'We can't. We don't know anything. Maybe they are going to take us to work in a secret factory or make us dig ditches. They can't be stupid enough to kill men who are useful to them.'

" 'The fascists are our enemies,' said the Ukrainian with conviction.

" 'The whole world is our enemy. Hitler may be more dangerous than the others, but he will lose the war some day. I want to live to see it.'

" 'As a slave?'

"The Ukrainian had asked this last question in a deliberately

27

cutting tone. The other man answered him with great gentleness and sadness.

" 'Even as a slave. What matters is to live. Let us leave heroism to the Polacks. We must live so we can tell what man is capable of doing to man. Perhaps this is God's will.'

" 'And where will the witnesses be, if you are all killed?'

" 'Others will tell how we died. Run away if you wish. You look strong, you will succeed.'

" 'I will stay with you,' replied the Ukrainian.

"The others left. He lay down in a corner of the room, my husband returned, and I fell asleep.

"The next morning we woke early. I talked to the Ukrainian. He told me that he was an officer in the Red Army and that he had stayed in Vilna at the time of the retreat to organize a group of guerrilla fighters. He was very ugly, but he seemed terribly strong. When I asked him what he was doing with us, he said that he had decided to stay with his people to try to organize them.

"In the afternoon a block of houses was surrounded and all the people in them were taken away. Our turn came the next day. We left for Ponar on foot. The Russian soldier was right behind me. I heard him trying to convince his neighbors.

" 'It's now or never,' he was saying.

" 'I hear they kill only the old and the sick. If we try to escape we will certainly be killed, but there we still have a chance,' someone said.

"It was shameful, but we all felt the same way. The Russian soldier was right, but he did not understand."

Dr. Ginsberg leaned forward and asked very gently, "What didn't he understand?"

Pessia seemed to be coming out of a dream. She looked at the doctor.

"He did not understand this desire to live. We were not afraid to die, but we wanted to live. You understand that, don't you, Doctor?"

28

Dr. Ginsberg, still half incredulous, answered "Yes" to keep from starting a discussion on this subject, so she would continue her story.

"Go on, Pessia," he said gently.

"Our column moved slowly, and the soldier's voice became more urgent. I turned around and saw that he had a bandage on his forehead. He must have been beaten during the raid.

" 'There aren't many guards. Let's kill them and take their guns!'

" 'Where would we go?'

" 'Into the forest.'

" 'And how would we live with our wives and children?'

" 'We have no right to die like this!'

"Nobody answered him.

" 'Rebel,' he shouted with rage.

"I turned around again. His neighbors were murmuring the 'Sh'ma Yisroel.' His face was contorted, his little close-set eyes burned. I was about to tell him to wait a while when suddenly, giving a shout, leaping sideways and shoving aside the people who were between him and the nearest guard, he jumped on him and grabbed his gun.

"When he had shouted the column had stopped, but no one understood what was happening. The guards had moved away and were aiming their guns at us.

"The soldier backed off slowly, using the guard as a shield. He brandished his gun in his right hand and shouted to us to attack the other guards, not to let ourselves be led to death like sheep. But all the men bowed their heads and murmured the 'Sh'ma Yisroel.'

" 'Jews!' cried the soldier. 'Fight back! Kill the Nazi murders! Look at them, they are afraid of us!'

"The guards did not know what to do. Then an S.S. man came forward, calmly shouldered his gun, slowly took aim, and fired. The guard whom the soldier was holding gave a cry and staggered. The soldier held him up. The S.S. fired a second bullet, and a third. The Russian soldier did not dare to fire, because we were behind the S.S. He yelled to us to lie down, but no one moved.

" 'Why did he do it?' murmured my husband. 'It's useless. He will die anyway and so will we. So why?'

"The soldier's voice was weaker. The S.S. man's bullets must have reached him through the guard's body. The S.S. advanced, gun in hand, ready to fire. After that everything happened very fast. The soldier released his human shield, jumped back, and began to run. The S.S. stopped, shouldered his gun, aimed, and fired with impressive calm. At the first shot the soldier reeled, at the second he fell. He was about to get up again when the third bullet struck him. His body gave a start and crumpled, motionless.

"The S.S. ordered two Jews to go and get the body and to walk at the head of the column, dragging it by the feet.

"We began to move again. The men said a prayer for the dead for the soldier. My little girl began to cry. Between her sobs she asked, 'Where are we, Mamma? I'm afraid, I'm afraid.'

"I rocked her and said, 'Don't be afraid, my darling, we are on the road to heaven. Sleep, my child, it's so pretty in heaven.' "

The doctor listened with great emotion, but this story, related in this dreamlike way, seemed almost unreal to him. His incredulity mounted when Pessia began the story of Ponar.

"We moved like a funeral procession, with those two men dragging the body in front of us and all the others singing 'El Maleh Rachamim.' The road was dusty and our exhausted feet raised a cloud of dust high above the ground. When the forest appeared in the distance, the men sang more loudly. The low murmur became a muffled roar from which now and then a stronger and finer voice emerged, full of supplicating love: 'Glory to Our Lord, glory to the Eternal, blessed be His Name!" The voice rose, harsh and fervent, then quickly fell and was lost in the thunderous background. In our thoughts we were already with the soul of the Just Man whose head was jolted by every stone on the road.

"I did not see the forest appear. Suddenly there were shouts, blows, barbed wire and a terrible smell. We stopped walking. I did not know how it would happen. I held my little girl tightly in my arms and closed my eyes, I opened them when my husband said goodbye to me. He was very calm and he looked at me intently.

" 'Forgive me,' he added, 'I was wrong.'

"Five at a time, the men stepped forward, walked fifty yards, stopped, and bent down. There was a volley of shots, and they disappeared.

"Then there was no one left in front of me and I walked forward myself. I was not afraid, I had already stopped living. Suddenly at my feet there was a huge ditch full of bodies. I did not hear the shots, but I felt a pain in my arm. I fell forward, thinking: This is it, I am dead. And I lost consciousness."

Dr. Ginsberg looked at this woman whom some miracle had saved. She was feverish. He thought that she was raving, or that she had gone mad. He could not believe this tale of terror which seemed to come out of a tortured mind.

"Calm yourself, Pessia," he told her. "You are feverish and you have had a nightmare."

But Pessia did not hear him.

"I opened my eyes. It was dark and cold. I tried to turn over but I could not."

The doctor motioned to Mrs. Ginsberg to bring boiling water, and he tried to untie the improvised bandage that encircled Pessia's arm. She was so tense that he could not move her arm away from her body.

31

"My little girl had died of suffocation. I do not know how I lifted all the bodies that covered me. I remember that I crawled. There was barbed wire, I managed to crawl under it. I was so afraid that I kept crawling for a long time, then I got up and began to run. Soon I met a peasant woman. She gave me this dress and this bouquet, put a rag around my arm, and told me to get back to the ghetto by pretending to be a peasant coming to sell flowers. When I got here, I asked where you were. Nobody knew. I don't remember how I got here. But I was sure that it was here."

Pessia's face grew calm and her body slackened. Dr. Ginsberg caught her just in time. He laid her on the floor on a blanket.

"The poor girl must have been beaten," he said to his wife. "She is burning up with fever. But where on earth did she get that story?"

"What we are going through is too hard for children like her," answered his wife.

The doctor was removing the bandage that encircled Pessia's arm. He saw that it was red. He drew the arm away from the body.

"She is wounded," he said.

His wife brought a saucepan of water. He put Pessia's arm on his knee. There was an ugly blackish hole on the upper part.

"It looks like a bullet hole," he murmured.

He dipped a handkerchief into the water and leaned over to clean the wound. Something stirred inside it. He leaned closer and suddenly stammered, terrified, "Sarah! Red ants from the forest!"

FOR A LONG TIME Dr. Ginsberg sat stunned, unable to utter a word. At first he could think only of all those who had gone and who would never return. He felt a profound grief for them.

"Why?" he asked aloud, but as if talking to himself. "Why were they killed?"

He recalled all the raids since the beginning; he pictured the faces of those who had been taken away. Had they known?

"David!" his wife called softly. "What will become of us?"

He looked at her questioningly.

"What does it mean?" she went on. "Why them? I don't understand. What had they done? Why were they massacred and why have we been spared?"

"I don't know, Sarah. I don't understand," he answered absently. He was picturing himself in the crowd during the march to the ghetto. Suddenly he understood, it was like an illumination.

"But"—his voice trembled slightly—"they were not chosen!"

"Which means that . . ." She did not dare to finish her sentence.

"Yes, we are all doomed."

"What will become of us?" she repeated in a flat voice.

Dr. Ginsberg pulled himself together. "We must warn everyone, so that from now on no one will let himself be taken away. Then we must decide: either to resist in the ghetto, since in any case we have nothing to lose, or else to try to escape. But we will see about that later. Now the important thing is to warn as many people as possible. You take care of Pessia while I go and tell people her story. News travels fast in the ghetto. By this evening everyone will know."

Although he was a young practitioner, Dr. Ginsberg was already an important figure in the Jewish community of Vilna. As a student he had taken part in the Zionist movement and from it he had retained not only great integrity, but a spirit of determination and readiness that inspired great confidence in all who knew him. Physically strong himself, he could not imagine how a man could let himself go. Even when he had been seized with occasional doubts, he had never given any indication of them. The events had appeared to him only as a terrible moral test for the Jewish people.

As he came out into the street, he was calculating how many people he could speak to in the course of the day. Ten, fifteen at the most, he thought, especially since I will have to tell them not to do anything foolish, to await orders. Only then did the idea occur to him that the revelation of the massacre of the Jews at Ponar might set off a riot.

All these problems assailed him at once as he strode along. The ghetto was calm, the street empty. They must all be on the square in front of the new Judenrat, he thought; and he decided to go there. That way, I can talk to several people at the same time.

The square was four hundred yards from where he lived. Quickening his pace, he began to prepare his speech: "My friends, we have been deceived. Ponar is not a work camp—"

"Good morning, Doctor!"

A voice interrupted his reflections. It was an old man who had greeted him. He was sitting on a chair in front of a door. The

34

doctor did not recognize him and was reluctant to stop. He was about to walk on when the old man said, "I think you were right, Doctor. Peace seems to have returned now that we are in the ghetto. There wasn't even a raid yesterday."

Understanding that the old man was saying this more to hear his hopes confirmed than from conviction, Dr. Ginsberg felt it was his duty to tell him the truth. Better that I should tell him. He seems to have so much confidence in me, and maybe I can keep him from despairing completely and doing something foolish.

"Listen, I must tell you something, it is very serious," he began.

"Well?" asked the old man in a voice that was deliberately cheerful.

"Ponar is not a work camp."

He stopped. The old man's face was impassive, as if he did not understand what the doctor was telling him. The old man's silence troubled him. He felt that something in his attitude eluded him. Ill at ease, he continued, "No one could have imagined, because it is absurd; only insanity could conceive such a plan. And Germany seemed like such a civilized country. Now there is no more doubt. This morning a young woman came to my house; she had escaped from Ponar. It is a miracle that she made it. All the others were massacred."

The doctor had lowered his voice at the end of the sentence as if to soften the meaning of the last word. The old man's eyes had blinked and his face had quivered for a fraction of a second, and then he had recovered his impassivity.

The doctor thought he had spoken too softly and that the old man had not heard him.

"All the others were massacred," he repeated, stressing each syllable.

The man did not move. The doctor thought for a moment that he was deaf.

35

"Massacred!" he shouted.

The old man did not react. Then Dr. Ginsberg was seized by a terrible doubt. But the old man's silence unnerved him, and he stopped trying to spare him.

"Ponar means death! All the people who have been taken there have been exterminated, and so will we! We will all be massacred!" Surprised at his own violence, the doctor stopped.

Then the old man's mouth opened and obstinately, like a child, he said, "That is not true."

Dr. Ginsberg looked at him, stunned. So he had known from the beginning; so he had understood immediately, perhaps even before the transfer to the ghetto. But this truth was too terrible for him, at his age, and he had decided to play the comedy of hope. The doctor was suddenly aware of all that was odious in his own attitude. He looked at the old man and asked his forgiveness.

"It is not true," said the doctor, and he left.

He walked more slowly, thinking over the scene. He had recovered his control, but he now saw the problem in another light. He saw that he had been doubly blind, that many must have suspected the truth but had preferred to remain in uncertainty. This uncertainty was what protected the weak from despair, and he did not have the right to take it away from them. He decided to speak of Ponar only to reliable men.

On the Judenrat square he met a lawyer with whom he had gone to school. He took him aside and told him Pessia's story.

"Why create an atmosphere of panic?" said the lawyer. "We are here to reassure the people and encourage them."

"But how can we encourage them when they are being massacred?"

"Who told you this? A girl who is half mad. We can't start an insurrection that might cost us all our lives because of a woman's nightmare. As long as we have no certainty, we must do nothing!"

Dr. Ginsberg asked him to come and hear Pessia's testimony. At first the lawyer refused, but since the doctor insisted, he finally agreed.

The lawyer, who was a member of the Judenrat, had opted for order. He was a good Jew and an honest man, but he thought this story might cause trouble. He was determined to suppress it. He believed that Jews had been killed, but not as systematically as his former classmate had said. This girl was mad, or else she was trying to create a panic in the ghetto, but you could not give credence to her story.

They had arrived at the doctor's house without saying a word. Dr. Ginsberg felt depressed and he now wondered whether it was worth the trouble to continue. First the old man, now his former classmate had shown him, each in his own way and for completely different reasons, that it was not truth that mattered the most, but hope.

When he entered the room the doctor received a shock. Pessia was not there, and his wife was sitting on the floor with her back to the wall. She looked up when she heard him, but she did not have the strength to smile. He rushed over to her and helped her gently to her feet. She seemed very tired, and he did not dare ask her where Pessia was.

In a monotonous voice, she told what had happened. Some neighbors had come in and she had asked Pessia to tell them what she had seen. At first they had been very kind to her; but when she came to the part about Ponar one woman, some of whose relatives had gone to the right, had called her a liar. Pessia had insisted, so they all silenced her by asking if she did not think they had enough troubles already. Pessia had begun to cry and they had left. After their departure she had cried for a long time. "I didn't want to hurt them! Why did they treat me like that?" she kept repeating. Then she had decided to leave, and Mrs. Ginsberg had not been able to stop her. She must be wandering now through

37

the streets of the ghetto, rejected by her community after losing her own family.

"Did she say anything when she left?" asked the doctor.

"Yes," answered his wife. "She said that nobody returns from Ponar."

The lawyer had slipped quietly out. The doctor thought that the adventure he was living through was unique. He decided to keep a journal and to live so that some day he could tell the story.

He saw Pessia again a long time afterward. She was working in a dressmaking factory in the ghetto; she seemed to have forgotten everything and was laughing with the other girls. She had never dared tell her adventure again.

The Technicians learned of Pessia Aranovich's misadventures in the ghetto with the keenest satisfaction. It was the magnificent crowning of two months of effort and the proof of the excellence of their method. They were especially satisfied because Vilna was a pilot ghetto, an experimental ghetto. A master stroke on the first try! Thirty thousand Jews had already been killed and not a word had leaked out. The most perfect calm reigned in the town.

Others in their place would have been content with this and would have decided that the ghetto as a whole was ripe for extermination. But they had a thirst for perfection and a meticulous sense of detail. They believed, rightly, that in these matters it is not the first steps but the last ones that are most difficult, that there would come a time when the Jews would be forced to face the truth and that then, driven by despair, they might be led to rash gestures which would complicate the Germans' task and sow confusion among the Jewish population of Poland who had not yet been "treated."

Since the Technicians did not want to take any unnecessary risks, they decided not only to continue but to step up their policy of conditioning. To bring the Jews to a deathlike submissiveness,

they supplemented the tactic of the brain buster with the less
original ones of division and the decoy.

Part of the population of the ghetto worked in German busi-
nesses. To them the Germans issued work certificates, saying that
the bearers would have to present them only during raids. The
ghetto was divided into two camps: those who had certificates
and who were lulled by the sense of security they derived from
them, and those who did not have them and who felt vulnerable,
isolated, abandoned. The raids resumed, striking those "without
certificates." For the privileged, it was the beginning of compromise. By brandishing their certificates during a raid, they dissoci-
ated themselves from their own people, they lost the sense of the
oneness of the destiny of their people.

But soon the privileged themselves were divided, the certificates became of two kinds: with and without photograph. They
wondered which kind offered the best protection. "With photograph," concluded the majority, for the photograph made the
document seem more official. The Technicians distributed a large
number of these and carried out a small raid on those without photographs. Our point, thought those with photographs. Then the
certificates with photographs were abolished and replaced by
blank certificates bearing the seal of the labor bureau of Ponar.
The word caused alarm and the "blanks" did not have much success, until a second raid descended upon those without photographs and those without certificates, sparing only those with
blanks. Then the "blanks" were in turn divided into two categories—those with and those without the qualification "skilled
worker."

As you had only to state that you were skilled in something to
obtain the qualification, it was easy to choose. Some thought that
the qualification was a ruse and preferred certificates "without
qualification." Others reasoned more simply, telling themselves
that since a skilled worker was useful, he would be spared. And

they awaited the verdict. It came from an unexpected direction, revealing that the problem was much more complicated than had been believed. The Technicians announced that they had observed that certain skilled workers had not registered, while others who had no skills had succeeded in imposing on the good faith of their employers. "Consequently," they added with perfect bad faith, "all certificates are abolished."

A raid struck the population at random, and despair descended upon the ghetto, a despair that was all the more profound because many felt that they were guilty. With extraordinary naïveté they thought, They trusted us and we cheated.

At this point the Judenrat announced that it was going to distribute yellow certificates which would be good for the whole family. Our point, thought the Jews; our leaders still enjoy some authority with the occupying forces.

In fact, of course, this was merely a new trick whose purpose was to have all the work done by the Jews themselves. The Technicians did not act out of a fondness for games or aestheticism, but to set up between themselves and the population a scapegoat against whom the people's wrath would eventually turn when they realized they had been fooled. The reasoning was very accurate: people feel more ill will toward their own for betraying them than they do toward the enemy for killing them.

The second phase of the operation began as the first had: 3,000 certificates were distributed among the 23,000 survivors of the ghetto. Once again the Jews were divided into "privileged" and "pariahs."

Only the pariahs were the victims of the first raids. Then a new kind of certificate was created: a "pink" family certificate. This time the distribution was generous and there were enough for everybody. Now everyone wondered which offered the most protection. Some holders of yellow certificates thought that the "pinks," being newer, had more value and traded certificates with "pinks" who had adopted the opposite argument. Some thought that the wisest course was to have no certificate at all and to hide. All waited for the next drawing to find out who had won. The raid was of great violence. Both "yellows" and "pinks" were decimated.

This raid marked the transition to the third phase. The certificates went though all the colors of the rainbow—yellow, pink, then blue, then green, and finally red, before being replaced by a single red passport which was distributed to all registered persons. But the numbers were of two kinds: above 10,000 and below 10,000. The eternal alternative: which was better? The Technicians had already answered this question: "Below 10,000 I win, above 10,000 you lose"; but nobody could know this.

With the introduction of the family certificate, the brain buster had become a terrible weapon, a heartbreaker. For the problem was no longer merely to save yourself or possibly die; from now on the responsibility extended to the whole family and even to friends. When the family certificates had appeared, the problem had arisen of whether to register your relatives, thus designating them as useless dependents. Many were suspicious and chose to abstain. But a raid took place which struck the nonregistered: their point. So everyone rushed to register their relatives and even their friends as relatives. But in a certain number of work commandos the registered relatives were rounded up: their point. It was noticed that these commandos were the least good, and there was a rush to register one's family on the certificates of workers of the "good" commandos. Workers who were employed in the personal service of the Germans suddenly acquired families of twenty and thirty persons. On December 4, 1941, the relatives, both true and false, of the workers of this commando were sent to Ponar, while the least privileged, who had not been able to get registered, were spared. The temptation was strong to unregister one's relatives. But might not the next raid be aimed at the unregistered?

Children under sixteen registered on the certificates of workers

41

were not compelled to do the work, which was so arduous that it would have been difficult for them to endure. But this raised a problem: should you register a child of thirteen as under sixteen, thus designating him as a useless dependent, or as over sixteen and send him to forced labor?

The supreme art of the Technicians was in giving each person the opportunity to cheat. For the registration of the family no official paper was required; bachelors, widowers and orphans could register their mothers or friends as their wives. But others had to make a terrible choice which destroyed them either way.

"Whom do you prefer," the unconscious Machiavelli asks the child, "your papa or your mamma?"

"Whom do you prefer," the Technicians asked the Jews of Vilna, "your mother or your wife? If it is your wife, give us your mother, and if it is your mother, give us your wife."

How could a man answer this question? The Jews who tried impaled their hearts on it.

But what did the answers matter? They had all lost—"Under 10,000 I win, over 10,000 you lose; your wife, I win; your mother, you lose."

Before dying, the Jews of Vilna were crucified.

The conditioning process was reaching its apotheosis and the Technicians were getting ready for the kill when they learned that a resistance movement had sprung up in the ghetto.

Two girls had been arrested at the Malkinia station, on their way from Warsaw to Vilna. A message addressed to the United Organization of Partisans was found on them. They died under torture without revealing anything else.

The ghetto had become a powder keg and the Technicians immediately ceased all raids. The slightest incident might set off a revolt that threatened to spread to all the other ghettos of Poland, Lithuania, the Ukraine and White Russia.

It BEGAN ON the night of Yom Kippur.

Throughout the previous days, the improvised synagogues of the ghetto had echoed with fervent prayers and imprecations. In these days of confrontation with the Eternal, the Jews of Vilna had renounced their vain hopes. They had come before God in all their nakedness and, full of fear and supplication, had placed themselves in His Hands: "Hear my voice, see my tears, defend me, and tell me at last, 'I pardon you.' We are in Thy Hands like the clay in the hands of the potter, like the stone in the hands of the stonecutter, like the ax in the hands of the carpenter, like the rudder in the hands of the sailor. Thus are we in Thy Hands, Thou Who givest grace."

Then came Yom Kippur, the Day of Atonement, a day of wrath, dark and autumnal, threatening in its grayish silence. At the hour of the *Nielah* the whole ghetto became an immense synagogue, vibrant with a mystic ecstasy. "All the cities are firm in their edifice, the Holy City has sunk into the bowels of the earth," chanted the cantor and the crowd trembled, tense, sorrowful, suppliant. The exaltation reached its climax when the shofar was sounded, announcing the end of the fast.

43

That night thousands of people were rounded up and taken away in a glacial silence, still drugged with a mystical fervor which was hardly dissipated but had already become remote as regret. The silence was broken only by a few stifled sobs which echoed dully on the air.

That night, furtive groups had slipped out of the ghetto through the sewers to the forest to meet Mordecai Tenenbaum, who had called together the first nucleus of what was to become the United Organization of Partisans.

Not one of the participants was over twenty. All were members of Zionist youth groups. Since the arrival of the German troops they had been living in hiding, refusing to take an interest in what was going on around them. They felt that whatever might happen to the Jews of the Diaspora did not concern them, that their own lives and all their efforts must be oriented toward the land of Israel.

The meeting was brief. Mordecai Tenenbaum asked them one question: "What is the meaning of Zionism if there are no more Jews?" It was the first time the problem had been stated in these terms. Mordecai asked each of them to think about it and to base his attitude on the answer he made. Then he went off into the forest.

A few weeks later in a Benedictine convent on the outskirts of Vilna, a meeting of the Hashomer Hatzaïr movement was held. The problem was debated. Chaika Grossman opened the discussion.

"We are coming to the end of a period in which all our efforts have gone toward saving the members of our movement. Have we been right in acting this way? Should we continue to ignore the destiny of our people? As a movement the Diaspora does not interest us; but as Jews?"

Dan Ariel, whose role was later to be dominant, was the first to reply. "I am going to review the facts," he began. "You have all heard about Pessia Aranovich, the young girl who escaped from Ponar. Since then, we have had other eyewitness accounts. We can no longer close our eyes and believe that those who have been deported are still alive. The truth is that they have been taken to Ponar—that is, to their death. . . ."

Dan Ariel spoke in a dry voice, without emotion. He was proving a case, and his short, choppy sentences swept away the last vestiges of hope.

"And if this is not the whole truth, the whole truth is even more terrible. The extermination of a few thousand Jews is only the prelude to the extermination of millions, that is, to our complete annihilation.

"I do not understand why Vilna is bled to death and Bialystok continues to live in untroubled peace. The messengers we have sent down there have come back confused and almost wondering whether we have not been imagining things, so completely does calm prevail in that town. The same goes for Warsaw and all the towns of Poland. I do not know why things are happening this way, why it is not Bialystok that has been bled and Vilna that has been spared, or why all the towns have not been bled at the same time. But one thing is clear to me: The lesson of Vilna does not apply to Vilna alone. Ponar is not a whim of the Germans. The Yellow Star is not the invention of the local *Kommandantur*. All this is part of a whole system. The rest is pure Machiavellianism. We are in the presence of a well-mounted mechanism whose key we do not yet possess."

During the night of Yom Kippur all had asked themselves the question; but many, even if they accepted the truth about Ponar, had not wanted to believe that they were witnessing the extermination of the Jewish people. Every sentence Dan Ariel uttered struck them painfully.

"Is there any way to escape? No. If this system is coherent, to flee from one place to another is an illusion and, like every illusion, is stupid. For who will escape from Vilna to go to Bialystok and Warsaw? The young, the swift, the healthy! Whereas the weak, the old and the children will remain in the town, doomed to destruction. And when the tragedy reaches those towns in which we have taken refuge, it will find us uprooted, completely disoriented and morally broken by the useless act of cowardice we have committed in abandoning our people. Perhaps we have already been guilty enough of cowardice as it is. This is why our first response must be, 'Running away is no solution.'

"What are the chances of the Jewish people? We must answer clearly, however cruel the answer may be: they are nonexistent. The Jews do not have the slightest chance of escaping. A few dozen, a few hundred may manage to survive. But for our people as a whole, for the millions of Jews living in the territory occupied by Germany, there is not the slightest chance. What must we do, then, since on the one hand we cannot run away and on the other hand we are being exterminated?"

Dan Ariel left the question in the air for a moment and then, in a different voice, he said, "Our only alternative is to prepare to fight before we die."

There was a long and painful silence. There are truths which are difficult to endure. Some could not yet bring themselves to accept this one. Yaakov was the first who was capable of answering:

"Our whole life," he said, "is turned toward the land of Israel; it is only an accident that we are still in exile. European Judaism is undergoing a catastrophe at this time, but we broke with it the day we joined the movement. We have been brought up to work and fight in the land of Israel, and not here. To this training we have sacrificed everything: our pleasures, our nights, our rest. and even our families. I am not a coward, but I ask: Have we the right to sacrifice the land of Israel for a useless combat here? Are we romantic dreamers or builders? For me the only future for the

Jewish people is in the land of Israel, and it is by building this land that we shall save our people—"

"Yaakov," interrupted David Rosen, "I want to ask you one question: What will you say to the children of Israel when they ask you what you did while thousands and millions of our brothers were being assassinated?"

"Well, I—" Yaakov hesitated.

"Will you tell them, 'We saved our skins, we became the kings of the hideout; it was not very heroic, of course, but it worked'?"

"No, David," Yaakov answered slowly, "you do not understand. I am not afraid—at least, no more than the next man. I am not a coward either, but this death that Dan proposes seems so absurd, so useless."

They were not twenty years old and they talked about death like veterans or philosophers. But this death was neither a possibility nor a hypothesis; it was a certainty—only the manner of dying depended on their choice, and this choice was difficult. David continued:

"You are right, Yaakov, to think only of the future, since the present is already dead. But a double threat hangs over our people. The physical threat is extermination. But there is a moral threat which is even graver and has to do with how we are exterminated. If not a single Jew resists, who will ever want to be a Jew again? Since the destruction of the Temple and the heroic defense of Massada, our whole history is nothing but massacre, extermination and helplessness. If we submit, what hope will we have that the new generation that will be born in the land of Israel will be strong and courageous? Where will it find its sources of heroism? It is up to us to provide them. We must fight for the honor of our people, and this way our death will not be useless."

Everyone was silent and tried to imagine what death was like. Suddenly Nahum Epelbaum cleared his throat.

"I don't mind dying," he began in his rough voice—

He was seventeen and looked thirty. Tall and powerfully built, his body was covered with a thick layer of black hair. Nobody had ever seen him either upset or tired. His strength had earned him the nickname "the bull."

"—and I don't mind if they put up a statue of me in the land of Israel, but we don't want to act like fools—"

His earthy language contrasted with that of the others.

"We have a responsibility to the future, but we also have a responsibility to the twenty thousand Jews who are still in the ghetto of Vilna. According to Dan, they've had it. Me, I'm ready. I think he knows more about these things than I do, but still we can't be sure. We wouldn't want to start something that would cause their death, because history might not forgive us for that."

By returning to more practical problems, Nahum had eased the atmosphere, and the discussion became general.

Then Dan Ariel, slight and tense, continued:

"Sure proof that our people is doomed to extermination can be provided only by the last Jew, and then only as he falls mortally wounded. But it is today that we must choose either to prepare ourselves and the Jews of the ghetto to fight, or to throw ourselves on the mercy of the invader."

"And supposing the Jews do not want to fight?"

"It will be our job to make them want to. We will take away their illusions and give them their choice: to die in dishonor or to die fighting."

"Of two solutions I always choose the third," muttered Nahum.

"What's that?" asked Dan Ariel.

"Nothing. My father used to say that all the time: of two solutions I always choose the third."

The idea of armed resistance had been born. Zionist youth had rediscovered a reason if not to live, at least to fight. While certain members made contact with the other Zionist movements and with Communists. Dan Ariel was assigned to take charge of the unorganized youth and more generally all those in the ghetto who were capable of taking part in the fight. The task was difficult, for in order to persuade the men to fight, it was first necessary to deprive them of hope. What did he have to offer them in exchange for their illusions? An honorable death—not very much. And yet he spoke with so much faith that soon the idea of self-defense took shape in the ghetto.

The first public meeting was held on the night of December 31, 1941. The snow that had been falling uninterruptedly for a week covered everything, and even the ghetto looked clean. From the Aryan town came shouts, laughter, singing. Snatches of the "Horst Wessel Lied" occasionally emerged and assailed the ears of the groups who came furtively to Number 2 Strachun Street, where the meeting was to be held. "When Jewish blood flows under our knives," they heard, and they bowed their heads a little lower, as if they felt the chill of the blade at their throats. The sense of their helplessness no longer even aroused their anger. They had suffered too much. They felt ground down, the pawns of a diabolical will that was infinitely stronger than they were. They were going to this meeting in order to feel less alone, to feel for a few hours a presence, a bit of warmth.

Dan Ariel was very moved. The room filled rapidly. There were already over two hundred young people standing, astonished. They were talking in low, fearful voices, and the room buzzed softly. Everything about them bespoke poverty, fear, and confusion: their oversize caps which came almost to their eyes, their gaunt faces and, above all, their eyes, which were enlarged by hunger and dulled by fear. An extraordinary feeling of love impelled him toward them and for a moment he wondered whether he would have the courage to rob them of their illusions, whether it would not be better to let them die peacefully in their stubborn

49

stoicism. They seemed to him at once very close and very remote —close because of their distress, remote because of their resignation. But this infinite possibility of suffering revolted him. "The Jews are too good at suffering; it is our downfall," he thought. His decision had been made: he would make fighters of them.

"Jewish brothers," he began. He had barely raised his voice, but it was so intense that everyone stopped talking. "Stop listening to those who are deluding us. Of the sixty thousand Jews in Vilna, no more than twenty thousand are left. Where are the hundreds of people who have just been deported, where are the women and children who were taken away, where are the thousands rounded up on Yom Kippur, where are all those who never reached the ghetto? Not one of all these people has ever returned, for they have been taken to Ponar. And Ponar means death."

He paused and cast his eyes around the room. Everyone was watching him, motionless, mute, inscrutable.

"Give up your illusions! Your children, your husbands, your wives are dead! Ponar is not a transfer camp, no one leaves it alive. Hitler intends to exterminate all the Jews in Europe, and he has begun with those in Lithuania. We are weak and unarmed, but must we therefore let ourselves be led to slaughter like sheep?"

The image had struck home and the room rustled.

"There is only one way to answer the butcher: rebellion. Let us not allow another Jew to leave the ghetto, let us return blow for blow and blood for blood, let us at least defend our honor, since our lives are no longer our own."

The room seemed stupefied. No one could speak. All eyes shone, but many with the dull brilliance of tears. Dan Ariel, who was just as moved as his listeners, remained petrified in his last position. He had no way of knowing whether he had won or lost, and he awaited the verdict rigid, as an athlete remains immobilized until the weight hits the ground. Suddenly a voice rose, solitary and wavering. It seemed to Dan Ariel that no one was going to take up the song, when a second voice rose and almost immediately a third, and the miracle happened. All at once the room exploded; it was no longer a song, it was a shout. The "Hatikvah" had become a cry of hate, a song of fierce hope answering the German song.

The next day a new atmosphere reigned in the ghetto. Everyone who had been at the meeting had become a propagandist for the idea of resistance. Some listened to them with sympathy, but others thought the adventure would end badly. Some saw the drama that the Jewish people was living through as a divine punishment and thought these young Zionists who talked about the honor of the Jewish people and did not even believe in God were irresponsible youngsters. What did they know about the honor of the Jewish people or its mission? But the majority were still too beaten down to listen or argue. For them only one thing mattered —to live, to survive—and the more threatened they felt, the more it mattered.

Complementing this work of propaganda, contact had been made with all the other organizations Poale Sion, the Zionist Socialist-Worker party; Bund, the non-Zionist Socialist party; Betar, the extremist Zionist youth group; and the Communists.

On January 23, in an attic at Number 6 Rudnitzki Street, the first general meeting of the resistance was held.

The first topic discussed was the calm that prevailed in the other ghettos and the skepticism of the Jews. It was decided to send a message to all the ghettos to alert them so that the lesson of Vilna would not be in vain. The two Silber sisters, Sarah and Rose, who were very blond and did not have Jewish features, were entrusted with carrying the message. It was their arrest on their way back to Vilna that revealed to the Technicians the existence of a resistance movement in the ghetto.

There was a long discussion about whether they should fight in the ghetto or in the forest. The idealists wanted to fight in the ghetto to involve the Jews in a final demonstration of honor. The realists thought that combat would be more effective in the forest.

In the end Itzak Wittenberg, a Communist worker who was to become commander in chief of the United Organization of Partisans, proposed that they remain in the ghetto until liquidation, to wage a final combat and then flee, taking along as many "civilians" as possible by itineraries prepared in advance. "As a Communist," he said, "I believe that combat in the ghetto is heresy, but as a Jew, I feel responsible to my brothers."

But how were they to know when the ghetto would be liquidated? It was decided to place a young girl with Aryan features in the headquarters of the Gestapo. This plan was not without audacity, which may have been why it succeeded.

When Wittenberg had mentioned a beautiful young girl with Aryan features, everyone had thought of Lydia. There were few men in the Jewish community of Vilna who had not been a little in love with her. She was an only child, and her mother had died in childbirth. Her father had been one of the first to be taken to Ponar and after that she had disappeared. It had just been learned that she was living in the Aryan town. A non-Jewish Lithuanian had taken her in and registered her as his daughter. When it was proposed to her that she enter Gestapo headquarters, she agreed, and her eyes became almost frightening. Itzak Wittenberg had personally assumed the responsibility of asking her. He was alarmed by the tone in which she answered him.

"Lydia," he told her, "it is very dangerous."

She gave him a long look. For the first time, she had the eyes of a woman.

"I like danger," she answered. "No danger can make me forget what they did to my father."

"But you are still a young girl, Lydia!"

"I am nothing. I am neither girl nor woman. I am only hate, I live only for vengeance. I shall not go to Israel, I shall never fall in love, I shall not have children or a home."

Wittenberg was a hard man and was not easily moved. He knew that the fight he had undertaken, the revolt he had chosen could end only in his death, and he asked the supreme sacrifice of all the men under him; but even so, deep down he retained a vague belief in life, in Man, in the future. He was ready to die, but he sometimes said "afterward" and "later." Lydia, on the other hand, had settled her account with the world and no longer expected anything from anyone. He regretted having entrusted her with this mission.

"Listen, Lydia," he told her, embarrassed. "You are destroying yourself. It would be better if you went to the forest and worked down there."

"There is no more forest, Itzak, there is nothing. The world is dead."

"You cannot carry out this mission in such a state of mind. You will get caught immediately."

"You want to know when the ghetto will be liquidated," she interrupted impatiently. "I will let you know a few days before. Goodbye, Itzak!"

Wittenberg looked at her briefly. Then, in order to say something, he murmured, "Goodbye, Lydia. Be careful anyway."

He saw her again a month later. She was blond and was wearing a German uniform. She was "inspecting" the ghetto along with an S.S. officer. He thought she had not recognized him, but as he passed close by her he heard her ask in a voice as harsh and deep as her eyes, "And the Jews still don't fight back?"

"Can't. Too cowardly," growled the officer.

Wittenberg had already passed them, but he felt someone's eyes upon him. He turned his head. Lydia was looking at him with her inscrutable eyes.

53

The purely military organization of the resistance movement was established a few days later. It was composed of a central staff of five members. The oldest, Itzak Wittenberg, was twenty-three. The troops were divided into two brigades of eight sections, each composed of three groups of five men. The two brigade leaders were members of the central staff. Each brigade was to detach a section of general reserves at the disposal of the central staff. All had a single duty: as soon as mobilization was announced, each man was to hold the position that would be assigned him with a sidearm when he had no more ammunition, and with his bare hands if he had no sidearm.

"What about strategic retreat?" someone had asked in the course of the discussion.

"We are not making strategy, we are making war," Wittenberg had said.

It was not an answer, but everyone had understood. They were not fighting either to win or to survive, but to send a message to the future, to history, to mankind, or to God, each according to his convictions.

They were about to overlook the problem of weapons when someone asked absent-mindedly, "And what will we fight with?"

"With this," replied Dan Ariel, tossing a gun on the table. "Baruch Goldstein stole it from a German who won't be needing it any more. We will have to take our weapons where we can find them!"

After an initial phase of preparation—creation of special groups like scouts, dynamiters and mine layers, installation of a receiving station, writing of an underground journal, *The Flag of Freedom,* fabrication of improvised weapons and explosives— the organization decided to go on to the offensive. Sabotage was to be a way of training the men while allaying their impatience. There was an orgy of accidents in which audacity and ingenuity were combined. Suddenly trucks refused to start and guns to fire, gas stations began to blow up, fur factories burned, powder magazines exploded. Then one day it was the turn of a munitions train which was leaving for the front. The explosion broke all the windows in town. Hundreds of Poles and Lithuanians were arrested, but the investigation came to nothing.

The Gestapo were about to close the file on the incident when the Malkinia brigade reported the arrest of Sarah and Rose Silber.

IV

THIS BUSINESS OF resistance raised a new problem for the Technicians. They were not really worried, for they could reduce the ghetto of Vilna to ashes without risking a single man, simply by shelling it with artillery. Of course, it would be ridiculous to ask for siege guns against Jews, but ridicule doesn't kill you. The Technicians were only embarrassed. This painful affair forced them to reconsider their whole strategy, which was based on the "good will" of the victims, a good will that served everyone: the killers, whose work it facilitated, and the victims, whose death it simplified. Indeed, the reasoning of the Technicians was not lacking in logic: since the Jews had to die anyway, it might as well happen rapidly, without protest, without useless rebellion—in a word, without disorder. For on this point the Technicians, who were actually lax about many things, were intransigent. "Order and efficiency" was their motto. In return, their victims were assured of a quick death with a minimum of suffering. This assurance was based on an argument just as logical as the first: "Why should the Jews be made to suffer when animals are not?" Apart from a few exceptions arising from human weakness, the Technicians were not sadists; they were merely "technicians."

56

So, it was as men bent on efficiency that they addressed themselves to the problem raised by this unforeseen resistance movement. One thing argued for the method of preliminary conditioning: the facility with which they had already exterminated two thirds of the ghetto. A method that had obtained results like these could not be bad. Consequently they decided to keep on using it, adapting it to the new conditions. Its principle had been the moral disarmament of the victim by means of skillful doses of panic and uncertainty. This disarmament forced the victim to make a certain number of minor concessions which led to others, which in turn brought him to a third stage, and so forth, until he received a bullet in the back of the neck with head bowed and hands joined in total submission.

Viewed from this angle, the problem was not to destroy the core of resistance but to cut off its power over the populace. To do this the flock would have to be led to reject its "bad shepherds," the ideal condition being that it betray them itself, for this way not only would it be stripped of its defense, but it would be morally compromised to the point where death would assume the guise of a justified punishment.

Having established the principle, the Germans began to put it into effect.

The first measure that had to be taken was to restore confidence to the ghetto. To do this it was necessary to make the Jews believe that the deportations were over and that life was resuming its normal course.

Accordingly, Jacob Gens, the Jewish Chief of Police of the ghetto and the leader of the Judenrat, was summoned by the Technicians. "My dear Gens," they told him, "the time of the raids is over. We have need of your Jews for our war production. Make them work, and we guarantee that there will be no more deportations." Then he was named president of the Judenrat.

Jacob Gens was a disturbing person. Of humble extraction and extremely limited education, he had started his career at the beginning of the occupation of Vilna as a lowly Jewish policeman. When the first Judenrat, who had understood the role they were being asked to play, had been jettisoned, Gens had called the policemen together and made an insane speech in which he explained that it was their duty to remain and keep order, otherwise the Germans and the Lithuanians would do it themselves. This speech marked the beginning of his vertiginous rise to power. This "responsible" attitude had earned him the appointment of Chief of Police in the second Judenrat. In carrying out his functions he directed the Jewish police during the raids and counted those leaving for Ponar at the gate of the ghetto. He seemed to display so much zeal during these operations that the whole ghetto began to hate him. He suffered greatly from this, and one day he tried to justify himself at a literary soirée. Leaving his Praetorian guard at the door, he walked alone into the room, which greeted him with hostile silence.

"Many of you think I am a traitor," he said. "Others wonder what I am doing at a literary demonstration in the ghetto. Me, Gens, I blow up the underground shelters in which the Jews hide to escape deportation and me, Gens, I go to a lot of trouble to get papers and certificates for inhabitants of the ghetto. Me, Gens, I keep track of Jewish blood, but not of Jewish honor. When they ask me for a thousand Jews, I turn them over, for otherwise the Germans would come and help themselves, and they would take not one thousand but many thousands. By giving them a hundred Jews I save a thousand, and by giving them one thousand I save ten thousand.

"You who devote yourselves to the things of the mind, you aren't involved in the dirty work of the ghetto. You'll leave it clean, if you're lucky enough to leave, and you'll be able to say, 'Our consciences are immaculate.' Me, Jacob Gens, if I leave, I'll

58

be dirty and my hands will be covered with blood."

It was after that day that he was called the False Messiah.

After he became the leader of the Judenrat, he began to take an interest in all aspects of the administration of the ghetto, and his prose flourished in the local newspaper, *News of the Ghetto*. It was one of his editorials, published after the deportations stopped, that caused him to be chosen by the Technicians. "In the administration of the ghetto," he wrote, "as well as in the work commandos, it is our duty to prove that the prejudice about our unfitness for work is fundamentally false. We must prove that we are indispensable to production, and that it would be impossible to replace us under present wartime conditions. At this moment there are in the ghetto 14,000 workers. We must make it our objective to raise this figure to 16,000. We must make a selection among the workers so as to increase our common output, which will increase our right to exist accordingly. Therefore, our workers outside the ghetto must give up their jobs if they are too comfortable and take others which are more useful, in the general interest."

As he left Gestapo headquarters, Gens was beaming with pleasure. He was sure that the Germans had understood the implicit appeal made by his last article. He, Jacob Gens, had succeeded in making the oppressors listen to reason. He was the new savior of his people. Determined to begin his reign lavishly, he organized a large banquet for that very evening. In the course of it the policemen presented him with enormous sheaves of flowers which they had picked themselves during the day. The party went on all night, punctuated with resounding toasts to "Jacob Gens, savior of the Jews."

The next morning the Germans sent him a goose. "Gens, *Ganz,* it's the same thing," the messenger explained. "This goose will be your emblem." Without suspecting the irony, Gens thanked him profusely. He had a huge cage built in front of the Judenrat, and he assigned a special policeman to take care of the bird. And evil tongues muttered that it was better fed than the poor people of the ghetto.

On the same day he had announcements of his appointment posted on the walls of the ghetto, and he took advantage of the occasion to issue his first official proclamation. Everything is in it, from amnesty to peace for the good offered to members of the resistance. The proclamation opened with what was to become his motto:

The watchwords of the ghetto are: Work, Discipline, and Order. No one among us must scorn work or take the bad road which leads to crime. Counting on the understanding of the ghetto as a whole, I have given the order to release all persons now being detained anywhere in the ghetto. By decreeing a general pardon, I am giving criminals an opportunity to redeem themselves by an honest existence. It should be known, however, that in case of necessity I shall not hesitate to take the severest measures in my campaign against criminal elements and their actions.

[Signed] JACOB GENS,
President of the Judenrat and Chief of Police

In this absurd world of the condemned, an enlightened dictatorship had been born.

Next, Gens remembered those "pillars" of his regime, the policemen. He had new uniforms and caps edged with gold braid made for them. For himself he chose an admiral's uniform. His cap was trimmed with five rows of gold braid.

At first the ghetto remained stupefied by this masquerade. Then, as calm continued to reign, people began to believe in Gens. Jews who had fled the town returned to it and even went to work. The members of the resistance smiled at this comedy. They found Gens more ridiculous than dangerous.

The ghetto was lulled by the peace. Once again people began

to hope, so strong is the will to live in creatures who have suffered too much. Spring had been premature, and the days were getting longer and warmer. The nightmare was receding. Ponar was only a dream. By tacit agreement, no one ever mentioned those who had disappeared.

The state of bliss lasted for a long time. The Technicians, who shrank from no sacrifice, appointed Gens chief of all the ghettos of Lithuania and White Russia. Another bacchanal marked this occasion. The new "emperor," who took his duties seriously, delegated officers to all the ghettos of his empire so he could organize them on the pattern of the Vilna ghetto: "Work, Discipline, and Order." Vilna became the toy capital of this make-believe empire.

All this amused the Technicians very much, but the problem of the liquidation of the ghetto was at a standstill. Members of the resistance whom they captured committed suicide before they could be interrogated. Each man carried an unpinned grenade wedged under his belt, and could set it off merely by pulling in his stomach. A dangerous group of fanatics.

The Technicians were not asking very much: one name, that was all, that would be enough, the name of the leader. They knew that if they asked for the whole resistance movement they would not get it. Too many family ties bound its members to the Jews of the ghetto. But if they asked only for the leader, one man in exchange for twenty thousand, with the help of Gens they would get him. It was not the man himself that interested them, but the idea that the ghetto should betray him. There are betrayals from which one never recovers. The Technicians knew this.

At last fortune smiled on them. A Lithuanian partisan revealed the name of the leader of the resistance: Itzak Wittenberg.

The "infernal machine" had been ready for a long time; they had only to light the fuse. To do this they sent for Jacob Gens.

"My dear Gens," they told him, "we made an agreement. We

have respected it meticulously. You, unfortunately, have not had the same scruples."

Gens was terrified and had no idea what was happening. He thanked the Technicians profusely for the way in which they had kept their word, assured them that everybody was working enthusiastically and unstintingly, and finished, "If anything has displeased you, be good enough to tell me what it is, and I will correct it at once."

The Technicians were ahead of him.

"Jacob Gens, Jew and son of a Jew, you are a swindler like all your people."

They had touched his sensitive point. Gens, since his elevation, was inclined to try to imitate the "honesty" of his masters, but not knowing what they were driving at, he could only stammer insipid protestations regarding his honor.

The Technicians let him flounder in the dark for a while. When they saw the sweat begin to bead his brow, they decided that he was ready.

"Of course, as far as work is concerned," they told him very gravely, "we all have reason to be satisfied with your administration."

Gens beamed.

"But, we have just learned a serious piece of news which proves your incompetence or your treachery, which is just as serious."

By this time Gens, like Abraham before his God, was ready to sacrifice his son to prove his good faith to his lords and masters, and they knew it.

"We have just learned that an agitator is trying to stir up the ghetto against us."

Gens feigned astonishment. "An agitator? No one would dare!"

"We even know his name!"

Seeing a way to get off the hook cheaply, Gens rushed blindly into the trap.

"Tell me the name of this man, I implore you, and I will turn him over to you tomorrow."

"We expected no less of you, my dear Gens," replied the Technicians with smiles that hinted forthcoming reconciliation. "His name is Itzak Wittenberg."

As he returned to the ghetto, Jacob Gens cursed the resistance movement—"these imbeciles who almost ruined my whole strategy." He walked briskly, muttering under his breath, "At least, I managed to avoid the worst, thanks to my good relations with the Germans. But Wittenberg won't get away, I'll see to it personally." The policemen who were with him heard him pronounce Wittenberg's name, and one of them ran to warn him that something was afoot.

When he learned the news, Wittenberg immediately called together the leaders of the movement. Night had already fallen. A great calm reigned over the ghetto. Everyone felt that the cold war was over and that violence was about to erupt. The meeting had just started when an emissary from Gens arrived and said that Gens wanted to see Wittenberg and the principal leaders at once. The two parallel authorities of the ghetto knew each other and even saw each other occasionally; but under the circumstances, this summons looked suspicious. Sensing the trap, the directors at first wanted to refuse, but Wittenberg insisted. With his two hundred and fifty men well trained and ready for anything, he felt he was the master of the ghetto He decided to give the order for general mobilization and to go to the Judenrat, where Gens awaited him.

In a quarter of an hour each man was at his post. A sense of pride filled Wittenberg at such efficiency. The two special sections had been ordered to take up positions around the Judenrat building and quietly to disarm the members of the Jewish police who were there. Meanwhile Wittenberg and his staff reported to Gens.

The room was full of policemen.

"Itzak Wittenberg, you are under arrest," said Gens, motioning to his men.

Wittenberg offered no resistance. Gens had expected a scuffle and he was so surprised that he stammered an excuse.

"Excuse me, but the Germans know of your existence and they are threatening to destroy the ghetto if I do not turn you in. Twenty thousand for one. I have no choice."

Wittenberg despised Gens, but he knew that if it had not been Gens, the Germans would have found someone else to do his work. There was no lack of scum in Vilna. He despised him, but he knew that he meant well and that he thought he was acting for the good of the Jewish people, just like himself, Wittenberg, but while one had chosen collaboration, the other had chosen resistance.

He wanted to give him one last chance to undo his terrible mistake, which was driving the Jews to degradation and death.

"Listen to me, Gens. I know you believe you are acting for the good of the Jewish people, but you are wrong, for the Germans have condemned us all. All your acts of cowardice, all your betrayals may postpone the end, but the end is inevitable. We have always suffered greatly, and pogroms have been our daily bread, but what is happening now exceeds the worst we have ever known. Before, they killed us with hatred and without method; today they are exterminating us without hatred but with method, and this is serious. It is no longer men we are up against, it is machines."

Overjoyed to have his prisoner, Gens allowed himself the luxury of listening to him.

"If they still hated us we might try to talk to them, if they had something in particular against us we might try to show them that they are wrong, but they no more hate us than you hate spiders.

64

Our only fault in their eyes is that we exist. We are all dead, Gens—you, me, your son and mine. It is merely a question of chronology. But we still have one thing left to save: our honor."

Gens was moved. He felt very close to Wittenberg, for his concern for the Jewish people was just as great as his own.

"The future may prove you right, Itzak," he answered with sympathy, "and my name may be cursed; and yet something tells me you are wrong. You talk about honor like a Gentile, not like a Jew. Honor for a Jew is honoring God as Moses commanded us to do. In Spain when the Gentiles tried to make us deny our God, we died at the stake. But today it is not our honor that is being threatened, it is our lives."

There was something extraordinary in this discussion about the meaning of honor between two men who were to become and indeed who already were mortal enemies, for circumstances had decreed that one of them must die for the other to live. Gens, if he did not betray Wittenberg, Wittenberg, if Gens betrayed him.

"Therefore, Itzak Wittenberg, I say that you are wrong, because you are mistaken when you talk about Jewish honor. Why God has imposed this punishment on His people I do not know. But one thing I do know, and that is that God cannot want His whole people to be exterminated, for if He wanted that, He would be denying His Word, He would be breaking His Covenant. This is why I know that I am obeying Him even when I betray you in order to save Jewish lives. Moses delivered the Jews from Pharaoh's clutches and Esther from Haman's; perhaps God has chosen me."

Wittenberg looked at him dumfounded, and he felt anger well up in him.

"You are mad, Gens! Mad with pride! You are nothing but a puppet in the hands of the Germans, and you think you are the savior of the Jewish people!"

Hurt, Gens was immediately the "dictator" of the ghetto again.

"I may be mad, but I am master of the ghetto," he said, standing up.

"Not even that," answered Wittenberg, contemptuous.

"Take him away," roared Gens.

The policemen hesitated before Wittenberg's assurance.

"Look who is master of the ghetto," answered Wittenberg, walking to the window and opening it.

Gens came over to his side and whistled softly as he looked out. Silhouettes emerged from all the dark corners. Gens drew back quickly.

Wittenberg motioned to his staff and they walked to the door. As they crossed the threshold Gens shouted with hatred, "I'll get you, Wittenberg! It's you or me!"

War had been declared. The leaders of the resistance proclaimed general mobilization.

Gens did not sleep that night. He saw his whole strategy collapsing because of only one man, when forty thousand had been exterminated in Ponar. What was one man compared to the forty thousand already dead and the twenty thousand who were going to die? He did not care about his own life, he had already sacrificed it for his people, but all his efforts reduced to zero, the ghetto liquidated because of this imbecile who should have gone to the forest if he was so determined to fight! Since he could not count on his police, he considered setting the ghetto against him, but he remembered what the sages had written: "When the idolator says, 'Deliver one of your people to us, we will kill him, but if you refuse we will kill you all,' let all consent to perish and let not one soul of Israel willingly be delivered to the idolator," and he was shaken for a moment.

"It is not possible, it is not possible," he repeated to himself, pacing up and down his room in front of his assistant, who found his chief's scruples pointless.

"Did you say 'not one soul'?" he asked suddenly.

66

"Yes, why?" answered Gens, stopping.

"Well, it isn't his soul they're asking you for, it's his body!"

Gens looked at him, smiling with a certain respect. Then, pensive again, he asked, "Do you think the people will accept your interpretation?"

"They're so afraid, they won't look too closely."

Gens spent the rest of the night preparing the speech he would make the next day to the population of the ghetto so they would betray Wittenberg.

The next day at dawn the police drove through the town, summoning the population to the square in front of the Judenrat. The rumor that the Germans were asking for Wittenberg had already spread, and everyone was terrified.

When Gens appeared at the window of his office, everyone looked up and a great silence fell.

He began with a history of the ghetto. He recalled the terrible raids, the missing relatives, the fear that had reigned, then the calm that the ghetto had known for several months. Then, adopting a tragic tone, he said, "Today this calm is threatened." (The crowd trembled.) "Threatened because of one man." (All bowed their heads, they already knew whom he meant.) "I had warned this man and all his friends, I had shown them the path of duty, but they chose not to listen to me. I left them in peace, for they are Jews like us. But today their imprudence places the life of the whole ghetto in danger. Yesterday I sent for this man and asked him to give himself up to save the ghetto. He refused, thinking, perhaps, that his life is more valuable than ours."

The crowd already knew what he was going to ask of them, and they held their breath. Gens ran his eyes over them for a moment to convey the drama that was taking place inside him. Then suddenly in a different tone, drier, undramatic, he continued,

67

"Yesterday the Gestapo sent for me. They offered me this choice: Wittenberg or the ghetto. Today it is your turn to choose: One man or twenty thousand. Before this evening."

A few shouts of "Kill Wittenberg!" were heard, but they were not echoed.

Wittenberg arrived in the building where his staff had gathered a few minutes after the end of the speech. Everyone knew about it already. People walking in the street had turned their eyes away as they passed him. He was pale.

"The poor people," he said as he sat down. No one answered.

"They are going to desert us. It's insane how the will to live can blind the most lucid." Suddenly he stared at them.

"I can count on you, at least?" he demanded aggressively. They all protested their loyalty.

"Good, then we must work out a strategy."

"We are cornered," someone said. "The revolt has no meaning, now that the ghetto is against us."

"In any case, it will be liquidated some day," interrupted Wittenberg. "Today or in six months, what's the difference? Let us prepare to carry out the prearranged plan."

"The population will blame us for their massacre," said someone else.

"I don't give a damn. What I want is for the Jews to fight back."

Just then a windowpane burst and they heard shouts. "Wittenberg is a coward, he loves his own neck better than the ghetto!" In the street, a band of rowdies had stationed themselves in front of the house.

"Listen, Itzak," said his assistant, "you'd better not stay here. If they found you, we'd be forced to fire to save you, and I'm not sure the men would be capable of firing on Jews."

"You're right," replied Wittenberg. "I am going to disguise myself and I will leave by the secret passage."

He asked for a black dress and a kerchief. He did not say a word as he dressed. But just as he left the room he turned and looking at his comrades, said in a cold voice, "Let one thing be clearly understood between us: I will not give myself up."

They looked down without replying.

When he had gone, someone went to the window and said that Wittenberg was not in the room, that they could come and see for themselves. Then he came back to his chair and sat down.

The silence lasted for a long time.

The youngest broke it to propose that the staff go down into the street and commit suicide.

The silence fell again.

Wittenberg did not dare return to his house. He kept wandering through the streets of the ghetto, gripping the butt of his pistol.

At noon Gens's assistant sent word that the Germans had ordered tanks and planes. The news spread throughout the ghetto. The streets were now being combed by packs of unleashed dogs. The manhunt was beginning.

At two o'clock word was given that the tanks had arrived, and half the ghetto took refuge in their hiding places.

Dr. Ginsberg was coming home when he met Wittenberg's wife with her child. She was crying. She had managed to get away when the Jewish police came to take her as a hostage.

"Hide me," she begged him.

Her son looked at the doctor, his enormous eyes brimming with misery.

The doctor took them to the hiding place in his building. Without recognizing her, the other tenants looked at her with hostility. But the doctor reassured them, saying that he would answer for her.

The roar of the street could be heard even in the shelter. Nobody dared move.

69

Suddenly a voice rose about the din: "Jews in all buildings! In one hour, if Wittenberg is not turned over, the ghetto will be destroyed. Look for him. He is disguised as a woman; he is wearing a black dress and a kerchief on his head. Jews in all buildings! . . ."

The voice moved on, and was replaced by cries of hate. In the shelter a woman said, "My God, make them find him."

Mrs. Wittenberg looked around and read mute consent on every face. She pressed her son's face to her breast. Her eyes were dead. A dry sob broke in her throat.

Wittenberg followed the crowd, trying to camouflage himself. He felt hemmed in. Suddenly, he saw two policemen advancing toward him. He turned around; two more had cut off his retreat. He took two more steps and quickly drew his revolver. He fired and rushed forward. The policemen, surprised, did not have time to react, and he ran past them. But the two who were behind began chasing him, shouting, "It's Wittenberg, catch him." And the crowd rushed after him, yelling. He turned around and fired blind. The din became still louder.

Then he decided to return to the source of the movement.

By the time he arrived he had managed to lose his pursuers, but something had snapped inside him. He walked up to the room in which the staff had been gathered since morning. His assistant came to him and helped him to a chair.

"Itzak," he said, "you must give yourself up."

Wittenberg could not catch his breath. Suddenly he remembered Lydia: "There is no more forest, Itzak, there is nothing, the world is dead." Now he understood what she had meant. What a dream he had had! Honor, heroism—all that had lost its meaning. There was room only for hate, an immense, inextinguishable hate which nothing could ever overcome. But he felt empty even of hate. You must be alive to hate, and he was already dead.

He looked up. His respiration had become normal again.

"You're right," he said in a voice that was already remote. "We don't even have the right to die fighting. We were children, all this is much too big for us." Then, lowering his voice still further, he added indifferently, "Go and find Gens."

During the long silence that followed, his assistant handed him a vial of poison.

Wittenberg looked up as if he were coming out of a dream. "Thank you," he said, and put it in his pocket.

The streets of the ghetto were empty as he walked through them. A Gestapo car was waiting for him at the gate. As he leaned over to get into the car, he lifted his hand quickly to his mouth. A cracking of broken glass was heard. The car door slammed and the car drove away.

Some time later, the ghetto was liquidated.

V

IF THE "PILOT GHETTO" of Vilna had been a success in the "pre-treatment" of the Jews, Ponar, on the other hand, had not completely satisfied the Technicians. The weaknesses of the system had rapidly become evident, and it was condemned as suitable only for such local camps as Babi Yar, for the treatment of the Jews of Kiev, or Janowska, for the Jews of Lwow.

The inadequacies of the system, which were of two kinds, technical and psychological, had to do with the method of execution, shooting. In the first place, shooting produced a low output, and in the second place, it created a relationship between the executioner and the victim which was prejudicial to the former's morale.

The method of shooting in itself gave rise to controversy among the Technicians, who were divided into two schools: the "classics" and the "moderns." The first were advocates of the regulation firing squad at twelve paces and the *coup de grâce* given by the squad leader. The second, who felt that this classic apparatus did not correspond to the facts of the new situation, preferred the simple bullet in the back of the neck. The latter method finally prevailed, because of its efficiency. It was here that the psychological problems vividly emerged.

With a firing squad you never knew who killed whom. The new system, on the contrary, personalized the act. Each executioner had "his" victims. It was no longer squad number such-and-such that acted, but rifleman so-and-so. Moreover, this personalization of the act was accompanied by a physical proximity, since the executioner stood less than a yard away from his victim. Of course, he did not see him from the front, but it was discovered that necks, like faces, also individualize people. This accumulation of necks—suppliant, proud, fearful, broad, frail, hairy, or tanned—rapidly became intolerable to the executioners, who could not help feeling a certain sense of guilt. Like blind faces, these necks came to haunt their dreams. Paradoxically, it was from the executioners and not from the victims that the difficulties arose. Hence, the Technicians took them seriously

Thus there arose, no doubt for the first time in the world, the problem of how to liquidate people by the millions. Today the solution seems obvious, and no one asks himself the question. In 1941, it was quite otherwise. The few historical precedents were of no use, whether it was a question of the extermination of the Indians by the Spaniards in South America or by the Americans in the United States, or again of the Armenians by the Turks at the beginning of this century. In these three cases, no attempt had been made at a new technique, no advance beyond the time-honored hanging and shooting which, as we have seen, did not satisfy the Technicians.

It was necessary to invent a killing machine. With a methodical spirit that is now well known to us, the Technicians defined its specifications. It had to be inconspicuous to avoid arousing anxiety in the victims or curiosity in the witnesses, and efficient enough to be on a par with the great plans of the originators of the Final Solution; it had to reduce handling to a minimum; and finally, it had to assure a peaceful death for the victims.

Long months passed before the legendary "Eureka!" was heard. It was a certain Becker who uttered it. He had devised a van in which the exhaust pipe fed into the interior of the back part, which was hermetically sealed. The victims were killed by carbon monoxide. Becker, who had made a certain number of experiments before sending the plan through official channels, had calculated that by observing a certain ratio between the cylinder capacity of the motor of the van and the volume of the sealed chamber in which the victims were imprisoned, the latter should die peacefully by going to sleep within ten to fifteen minutes, given a motor running at moderate speed. Consequently, he suggested that ditches be dug about ten miles from the points of concentration of the Jews, which would allow the vans, driving twenty-five miles an hour, to reach them with a security margin of five to ten minutes. Finally, he proposed a certain number of details, such as *trompe-l'oeil* windows painted on the inside of the van to bolster the credulity of the victims on the very threshold of death. Becker claimed that thanks to his system the victims would die without anyone being aware of it, not even the "parties involved."

The Technicians were immediately attracted by the simplicity and rationality of the plan. They began to carry it out at once. The first gas vans were put into service in early spring, 1942. Their brief career was to be a series of disappointments for poor Becker.

Less than a month after the vans had begun to replace shooting, reports of complaints began to reach Berlin. The grievance that cropped up in all the reports charged the gas vans with killing the victims badly. The spectacle they presented when the doors were opened was so hideous, the reports specified, that the S.S. men had to get drunk to stand it. Becker, to whom the complaints were passed on, his creative pride wounded, decided to visit the scene. What he saw convinced him that it is more difficult to kill people than one might suppose. Here again, it was not the ill will of the victims that was at issue, but the human inadequacy of the executioners. The drivers of his vans, affected by the nature of the trip they were providing for their passengers, covered the required distance by pressing down on the accelerator, in order to rid themselves more rapidly of their sinister cargo. Thus the victims, instead of going peacefully to sleep, died in terrible agony and offered after their death the indecent spectacle of which their executioners complained.

After trying in vain to reason with the drivers by explaining that in the interest of the victims as well as of their comrades, they must drive slowly, Becker was preparing to modify his invention by mounting the back portion of the van on a tilting platform, when he was dismissed.

This problem with the drivers had made a very bad impression in high places, where it was felt that there was no point investing so much money in a method which in no way solved the psychological problems raised by the technique of shooting. Becker's star waned. It disappeared altogether when the order was given for the liquidation of the Warsaw ghetto.

The ghetto of Warsaw was a formidable concentration of four hundred thousand Jews. Its extermination required the creation of installations equal to its size. The Becker truck, with its fifteen to twenty seats according to the type of the truck, could not possibly assume such a task. The Technicians began looking again. But they were no longer working from scratch: they had two files at their disposal, that of the local camp of the Ponar type, and that of the Becker truck. They compared them. The Technicians of Ponar had solved the problem of handling of bodies by entrusting the job to Jews especially selected for the purpose. But this was possible only within the context of a fixed installation. Becker, on the other hand, had solved the problem of the confrontation with the necks of the victims. The solution came in two stages. A "researcher," whose name history has unfortunately lost, had the idea of putting the Becker truck in a camp of the

75

Ponar type. This solution, which solved the theoretical problems, also took care of the question of output. The limited size of the sealed chamber was due to the fact that it had to be mobile, but as soon as it was no longer the chamber that came to the Jews but the Jews who came to the chamber, nothing prevented its being enlarged, and nothing obliged it to remain on wheels. In short, what had to be constructed was a hermetically sealed building supplied with gas by a motor. The first gas chamber was born. It was still a long way to the ultramodern chambers of Auschwitz using Zyklon B gas, but the road was open. The rest was only a matter of working out the details.

With the gas chamber, amateurism, guesswork and the mistakes inherent in all innovations came to an end. The Final Solution entered the era of modern technology. The machine came to man's aid, engineering took over where good will left off. An almost perfect system had been created. A new world was about to be born.

Before the war, on the Siedlec-Malkinia Railway not far from the great axis running from Warsaw to Bialystok, there was a forgotten little station with the strange and beautiful name of Treblinka. It rose unexpectedly in a damp, sandy plain dotted with little pine woods and marshes. Situated near the German-Soviet boundary drawn by the armistice of September 28, 1939, it had been snatched from oblivion by the preparation for the invasion of the U.S.S.R. in June 1941. At that time its strategic position had earned it a visit from a certain number of German military leaders. As luck would have it, they were accompanied by a few Technicians, who were immediately struck by the site of this mysterious and abandoned region. So it was that in August 1941, near a gravel quarry served by a special branch of the Siedlec-Malkinia Railway, they set up a mixed work camp for Jews and Poles.

In the spring of 1942, when it was necessary to create a large extermination camp for the Jews of Warsaw, the Technicians remembered this little station lost in the middle of the wasteland.

After a rapid inspection of the premises, they settled on a piece of land some eight acres in area, bounded on the south by the branch line serving the gravel quarry, and cut off from the Siedlec-Malkinia Railway and the Kossow-Malkinia highway to the north by a little oblong hill covered with pine trees, which screened it from prying eyes.

Since D-day for the deportation of the Jews from Warsaw had been symbolically set for the ninth of the month of Ab, the anniversary of the destruction of the Temple, which corresponded that year to the twenty-second of July, work was begun immediately.

The heavy work was assigned to the prisoners of the work camp. They constructed a second set of tracks starting from the ones that led to the quarry, a row of barracks, and a substantial building containing three gas chambers, and dug some large ditches. The prisoners erected a barbed-wire enclosure around the whole. Then they were executed and replaced by Jews whom the Technicians selected especially in the neighboring hamlets of Wengrow, Stoczek, and Wingrowski. These Jews, who were earmarked from the start to take care of the functioning of the camp, the handling of the bodies and the maintenance of the installations, formed the first nucleus of a new class which would be condemned not to die, but to suffer the passion of the Jewish people beyond extermination. As the witnesses and accomplices of this extermination, only one thing mattered to them at the time: to live, no matter what the cost. Morally broken by the conditioning process they had been subjected to in the ghettos, they were ready to do anything in order to live. But this will to live was more than the manifestation of an instinct of self-preservation, and it was by failing to understand this that the Technicians made their first mistake.

For a Jew, survival is more than a desire, it is a duty. Rabbi

Isaac Niessenbaum of Warsaw, one of the shining lights of Polish Judaism, had formally defined this duty. Within the context of their campaign of demoralization, the Technicians had set up a large number of arms factories in the Warsaw ghetto. In order to escape the raids, the Jews had to have work certificates. To obtain these they had to be hired by one of these factories, and thus help their enemies in their war effort. What should they do? Help the enemy in an effort to survive, or agree to die rather than compromise themselves by helping the enemy? They asked Rabbi Isaac Niessenbaum this question. "To live is a *Mitzvah*," he replied. "When they attacked our souls, we joyously mounted the funeral pyres for the sanctification of the Name. But now that it is our bodies they are after, the time of the sanctification of Life begins."

Was there an element of cowardice in the attitude of the Jewish masses, who preferred to suffer the worst degradation rather than revolt? Given the terrible conditions created by the fierce anti-Semitism of the local population and by the science of the Technicians, the masses had little incentive to resist. A revolt in the name of the honor of the Jewish people, which the young Zionists urged, did not touch the deepest chords in them: the people of the Bible placed their self-respect on an infinitely higher level. But revolt may also be born of despair, of the feeling that there is nothing left, that life has lost its meaning. In this case it is no longer a revolt for the sake of something, some ideal or other, but a revolt against nothingness. But the Jew, the real Jew, raised only on Jewish culture, though he may be susceptible to anguish, is inaccessible to despair.

Lydia had died after assassinating an S.S. officer.

Itzak Wittenberg was dead, betrayed by those for whom he had chosen to die.

Dan Ariel managed to leave the ghetto before its liquidation with the remnants of the organization. In the forests of Lithuania he waged a fierce and desperate struggle to prove to the Germans, the partisans, the Poles, the Jews, to history, and also to himself that the Jews were not cowards. But the real enemy he was fighting was inside himself, and he put as much passion into dying as the others put into surviving.

Those who wanted to live realized that humiliation was only one method of the Technicians, and that it was not against humiliation that they had to struggle, but against death. This choice was a dangerous one. It opened the way to all those repudiations that made the Jews the Germans' accomplices in their work of extermination. The consequences of this choice threatened to compromise the name of Jew so irrevocably that some day not a single Jew might want to bear it. On that day, the victory of the Technicians would be complete.

The first convoy left Warsaw the evening of the twenty-second of July and reached Treblinka the morning of the twenty-fourth. It was a beautiful summer's day and the air was still heavy with heat when the first train of twenty cars left the section of track serving the quarry and pulled slowly into Treblinka.

As soon as they had landed, the men were separated from the women and children. As nonsalvagable material, the latter, after they had undressed, were taken to the "shower." Everything happened very quickly and without incident.

For the men it took a little longer, because S.S. Untersturmführer Max Bielas wanted to select two hundred to help with the functioning of the machine. He could have taken the first two hundred or the last two hundred or even two hundred at random, but this would have been acting indiscriminately. He wanted the two hundred slaves to be of a certain kind: driven by a powerful desire to live, very strong physically, and finally, workers. This is how he had defined the dominant traits of the last Jews, the Jews of Death. To carry out this selection he had devised four aptitude tests. The final game was to be played in four heats.

79

The first ordeal was easy, it was a test of minimum education. "Skilled workers, take one step forward!" The majority realized that skilled workers, being useful, had a better chance of being well treated than the others. As obviously no diploma or certificate was required, only those who had already been too broken by the period in the ghetto to have any desires left stayed where they were. They were led to the gas chambers, where their wives were finishing their showers.

The second test, designed to confuse the candidates and eliminate shirkers, was much more difficult: "All those who speak German, take another step forward!" Actually all could claim to speak German, since they knew Yiddish. The shrewdest sensed the trap; the others, foreseeing jobs as interpreters, moved forward: "No dice!" They were taken away in turn.

Four hundred candidates reached the third ordeal. It was a test of psychological and physical resistance. Lined up in five rows, they were surrounded by Ukrainians armed with whips and guns. Max Bielas, planting himself in front of them, explained the idea of the maneuver.

"Jews," he told them, "you are going to be beaten with whips and rifle butts. Those who fall will be shot; the others will be spared. If any of you prefer to give up now, they have the right to do so. I disapprove of unnecessary violence and I authorize them to step out of line. When I count ten, we will begin."

There was a profound silence. Every man was tempted to step out of line and join his family, to be done with it once and for all, but a mysterious force impelled them not to move, to wait, to play the game of survival to the very end. Max Bielas, rigid and impeccable in his black uniform, stared at them. His slightly bloated face gave him a look both elegant and depraved. From a distance, his washed-out-blue eyes resembled those of a blind man.

Fascinated, Meir Berliner studied Max Bielas. In the two years since he had returned to Warsaw to look for his parents, he had still not grown used to what was happening to him. Born in Warsaw, he had left the Polish capital at the age of thirteen after secretly reading a letter from his uncle to his father in which he said to come and join him in Argentina. As his father never mentioned the letter, Meir had understood that his parents did not want to leave, and he had run away one morning without saying goodbye and with his uncle's address scrawled on a scrap of paper which was his sole possession. It had taken him two years to reach Buenos Aires, but he knew English and Spanish by the time he arrived. At twenty he had made his first million, and at twenty-five he had had his first son. His wife was expecting a sixth child when he left Argentina to come and look for his parents. The nightmare had begun when the war caught him in Warsaw. With his Argentinian passport he could have left Poland, but he had not wanted to leave without his parents, because of the way his mother had looked at him when he came home. She would not have welcomed him so warmly if he had been the Messiah himself. While she kissed his hands, his father had stared at him, muttering incoherently. That night he had slept in his old bed again. After that, it had been the ghetto. Thinking that his passport would protect him from the raids, he had not taken any precautions, even when troops of Ukrainians and S.S. had overrun the ghetto. He had been arrested in the street and had received nothing but blows in exchange for his recriminations. On the *Umschlagplatz* they had taken away his passport, his watch and his money, and he had understood.

As he looked at Bielas, Meir Berliner again saw his parents, his wife, his children. Suddenly he saw Max Bielas grow rigid and slowly begin to raise his arm. He pulled in his head, his ears began to ring. He heard a hoarse shout and his head exploded under the blows.

So great was the Jews' will to live that the third ordeal lasted over a quarter of an hour, and by then it was not necessary to shoot those who had fallen. Combatants in a new war, they had died on their feet.

The final test lasted until evening. Survivors of the third ordeal were divided into two groups. One was sent to transport the bodies from the gas chambers to the ditches, the other to carry the clothing to a large open place where it was to be piled. They had to do everything while running, without stopping once. Those who faltered or who did not carry large enough bundles were hit on the face, marked like trees that are to be felled—which they were at the end of the day.

Night fell as the last body was thrown into the ditch. Unconscious, the survivors, who were no more than two hundred, were each given a tin of warm water in which there floated a few pieces of potato. Few could eat. Then they were shut into a barracks with a sand floor. Treblinka was one day old.

After the blows had begun to fall, Meir Berliner had lived like an automaton. He had felt strangely calm and lucid. He had had a sense of having arrived—he had not known where or why, but he had felt that it was all over, that even if he managed to survive for a few days, he would never leave Treblinka.

A group of men collected in one corner of the barracks and began to recite the evening prayer. Their voices droned in the profound calm that had succeeded the tumult of the day. Berliner dozed off.

Gradually other voices mingled with those of the group; everyone wanted to say the *Kaddish* for the members of his family who had died during the day. By reawakening their pain, the prayer brought them a kind of consolation. Men who had long since ceased to believe or to pray rediscovered the words of the prayer for the dead: *Yiskaddal veyiskaddash* . . . The words flowed soothingly, like tears. God had become a necessity and they reinvented him, revived him from the bottoms of their memories.

God lived in the prayers, and because they did not want to leave Him, they did not want to stop praying. But the moments of relief were interrupted by sudden relapses into pain, and the voices rose, threatening, questioning, accusing.

Meir Berliner awakened with a start, his face drenched with perspiration. It took him a few seconds to remember where he was and to realize where these voices came from. Suddenly a terrible fury seized him.

"Shut up," he shouted. "Stop going through these ridiculous motions. To whom are you addressing this *Kaddish?* Whom are you glorifying?"

The murmur which had paused for an instant, resumed.

"What God? What mercy? Fall on your murderers if you want to do something, but cease these useless prayers."

The unbroken murmur exasperated Berliner. He wanted to hurt them.

"Is it for taking our fathers and mothers, for killing our children that you are blessing His name? No, it's not true, God does not exist, for if He did exist and could allow such a tragedy, He would be the Devil."

In the dark a man had come over to Berliner and grabbed his arm. His name was Pinhas Alter, he was a Hasid. His whole family had been gassed during the day. His faith was so great that he saw this ordeal as a further mark of God's concern for men. He had decided to live in order to discover the mystical meaning of this catastrophe.

"Our sages have taught us," he said in a dull voice, "to love the Lord, blessed be His Name, in the mercies that He grants us as in the punishments that He sends."

"Let me go!" exclaimed Berliner, turning violently away. "Keep your idiocies to yourself!"

But the religious man pressed him even harder. He had the inspired face of a fanatic. There was not the slightest trace of softness or gentleness in him. Berliner hesitated.

83

The other sensed this and said, "Too many Jews are abandoning Judaism. This may be a warning. We do not have the right to break the Covenant."

A few men had gathered around them, listening. Berliner's anger had receded and he felt consumed by despair.

"If God is punishing the Jewish people because they are abandoning the Law, why does He also punish those who observe it? Why are you here, you who live only in His Dread! If only unbelievers were punished I would understand, but no one is spared, neither wise men nor children."

He thought to himself that the argument was pointless, that this was neither the time nor the place to discuss theology, and he was surprised to see these men gathered around them.

The religious man argued by observing the forms of the Talmudic *pilpul*. He made frequent references to tradition.

"The old rabbis," he said, "believed that when a Jew leaves the community of Israel, the whole community is in mourning. We are all involved in what every Jew does."

Berliner did not feel like arguing any more. It seemed to him that they did not speak the same language. He fell back and closed his eyes. He felt even more alone and desperate.

The religious man had stood up again. He looked at Berliner as if he were hesitating and then said, "Treblinka is the abyss. One cannot live here without God."

Without opening his eyes Berliner murmured, "I do not want to live. *I want revenge.*" It was the first time he had thought of it, but suddenly this idea filled his whole being.

The next day they were awakened before dawn and chased out of the barracks with whips. Men whose faces were marked by the blows and who had escaped the inspection of the previous day were taken away.

The last survivors were standing in line before a portable field kitchen when they heard the whistle of a locomotive. The blows, which had stopped for a few moments, began to fall again. That day a new contingent was selected. It underwent the same tests. This would go on for months. But whereas you took the first three only once, the fourth was permanent. This was the era of the "black eye." Although very primitive, this system offered the Technicians a certain number of advantages. In addition to the obvious one of being able to recognize unmistakably and thus to eliminate poor workers, it created in the prisoners a kind of "face complex," which either led them to their own destruction or reduced them to a level of absolute subhumanity.

The prisoner had two ways to avoid being marked. The first consisted in demonstrating his zeal, in working without allowing himself a single second of respite. But since he could never know whether the bundle he chose would be considered large enough or the body sufficiently substantial (the "clever" at first chose women and children, which caused them all to be marked), the prisoner was inclined to go beyond his strength, whose limit was his only criterion. Given the living conditions—beatings, lack of sleep, inadequate nourishment, which often he could not even touch—this constant effort to outdo himself condemned the prisoner to death by exhaustion, and this all the more rapidly, the greater his zeal.

The prisoners quickly realized the danger and they perfected a technique of survival. Since they could avoid being marked only by knowingly condemning themselves to a death that was different but just as certain, they tried to protect their faces. This "ostrich strategy" lead them to the "face complex," which is precisely what the Technicians wanted. These prisoners, who were already without names or even numbers, lost their faces. They became "forked sticks." Slaves of an entirely new species were born. They formed a working force of two hundred units, which was almost completely renewed every week.

85

VI

THE DIRECTORS OF the camp were pleased with their human material. Conditioned in the ghetto, screened by Max Bielas' tests, obsessed by the fear of being marked, the prisoners could only be a malleable dough. One detail seemed significant to the Technicians. It was only a minor incident, but most revealing, in their eyes, of the abjection of the Jews.

The scene had been very brief. A child who had arrived in one of the convoys had recognized his father among the Jews who were carrying the clothing of the victims, and he had rushed over to him. The child, who was very young, must have been arrested alone on the streets of Warsaw, and he had no idea what sort of place he was in. From the way his face lit up when he recognized his father, the S.S. man who noticed the scene concluded that the child had been looking for him since their separation. There was no astonishment on the child's face, only joy. At the sight of such innocence the S.S. man had almost been moved, and he had walked over when the father, dropping the pile of clothing he was carrying, took his son in his arms.

"Papa," murmured the child, "I knew I would find you again. When you disappeared, they tried to comfort me, as if I would never see you again. So I ran into the streets to look for you. Then they took me away in a train. I was very thirsty and a little afraid. And now I have found you again. I knew I would!"

But the father had seen the guard approaching and he tried to interrupt his son. "Yes, yes," he murmured in a voice that was gentle and trembling with emotion.

The son had raised his head and was looking at his father. "You look sad," he said, "like the people in the train."

"No, it's nothing. But now you must go and take your shower with the others," replied the father in a voice which he tried to make reassuring.

"But I don't want to leave you again," said the son in his clear voice.

"Go, go, I'll see you in a minute."

The father stood up again and looked at the guard covertly. He was motionless. Life had come to a stop for the few seconds the scene had lasted. The child had gone away. The father bent down, gathered the pile of clothing, straightened up, seemed to hesitate for a fraction of a second, then suddenly pulled in his head and left at a run.

When the scene had been reported to the commandant of the camp, he had been very much impressed.

"The sacrifice of Abraham," he had murmured.

He was a former minister who had found his true vocation in the S.S. Tall, slightly round-shouldered, and balding in front, he had a handsome, intelligent face. He knew Hebrew to perfection and sometimes discussed certain contested points of translation with one of the prisoners. During the first ten days of Treblinka he had never laid a hand on a prisoner. His long black silhouette roamed pensively over every inch of the camp, showing a predilection for the exits to the gas chambers, to which he returned incessantly, as if driven against his will. He looked silently and left reluctantly. At these moments his face became confused and an intense struggle seemed to be taking place in him.

Then one day as he was returning from one of these visits, he had attacked a prisoner. He had hit him so furiously that he knocked an eye out of its socket. But he had calmed down immediately and had even seemed distressed. He had ordered that a doctor be found among the prisoners. The doctor had told him that the wounded man was doomed; the few days he could be kept alive would only be days of suffering. The commandant had answered that he would hold him responsible for his death, and strode away. That evening he had gone to see the wounded man and had finished him off with a bullet in the temple. Since then he had consistently attacked every prisoner he met. He had also devised a certain number of tortures whose refinement even impressed the other S.S. The rest of the staff of the camp did not like him very much. Kurt Franz, a young noncommissioned S.S. officer who was destined for a brilliant future, dismissed him as "an intellectual."

The former minister's Biblical interpretation had not, therefore, had much success among his colleagues, for whom the story was merely a commonplace proof of Jewish cowardice.

"Of their submissiveness," the commandant had concluded.

The theological sense being, strangely enough, somewhat rare in the average S.S. man, the discussion had ended there. All the Technicians were in agreement on the practical implications of such an incident, namely, that they had nothing to fear from the Jews.

Since the discipline problem was apparently solved, the Technicians addressed themselves to the material organization of the camp, in order to bring its output up to what was expected of it.

In the minds of its creators, Treblinka, like the five other extermination camps, Auschwitz, Majdanek, Sobibor, Belsec, and Chelmno, had a double vocation: extermination and recovery. Extermination of the Jews and recovery of their clothing, money, assets and various objects which they had managed to bring with them. For the Technicians, recovery was no less important than extermination, and Himmler himself personally insisted that it be handled with the greatest care. Having observed in the course of a visit to the General Government of Poland that "hundreds of thousands, even millions of watch crystals were being thrown away, when they could have been turned over to German watchmakers," and shocked by this waste, he wrote his colleagues Krüger and Pohl: "I believe that in each and every respect we cannot be too meticulous. . . . I beg S.S. Oberguppenführer Pohl to work out and regulate these matters in every detail, for the care we use now will spare us much trouble later on."

An auxiliary activity of extermination, recovery (which may be compared to the reprocessing of by-products in normal industry) required not only an excellent organization of the work, but also a more specialized and more extensive manpower. So it was that at Treblinka, where up to now nothing but chaos had reigned, the first suggestion of social organization among the prisoners was born.

Before that day in late August on which Treblinka celebrated its first month of existence, its society had been divided into three absolutely airtight classes: that of the masters, the Technicians; that of the assistant masters, the Ukrainian guards; and finally, that of the slaves, the Jews. This last class formed a completely undifferentiated subhumanity that had lost all notion of family, social life, time, and even of space. The units of which it was composed lived in an intermediate state which, because of its immobility, had every appearance of death, but was nevertheless bound, by a flicker and an imperceptible breath, to life. In this species of social and biological Nirvana the multiple divisions of time—past, present, future, hours, days, weeks, years—had been reduced to the simple distinction between night and day. Even pain had disappeared. Prayer had been stilled. Probably never except during mystical experiences had men been so utterly cut off from the outside world, enslaved body and soul. They were told to run and they ran, to dance and they danced, to speak and they spoke, to sing and they sang. If they had been told to kill they would have done so. *Perinde ac cadaver:* the Technicians had fashioned the absolute subhuman, the ideal slave, obedient as a corpse.

There was another side to the coin: the success was too complete. After a month of treatment, the Jews had reached such a point of insensibility and automatism that they no longer reacted to blows or threats. They were incapable of performing slightly complicated actions. If they were ordered to march, they marched; but as soon as the order was complicated by a second action, their minds ceased to register. It was impossible, for example, to order them to go to a certain place, get a certain object and take it to another place. To get such a simple action performed it was necessary to give three orders: "Go there!" then "Pick that up!" then "Take it over there!" And even then it was necessary to point to the object and not merely to name it, for the prisoners were incapable of the slightest judgment.

As for blows, they did not seem to feel them. Thus, a prisoner allowed himself to be chopped to bits with a shovel without a sound or gesture. The commandant of the camp had caught him, during one of his visits to the exits of the gas chambers, wandering through a pile of bodies with a pair of pliers in his hand, wild-eyed. Although up to then his job had been carrying clothing, that morning he had been chosen as a "dentist" to extract gold teeth. He had been a quiet, gentle man, a good Jew, a good father and a good husband. He had arrived in Treblinka with his whole family, and he had never understood what force had compelled him to claim that he was a carpenter. After spending his first night saying the *Kaddish*, he had fallen into a state of catalepsy in order to escape the horror of the situation. Since then, he had been sustained only by that mysterious and ancient will to live which had helped his ancestors survive all the empires, all the tempests, all their enemies, and all their friends, all those who had told them, "Die, Jew!" and all those who had told them, "Live, my brother. You are a man like all men!" No one remembers his name; the oral tradition of camp Treblinka has kept only the memory of a round face that seemed made to smile, two eyes with a lost expression, and a short and weary silhouette. He had been brought to this secluded corner where the bodies were piled after leaving the gas chambers and before being dragged to the big ditches. A pair of pliers had been placed in his hand, and he had been told to open all the mouths and to extract any gold teeth that might be in them, but he had not understood, it was much too difficult for him. With the pliers dangling from his hand, he had wandered among the bodies, murmuring the *Kaddish* for all these dead brothers. As they passed, the S.S. and the Ukrainian guards hit him a few times, which stopped his murmur for a moment.

The sight of him had plunged the commandant of the camp into a great agitation. He had asked him why he was not working, but the prisoner had not answered. He had ordered him to work, and the prisoner had not reacted. Then he had grabbed him and hit him with his riding crop, but the man had not even winced. The fury of the commandant, which was multiplied tenfold by the presence of the bodies, had then exceeded all bounds. He had ordered an S.S. guard to get a shovel and had had the Jew dragged to the middle of the yard. At first the prisoner had remained transfixed, but the first blow had knocked him to the ground. The commandant had ordered him to get up, and he had stood up. His severed arm hung limp, drops of blood fell swift and heavy from the tips of his fingers. The second blow landed on his head. The only sounds were the woodcutter's grunt of the S.S. guard and the impact of the blow on the skull. The other workers went by, carrying their bodies without a glance of curiosity, without a gesture of emotion. When he did not get up again, the commandant began to yell more and more shrilly, then he grabbed the shovel out of the S.S. man's hands and began to hit him. When he had recovered his calm, there was nothing left of the "dentist."

The incident proved that the ill will of the Jews was neither conscious nor contrived. On the contrary, it was evident that this human material was altogether inadequate for the work that was expected of it. This explains the emergence of specialization, the first outlines of social life at Treblinka.

This organization took place on two levels: the formation of social classes corresponding to the different tasks, and the formation of hierarchies within these classes. The tasks allotted to the prisoners fell roughly into three categories: the handling of the bodies; the handling of the living and their possessions; and finally, the upkeep of the camp.

Those who handled the bodies, those who took them out of the gas chambers, extracted their teeth, and carried them to the ditches, had jobs of a very special nature. Their administration required extreme vigilance. Indeed, the Technicians did not know what to expect from men living under such conditions. They decided to isolate them in a camp within the camp itself, in a kind of dungeon, sanctuary, or holy of holies. They were called the *Totenjuden*, "Jews of Death."

This second camp, which was of much smaller dimensions, was located in the northeast corner of the general camp. Bounded on the south by the building containing the gas chambers, it was surrounded by a sand embankment two and a half yards high, on which a barbed-wire fence was erected. Two exits led to this camp, one at the west reserved for S.S. personnel and Ukrainians, and another to the south to accommodate Jews going to the gas chambers, which the Technicians called the "road to heaven." Within this Camp Number Two a barracks was constructed in which the workers were locked up at night. Around this barracks was erected another enclosure, surrounded by a barbed-wire fence, in which the Jews were penned during lunch hour and between the end of the working day and lights out. It was decided that nobody would ever leave this triple enclosure, and the Jews called the western exit "the road of no return."

The great majority of the prisoners remained in Camp Number One, in the barracks between the platform where the convoys arrived and the gas chamber. East of this barracks was the "roll-call square," where shipments undressed; further east an enormous open space where the objects and clothing were stocked. This was called the "junk square," the "sorting square," or, more often, the "square." These prisoners acquired the name of *Platzjuden*, "Jews of the square." They were divided into a certain number of work commandos, which corresponded to the various activities which the Technicians decided to assign to them.

The work commando of the railway station, or "blue" commando, was in charge of greeting the convoys, herding the Jews out of the cars, collecting their baggage, and cleaning the cars. The task of the "red" commando was to help the convoys undress and to carry their clothing to the sorting square. The work of these two commandos obviously had an indelicate side, since they participated directly in the final process of liquidation. This method which consists in making the victims the accomplices of their own executioners was a kind of dogma to the Technicians. It was for the sake of this principle that they had made Vilna destroy itself, and it must be admitted that the results had been more than satisfying.

In their desire to push specialization to the maximum, the

Technicians set up as many sorting commandos as there were kinds of objects: a clothing commando, a linen commando, a dishes commando, a pen commando, a tool commando, a fur commando, et cetera. The variety of objects brought by these people who were coming to be exterminated may be surprising: it is the proof of the inability of the Jewish masses to accept the reality of extermination. This variety was even greater later on, when, after Poland had been "cleared" of Jews, the Technicians hunted them down in Czechoslovakia, Bulgaria, Germany, and Greece. At this time the sorting square became a kind of flea market, an amazing storehouse where clothing and musical instruments were found next to artificial legs and dentist's chairs.

The Jews in charge of the sorting of gold, money, various securities, deeds, jewels, et cetera, had a special status. They were called *Goldjuden*, "Jews of gold." Their center was a shed to which everything was brought in bulk, but they had a certain number of fixed or mobile stations from which they collected raw materials. The head office was located on the square where the men from the convoys undressed. This office had two branches, one in the shed where the women undressed and the other in the middle of the "road to heaven." On the square and in the shed, the *Goldjuden* merely went among the arrivals with suitcases and asked them to hand over their stocks, jewels, et cetera. On the "road to heaven" it was the final inspection. This advanced post consisted of a cabin in which men and women were subjected to an intimate search. Besides the head office, there was on the sorting square a secondary office whose employees had to pass among the sorting commandos, who turned over to them whatever gold, silver, securities, and jewels they found in the clothing and baggage. Only the mouths of the arrivals were exempt from the *Goldjuden*. The Technicians had decided it was easier to extract gold teeth from the dead than from the living. This arrangement necessitated a control operation at the exits from the gas

94

chambers. It was more reasonable, therefore, to have the "dentists," while they were at it, collect any jewels that the Jews had hidden in their mouths. This gold and these jewels which the commando of Camp Number Two collected were then sent back to the *Goldjuden* after the preliminary work of sorting and cleaning the gold teeth.

A certain number of other commandos were also set up: a "camouflage" commando, whose mission was to decorate the barbed wire with branches which it gathered in the forest, to conceal the existence of the camp from airplanes; a construction commando in an embryonic state which was, however, to have a brilliant future; a garbage commando; finally, a commando of woodcutters in charge of furnishing timber to the construction commando.

Many of these commandos existed only as cadres, with work forces varying from zero to fifty according to need, but the foundations of the future organization had been laid.

Finally, at the top of the social scale, a class of aristocrats was created: the *Hofjuden,* or "court Jews." These were the first Jews brought to Treblinka before its inauguration. Their responsibility was the upkeep of the camp and the personal service of the Technicians. They were lodged in huts several hundred yards west of the compound formed by the sorting square, roll-call square, the "road to heaven" and the building housing the gas chambers, which had acquired the name "the factory." This place was still wooded, and it was necessary to clear the land in order to construct the huts. Since the terrain sloped down slightly toward the huts, the place came to be referred to as "Below," whereas the compound was referred to as "Above." To indicate the horror of the situation of the Jews in Camp Number Two and their isolation from everything, it was called "Down There." Thus, parallel to the social structure, a geographic structure of the camp was born: "Below," "Above," "Down There"; "Court Jews," "Square Jews,"

95

"Jews of Death": aristocrats, masses, untouchables.

But the Technicians were remorseless organizers. Their great ambition was for the camp to run itself. In Vilna, as later in all the other ghettos, they had controlled the situation of the Jews in such a way that, whatever they might do or try to do, they would continue to advance in the desired direction. Now it was necessary to create an analogous situation at Treblinka. This desire for rationalization combined with a concern for detail clearly illuminates the grandeur of the machine and the disconcerting power of a technique which, in its constant and unsatisfied search for perfection, even utilized human imperfections for its ends. Carried to this level, technique becomes an art which engenders its own aesthetic, its own morality, and even its own metaphysic.

Kurt Franz, the great promoter of these reforms, had defined the goal to be attained as follows: "We must reach the point where we no longer have to do anything, not even press a button when we get up in the morning. We create a perfect system, then we watch it work. As masters, our role is not to do but to be." Of course the remark is mere rhetoric, but how revealing, in its infinite pride, of the Technicians' desire to recreate a world.

In order for the camp to run by itself it was necessary, as in Vilna, to organize it for self-administration. The Jews themselves had to become responsible for output as well as for discipline. The easy solution would have been to give the rank of *kapo* to a few bullies—easy, but limited, for to be obeyed, a leader must be respected. Now, the demands of output required of the prisoners a certain zeal which only respected leaders could impose. Besides, bullies, by their brutality and arbitrariness, might put pressure on the prisoners and, who knows, even drive them to some regrettable extremities. Of course, the solution of appointing respected leaders also had its dangers. Their rank of leaders, by more or less protecting them from physical violence, would release them from the perpetual pressure of fear and might one day

96

enable them to take the lead in some kind of movement. The Technicians had weighed the risk, but their experience with the ghettos had taught them that a man who had knowingly compromised himself did not revolt against his masters, no matter what idea had driven him to collaboration: too many mutual skeletons in the closet. Tcherniakow, president of the Warsaw Judenrat, had committed suicide in July of the same year when he had at last faced the true nature of the deportations. Gens, in Vilna, had refused to run away when he had learned that he was condemned to death. These were so many proofs of the absolute obedience that could be expected of men of honor who had drifted into collaboration.

Gens's end was even more characteristic, perhaps, than Tcherniakow's.

After the death of Wittenberg, the Technicians, who had no further need of Gens and decided to part company with him, sent for him. But, as they learned later, an indiscretion had been committed, and Gens had discovered their plans. His assistant had paid highly for the information, but when he had come to tell him to run away, Gens had replied in his rather pompous tone which ceased that day to be ridiculous and attained tragic nobility: "My dear Dessler, one must be logical with oneself. My whole policy could be justified only if I was right. Today, I realize that I was wrong. My life has no more meaning." Then he had put on his fine ridiculous uniform and his extraordinary False Messiah's cap, and had gone to his last meeting with the Technicians.

The blueprint for Treblinka provided for a Jewish commandant, two *kapo*-leaders (one per camp), and one *kapo* assisted by two foremen for each commando.

Kurt Franz took charge of the selection. He immediately encountered great difficulties, for if volunteers abounded among the riffraff, they were rare among the respectable Jews.

To make up for this semi-deficiency on the part of the leadership, Kurt Franz proved intractable on the choice of the "commandant," whom he wanted to be of first quality. After several unsuccessful tries, he thought he had found the rare pearl. He was an assimilated Jew who even claimed to have been converted. He was a reserve officer and had the bearing of a Polish aristocrat. A recent arrival at Treblinka, he seemed not to have understood what was happening. Although his pride had immediately displeased Kurt Franz, Franz had determined not to let any of this feeling show, potential commandants being too rare. He even took it upon himself to speak to this Jew as to a man.

"The German commandant of the camp has decided to appoint a Jewish counterpart. You seem to fill the required conditions and I offer you the position."

This almost friendly way of speaking surprised the Jew so much that suddenly he wondered whether he had been dreaming until then. He looked up in a way that said both "It's too great an honor" and "But perhaps . . ." Then, as one soldier to another, he asked what his duties would be.

In a voice whose exaggerated kindness should have put the Jewish officer on his guard, Franz explained.

"I do not feel absolutely Jewish," replied the officer coldly, "but I shall never agree to perform your work on these people. I beg you, sir, to permit me to make use of your pistol."

Kurt Franz looked at him and burst out laughing. Then he rose quickly, grabbed the officer, and threw him into the yard. In the evening, he called the camp together and summoned the Jewish officer.

"No doubt you thought I was not big enough to kill you myself, sir," he told him, stressing the "sir" mockingly. "Well, you were right," he added after a moment. "I am going to have several good Ukrainians do it for me."

After being forcibly undressed, the officer was beaten to death with rifle butts.

When there remained only a red and formless heap of flesh, Kurt Franz turned to the prisoners.

"If by tomorrow I do not have a Jewish commandant worthy of the name," he told them, "you will all be executed.'

The engineer Galewski spent the night thinking. The idea of becoming the leader of the collaborators was repugnant to him. He was already old, and his whole family had just been gassed almost before his eyes. The mere fact of surviving them struck him as a betrayal. But all the prisoners had pleaded with him. He had sensed so much fear in their voices that abandoning them also seemed like a betrayal. In the morning, when the door of the barracks was pushed violently open and the savage shouts of *"Raus"* rang out, he told himself that perhaps he might do something some day. He thought again and decided that this was a bad justification. Everyone crowded around him.

"After all," he murmured, "what difference does it make, at the point we have reached?"

When Kurt Franz asked whether anyone had been decided on, Galewski came forward.

Franz sized him up carefully: tall, a dignified air, without pride, obviously chosen by the others: it seemed possible.

He told him to approach. Galewski took a few steps. Franz looked at him for a moment and then slapped him twice with all his might. Galewski staggered, his shoulders slumped, and he lowered his eyes.

"That will be the last time, if all goes well," Franz told him.

Then, turning to the prisoners, "Behold your leader!" he shouted. "The leader of the subhumans! To me, he is a Jew; to you, he is a leader!"

Franz then turned to Max Bielas and saluted. "Mission accomplished."

It had taken the Technicians two months to create Treblinka. Now they thought they could rest.

VII

THE DAY AFTER HIS arrival in Treblinka, Meir Berliner forgot his resolutions of vengeance under the shower of blows that began to fall. You do not take revenge on the *golem;* you destroy him. One evening he found himself lying next to Pinhas Alter again.

"All empires are perishable," the latter said. "We have seen thousands of them fall since God called Abraham. We have seen them arise in labor, grow in injustice and die in pride, killed by other empires whose star appeared. This one will disappear like the rest."

"And we with it," Meir Berliner had added.

"This is why we must do all we can to survive."

"But how many of us will be left, and in what condition?" Berliner had asked sadly. "And what will be the value of a world that was capable of doing this, enduring this, and allowing this to be done?"

"It will be the world of redemption, and we will be the witnesses at its trial."

Pinhas Alter was a visionary whom nothing seemed to touch. The greater the ordeals, the more certainly he saw them as the will of God. His reasoning was simple: "God has willed that the others die and that I survive." His only problem was, "Why has God chosen me not to die, me and the few hundred whose tragic fate I share?" After considering this question at length, he had reached the conclusion that God wanted him to be witness to His Wrath.

He was a fanatic whom nothing touched. His fanaticism was even more intransigeant than that of his tormenters, but while they had devoted theirs to destruction, he had dedicated his to obeying God's Will. And nothing could reach him, neither beatings nor humiliation nor death. He went about staggering under the blows, carrying the dead bodies of his Jewish brothers which were yellowed by an atrocious death, and his heart praised the Eternal and his lips perpetually murmured *Yiskaddal veyiskaddash* . . .

Berliner, however, was a man, and he suffered. He suffered all the more because his extraordinary physical and moral resistance sustained in him a remnant of sentimental, social, temporal life.

"A world of redemption," he repeated with fear. "If God created the world, this is the proof that His Work is a failure."

"This is the most shining proof of the Love of God for His People! If He did not love us, would He take the trouble to raise up so many evil forces against us?"

Pinhas spoke with such conviction that Berliner was impressed. But on finding God in this hell, instead of loving Him, he began to hate Him.

"So be it! God wants it this way," he said, "but in that case I don't want God!"

"Then you will die!"

Berliner found himself ultimately alone, without God, without support, without hope, with only his fierce will to live in spite of everything, against all odds. He knew that he wanted to live, but he did not know why. He withdrew into himself, contracted around this senseless desire.

The next day he was assigned to the undressing of the convoys. The role of the workers of this commando seemed to be a passive one, but when the Jews from the convoys did not undress fast enough, the blows began to fall. When this happened they "helped" the Jews undress, tearing off their clothing if necessary. To keep the certainty of approaching death from plunging these Jews into a kind of inertia, they had tacitly decided not only to reveal nothing to their brothers, but to calm the fears of those few who suspected the truth. Thus the complicity had entered into its final phase. At that period the personnel of this commando changed every day; and yet, no one broke the rule.

Meir Berliner, like the others, obeyed it scrupulously. That day he saw an old woman who was having trouble taking off a long black dress that buttoned all the way down. He rushed over to her and with a furious gesture tore off half the buttons. The old woman, who had seen him coming and was about to thank him, slowly raised her head. Age had deformed her body, and her face had the slackness of dead flesh. Only her eyes were still alive. They said that she had understood. Berliner stopped, embarrassed, possibly ashamed, unable to go on while those eyes were turned on him.

"So it is all over," she said, with a resignation that was free from despair.

He looked at her and hesitated, but could not lie. He bowed his head.

"The old and infirm are put to death, then?" she continued.

She seemed to have accepted the fact without effort, without resistance, as a necessity that she had long suspected. Half bared, her bloated flesh hung from her torn clothing. She raised her hands to finish undressing. Berliner could not move. She was no longer an object to him, she was an old woman, she was a mother, all the old mothers in the world, she was his mother.

In the eyes of the old woman the expression of resignation

changed to one of interrogation. "It is not yet the end?" she asked.

If there had been a particle of hope in her tone, Berliner would have fled, but there was only a vague curiosity. He said nothing, and she understood.

"But the men are saved," she said.

Such disorder reigned in the shed where the women were undressing that their conversation passed unnoticed. Berliner still did not answer. A slow process began in the mind of the woman, and her eyes became confused. Her fingers plucked at the same button. Her mind skipped several questions. Then she asked, "But what about you?"

"We—" he pronounced. It was the first word he had uttered. Out of shame, and because he knew the words had no meaning here or at least not the same meaning, he said no more. But his tone implied, "For us, it is even worse."

His expression had become pleading. The woman took his hand and carried it to her lips.

"Jew! You are my son. Swear to me that you will stay alive."

Then she raised her arms, and her look, which was all determination now, said, "Go ahead!"

Turning away his face, he grabbed her dress and gave it a violent tug.

It was at this time that a convoy from Mezritch, near Bialystok, arrived. The trip had lasted a very long time under appalling conditions and without water. The only thing that seemed to preoccupy the deportees was getting something to drink. But although there was a well in the middle of the yard, they were not permitted to quench their thirst before they died. "Soon! Soon!" said the S.S. "Hurry up! You will drink under the shower!"

When he heard their moans, Berliner told himself that he was no longer a man if he did not go and get water. On that day he ceased to be a man. There was no room for men in Treblinka, either on one side or on the other.

Then he learned to hide his face, not to see the blows coming, to run like a blind man, to work like a robot. His world contracted. One day he thought of his family in Argentina, and he looked for someone he could talk to about them. It was evening in the barracks, the bodies of the other workers were piled together like corpses. He told himself that nobody would believe him. His villa in Buenos Aires seemed like a dream, a memory from a previous life. He never thought about it any more. During the day his hidden face kept him from seeing, and the outside world ceased to exist for him. The insensibility of Pinhas Alter had become intolerable to him and he also stopped talking. In order to survive he had drowned his own sensibility and it seemed to him that he had become someone else, living in a different world. Those who had not followed this course had died, by accident or from exhaustion. Meir Berliner had found in the old woman's eyes a reason for wanting to live. Until then he had survived by instinct; after that he felt he did so by reason.

Neither the blows nor the tragedy of the Jewish people who poured through the "road to heaven" touched him any longer. The more horrible the spectacle was, the blinder Berliner became. The louder the cries, the deafer he became. Only one thing mattered: to avoid the cadaver commando; for, since the burdens were heavier, you died faster. But even this was more an instinct than a conscious desire. Of course the scenes were more terrible with the undressing commando, but since he did not see them anyway, it did not matter. He had long since lost the ability to be moved. These naked men who tried to keep their dignity, these mothers who pressed their children to their breasts, these young girls who, with their arms crossed in a last gesture of shame, tried to hide their nudity, had ceased to matter to him. All these human reactions seemed to come from another world. He registered the most tragic scenes, but he did not react to them. At the very most they astonished him when, for an instant, their violence stopped the machine.

One day when he was assigned to undressing the women, he suddenly saw a naked girl no older than eighteen standing before him. If it was not until after the women had left that you had to run with their clothing to the sorting square, it was a "good" commando, for during the undressing you were not beaten much unless some scene aroused the Ukrainian guards or the S.S. on duty.

When the girl had appeared he had felt a vague annoyance. This had occurred on the reflex level. Like a Pavlovian dog, he had learned that a scene equaled more blows; and he also knew that a single blow on the face equaled death, a death which you might put off a whole day, sometimes two or even three, but which came inexorably. Those who were marked had a name in the language of the camp. They were called *clepsydras* (water clocks). Their black eye, bruised cheek, or cut face was an indelible stigma. Every evening the Technicians sent for the clepsydras. Those who came forward of their own will were entitled to a quick death—"as a reward for their honesty," according to Max Bielas: a bullet in the back of the head at the edge of the ditch in the "hospital," where a perpetual sulphur-fed funeral pyre burned. At the edge of the ditch, so that the body would fall by itself; a bullet in the back of the head, so that justice would be done all the same. But those who did not come forward when they were called were hacked to death with a shovel. It was often longer and always more painful. From the moment he was marked, the clepsydra blocked out part of his consciousness. The easiest death—which, however, was reserved for a privileged few —was the one that occurred during work, from being hit too hard with a rifle butt or a club. Of course, the clepsydra could choose to come forward when he was called, but in fact only the most desperate did this. Actually, since he possessed no mirror and had no communication with the other workers, a man who had been hit on the face during the day was never sure that the blow had left a mark. Thus, certain men who showed no trace of the blow came forward and were executed, when they might have gained a few more days. The clepsydras were faced by a cruel and insoluble dilemma: to come forward anyway, or to gamble that the blow had not left a mark and thereby risk a terrible death. Their fierce will to live generally drove them to play double or nothing, which further increased the fear of becoming a clepsydra.

The annoyance that Berliner felt was caused by a revulsion of his whole being. In his poor atrophied mind the pattern was clear: scene–blow–clepsydra–death. His sensibility was too deadened for him to feel this tragic pattern in a really painful manner, but a red light had nevertheless lit up far off in his hazy brain. This light told him, "Danger." But if he vaguely experienced the notion of danger, he was completely incapable of imagining the slightest defense, and, intrigued as well as annoyed, he stopped.

The girl was very beautiful, but her eyes had the gleam of madness. Her mother, who was still undressing, tried to restrain her, but she pushed her away with an imperious gesture that made her whole body vibrate.

"Let go, Mamma! Leave me alone now with your good advice, with all your wisdom!" Then she turned toward Berliner, proud and provocative.

Berliner looked at her without seeing her.

"Save me," she said, "and I will be your servant." Her voice was heavy with intensity; she pronounced each word slowly.

"Save me, and I will give you what I refused my fiancé."

Her mother began to weep slowly.

"Look at me, I am beautiful. Look at me, I am going to die. Look at my body, see how beautiful it is. It was made to love, it was made for life, for caresses. Look at it! Isn't it beautiful? Isn't it young? Isn't it firm? It wants to live, it wants to love! God intended it for love. But my fiancé is dead and I am going to die too, and everything is going to die and my body will never know love."

She dropped her hands which she had run along her hips and loins. After an instant of immobility, her glowing face was racked by sobs.

Two Ukrainian guards, attracted by the noise, took her behind the shed, and her cries of despair became cries of pain.

But Berliner, who had seen nothing, heard nothing either. Suddenly he felt a blow, and grabbing the girl's clothing, which was at his feet, he ran off, burying his face in it.

Pain—and consciousness—returned only at the end of a month after the Technicians had begun to reorganize the camp. At that time there were fifteen hundred prisoners in Treblinka. Many committed suicide, either with poison found in the baggage of those who were gassed or by hanging themselves at night in the barracks. The conditions made hanging very difficult, and many struggled for a long time before they were still. Later, when the beginnings of social life began to establish itself among the prisoners, the technique improved. You had a friend pull the box away; indeed, this became the greatest proof of friendship. The desperate man would get up on a box, put his belt around his neck and attach it to a beam. When everything was ready, he would say, "Now!" The friend would quickly pull the box away and then recite a prayer. When two friends were very close and both wanted to end it, they drew straws and the loser, after pulling the box away, would either have to hang himself or look for another friend.

It was a father and son who had been the first to utilize this method. The son was still a young boy, the father already an old man. They were the last remnants of a large family. The father had urged the son to live in order to perpetuate their name, but now the son was a clepsydra. When his son had asked him whether he was marked, at first the father had not dared to answer. The murmur of their discussion had lasted long into the night in the barracks.

"Tell me, Father, tell me frankly," asked the son.

"No, my son, there's nothing there," answered the father, running his hand over his son's face. "You will live, and you will perpetuate our name."

So powerful was the father's desire to have his lineage survive that he was ready to take the risk of having his son die in great agony.

"You will live, and you will go to the land of Israel, our land, you will marry and raise children, my children, the children of my father and my father's father. You will teach them our religion and the fear of God. You will also tell them how we died, so that the world will never forget it. You will make our land an impregnable citadel, which will fear the Lord, blessed be His Name, and be feared by its enemies."

The voice swelled like a prophecy.

"Yes, Father," answered the son timidly.

" 'And it shall come to pass that in all the land,' said the Lord, 'two parts therein shall be cut off and die, but the third shall be left therein. I will bring the third part through the fire, and will refine them as silver is refined, and will try them as gold is tried. They shall call on my Name and I will hear them. I will say: "It is my people," and they shall say, "The Lord is my God!" ' "

"You will be among the third whom the prophet Zechariah foretells," said the father, "and I will be cut off. But you will be refined like silver and tried like gold. So the Lord decided, blessed be His Name."

"Father," said the child suddenly, "I'm afraid."

The father said nothing for a long time. When he began to speak again, his voice was changed, softer, sadder.

"You do not have confidence?" he asked.

"I'm afraid."

The voice of the child tried to be steady, but it shook a little.

"I felt blood on my fingers."

For a long time the father stroked the face of his son who would not go to the land of Israel, who would not have children, who was the last of his name, and who was going to die.

"God does not exist," murmured the child.

This blasphemy, uttered with a pure heart, did not disturb the father.

"Yes He does, my son," he answered in a voice full of love, "but we do not understand Him. Our sins have stopped our ears and closed our eyes."

"I'm afraid," said the son again. "They are going to kill me. I don't want them to kill me. I don't think I can stand it."

And he fell against his father, who held him in his arms for a long time, murmuring prayers. Finally, as if coming out of a deep meditation, the father said, "Come, my son, prepare to die."

"Yes, Father," answered the child with total submission.

The father took off his belt and knotted it around the child's neck. Then he made him stand on a box and climbed up beside him to fasten the belt to a beam. When this was done, he embraced his son and got down. "Goodbye," murmured the son. "Until later," answered the father, and he pulled the box away quickly.

After a few minutes he came back, climbed onto the box, and took down his son's body. He laid it gently on the sand floor of the barracks and began to recite a prayer.

Voices had risen in the barracks, hushed, anonymous and fraternal, swelling each "Amen." But when the father put the belt around his own neck, no one made a move. He mounted the box, groped with raised arms to fasten the belt, then, with a sudden movement, kicked over the box. His body strained, shuddered, and was still. The funereal murmur resumed, profound as death, eternal as faith. That night marked the first sign of the rebirth of a social life among the Jews of Treblinka.

When the first reforms had begun and the prisoners had emerged from their abyss of unconsciousness, their first affirmation of freedom had been suicide. The rebirth of pain had liberated them. At this point they had ceased to be perfect slaves, since they could choose either to kill themselves or to continue to struggle. This freedom of choice released the prisoners from the hold of the Technicians, who lost their role of supreme judges. If they retained their authority over death, they had lost their authority over life.

The second victory had been the first demonstration of solidarity in death. This seems like very little, and yet it was from this first gesture that everything would follow. On the basis of this solidarity in death, life would begin again. In the life of this new world that was born in Treblinka, this gesture of pulling the box away represented a stage that may have been more important than the discovery of fire in the history of our civilization. Although this was not yet apparent, it set a limit to the power of the Technicians.

Meir Berliner, who had stayed in Camp Number One at the time of the division into two camps, was named foreman of the blue commando in charge of "welcoming" the convoys. He very quickly realized that he could not long survive in this world of death. He thought of committing suicide, but he remembered the oath that the old woman had made him swear. He did not understand this frantic desire to survive, but he felt himself bound by it against his will, as if by a force that was greater than himself.

The nights were even worse than the days, for the salutary numbness of the blows wore off. During the day the rhythm of work was such that you could not think, but when the doors of the barracks had been shut, it was despair that Meir Berliner found instead of repose. At this time the suicides were so numerous that when you got up in the night to go to the big tanks that served as latrines, you had to walk with your arms in front of your face to keep from running into the hanging bodies. Sometimes a man went mad. Some sobbed, others laughed hysterically, still others jabbered unintelligible phrases.

One night Berliner thought that he too would sink into madness. The day had been stifling and the barracks was still overheated. The smell of the bodies, combined with that of the latrines, was suffocating. From time to time you would hear the muffled order, "Now," and the barracks would shudder, living the agony of the hanged man—first a jolt, then vibrations that gradually subsided. Some lasted only a few seconds, but others seemed as if they would never end. As a rule, it was those who had seen their relatives exterminated during the day who hanged themselves at night, and the number of hangings was proportional to the size of the convoys.

Five convoys had arrived during the day, and Berliner told himself with strange lucidity that there would be many hangings that night. Despite his great fatigue, he could not go to sleep; each jolt reverberated through his whole body. Pinhas Alter had been sent to Camp Number Two, and Berliner was alone. Involuntarily he waited for the jolts, driven by a kind of morbid curiosity.

Suddenly, he heard a man talking right next to him. The voice was clear and precise, the tone indifferent: "Thank heaven," he said, "we're doing something too; that's it, we've left, we'll catch them in no time." Since the man was speaking softly, Berliner, who was listening for all the noises in the night, strained to hear.

The voice seemed to trip over the last words, wavering on the brink of incoherence. It fell until it was only a hoarse and weary murmur, a vague litany like the moan of a dying man. Berliner listened, fascinated. The voice recovered strength. The murmur became words again. But the words had no meaning, no connection. They were only the absurd punctuation of an incomprehensible murmur. Suddenly the murmur disintegrated into a sob of laughter which burst, savage and insane, upon the funereal silence of the barracks. Petrified, Berliner felt that he was going to laugh too. To break the spell he gave a savage yell and fled to the other end of the barracks.

That night, he decided to escape. His reawakened sensibility made it impossible for him to endure life in Treblinka, but he did not want to die. Between death and suffering, he chose flight. "Of two solutions, I always choose the third."

The next day, and for the first time since his arrival in Treblinka, Berliner had control over an event. It was not very much, but this renewed possibility of influencing the course of things seemed full of significance, and gave him the hope of being able to escape. While he was herding the Jews out of a convoy, he saw, coming out of the car he was standing in front of, Itzak Choken, one of his comrades from Warsaw.

Short and wiry, Choken was endowed with an extraordinary vitality and a physical strength that bore little relation to his build and appearance. His friends said that in his case the boldness of spirit and keenness of intelligence of the Jews had gone into the body. He loved to fight as Talmudist scholars love to argue. He fought with as much ingenuity as they talked. Berliner had got to know him on the occasion of one of his numerous brawls.

It was at the beginning of the ghetto. While walking down the street one day, Meir had seen some Ukrainian soldiers bullying little Choken. Still believing that his Argentinian passport protected him from brutality, he had walked over to intervene. Choken had taken the opportunity to make his escape, and the Ukrainians, furious, had turned on him. He had not had time to put his hand in his pocket to get out his passport before he slumped to the ground, half conscious. The rest happened even more quickly. Choken, seeing his unlucky defender in trouble, had returned to help him. How he had knocked out half the Ukrainians and chased away the others, Berliner never understood. He found himself half running, half carried by Choken, who was telling him, "Faster, faster, they'll come back." When they stopped at last, Berliner thought he was going to die of exhaustion. Lying at the foot of a wall, he tried desperately to get his breath, while Choken, his face calm, his forehead without a drop of sweat, regarded him with a vague smile that was ironic and affectionate at the same time. A long moment passed before Berliner could murmur, "Thanks! You saved my life."

When he saw Choken jump out of the car and look quickly around to try to figure out what was going on, Berliner remembered the loud guffaw with which Choken had greeted his expression of gratitude.

He walked over to his friend and cautiously murmured, "Are you alone?"

Without showing any surprise and without looking at Berliner, Choken replied in a whisper, "Yes."

"When you are undressing, say that you are a carpenter," Berliner continued in the same way.

Without asking any questions, Choken gave an imperceptible nod and ran off to avoid being hit.

That evening Berliner was standing in line to get his tin of soup when he heard a voice say, "*Shalom!*" He turned around. Choken was behind him.

"What's going on here?" Choken asked.

"Don't ask questions. I'll explain in the barracks."

"What can we do?" asked Choken, as soon as Berliner had finished explaining what Treblinka was.

The door of the barracks had just been closed upon another night of agony and nightmare. Choken had not asked questions, he had not burst into tears, he had not begun to rave, nor had he said nothing, mute with stupor. "Even with the blade of the sword at your throat you will not despair of life," says the Talmud. All those Jews who refused to accept the idea of death were following this teaching. But whereas they submitted to it with all their human weakness, Choken lived the commandment with a spontaneity that was almost inhuman. He had just learned that the fifteen thousand Jews who, like him, had arrived that day in Treblinka, were now dead, that millions of Jews were going to die like them, but he asked only one question: "What can we do?" He was one of those men whom only death can stop.

"We must try to escape," answered Berliner.

"Do you have an idea?"

"Maybe. But it will be difficult."

"Explain."

"It's this. For several days the clothing and possessions have been forwarded to Lublin. The convoys bring the Jews and take away what is left of them, piles of rags."

"Not bad for organization," commented Choken.

The tone was curt, crisp, without emotion. Berliner was both shocked and reassured by it. He continued:

"All the commandos take part in the loading. My idea is to hide in one of the cars. The Germans must be on their guard and I don't know how—"

"It seems feasible," Choken interrupted.

He was silent for a moment, then said casually, "By the way, thanks! You saved my life."

He felt for Berliner's hand in the dark and pressed it.

"It is I who should thank you," the latter replied with emotion. "I think it's you who have saved mine again."

"We'll talk about that when we're on the train. Good night."

"Good night," replied Berliner, and he fell asleep immediately.

A few days later two Jews who tried to escape by hanging onto the underside of the train were killed with shovels. They had hidden while the train was being loaded and had been spotted just as their car was passing the gate of the camp. Berliner had watched the scene. He was still upset when he told Choken about it that night.

"Two Germans were crouching on each side of the gate. When the car came opposite them, one shouted something and the train stopped. The German aimed his machine gun and shouted an order. The men must have been rigid with fear, for they did not move. Then the German leaned down and fired. One of the Jews fell off. The German shouted again and the other one came out. I will always see that face distorted by fear and those eyes overwhelmed with despair. When the train had started to move he must have thought they had made it. The other man was only wounded. They were both dragged to the middle of the platform. The Germans took a long time killing them. They screamed with pain to the end. Then two prisoners were ordered to search their clothing. They found a lot of gold and paper money. After this discovery, even though the poor men were already dead, the Germans went to work on their bodies. They held it against them for stealing the gold of the Reich."

Berliner paused. "I'm afraid," he added after a moment.

"I had thought of that way. We'll have to find something else," said Choken calmly. "But the idea of taking money along seems good."

Again Berliner had that sensation of mingled shock and confidence which he had felt the night before.

"Doesn't the way they died bother you?"

"I realized long ago that this would be a fight without mercy."

"For there to be a fight there must be fighters, and the conditions don't even permit us to defend ourselves."

"As long as a Jew wants to live, the fight will go on. Every man fights in his own way, but since the stake is the survival of the Jewish people, we are bound to win."

"Strange victory!"

"Listen! The Germans are like a mountain climber who wants to climb a mountain. If he succeeds in planting his flag at the top, people will say that he has conquered the mountain; but if he stops halfway up or even a hundred yards from the top, people will say that the mountain conquered him. Since the Germans will not succeed in exterminating all of us, in a thousand years the textbooks of Jewish history will teach that in the middle of the twentieth century the Jewish people faced one of the greatest threats in their history, but that they triumphed over it as they did over all the others."

Berliner looked at him, astonished by this extraordinary sense of the collective destiny of the Jewish people.

"But what if the survivors no longer want to be Jews after such a catastrophe?"

"Then we will be lost. For the danger is in us and only in us. This is why we must find a meaning in what is happening to us."

"And what meaning do you find in it?"

"That's not my business, I leave that job to our sages."

Just then they heard the brief command, "Now," and the barracks shuddered.

"What's that?" asked Choken.

"Someone who couldn't go on living and is hanging himself."

"But he is mad."

"That's what the Germans say too."

They had been talking more loudly for the last few minutes,

and a man who had heard them felt his way toward them.

"He's out of his misery," he said.

"That's what the Germans want too, to put us all out of our misery."

"You're right," said the man who had just come over. "I think we should try to do something."

Berliner hesitated a moment, wondering whether he could reveal their plan to the stranger. He knew he had to be careful, but the man inspired his confidence. He decided to ask him to join with them.

"We want to escape. If you want to try with us—'

"No, I can't. I've already thought about it, but it's impossible. I was with my wife and children when I arrived. I will never leave Treblinka. There is no room in the world for a man like me. All I can do to give meaning to my survival is help others. I will not leave with you, but I will help you if you wish. My name is Galewski. I was an engineer in Warsaw."

"My name is Berliner. I was a businessman in Buenos Aires."

"My name is Choken. I was a Jew."

By a kind of reflex, each put out his right hand. Their hands joined in a confused knot.

The Committee of Resistance of Treblinka was born.

The three men formed the habit of meeting every evening. The first job they assigned themselves was to try to prevent suicides. As soon as they heard the command "Now," they rushed toward the sound. They did not always arrive in time, and even when they managed to get the poor man down before he died, they often had to fight to keep him from getting back on the box. While Berliner and Choken held him motionless, Galewski would talk to him.

He had tried a certain number of arguments before finding the most effective one, the argument of testimony. "We must live to tell the story," he explained. "You are like damned men who are kept alive by some magic power in the very heart of hell. You must have only one thought: to get out in order to tell the living, to warn them. Think of all those who sin inadvertently, without being aware of it. Think of all those who make decisions lightly, without knowing where they will lead them. Think of all those who seal their eternal doom with a carefree heart, like blind men heading for a precipice. Won't you do anything for them?" At this point in the argument, the desperate man usually became angry. His response was, "Why should I think about people who didn't think about me? The whole world is a party to our extermination." Against this argument Galewski had found a good answer: "The world is a party precisely because it does not know." When the would-be suicide began to complain about the difficult role the world assigned to the Jews, Galewski knew that they had won.

For them the extermination took on a mystical dimension that connected it with a past too laden with promises and ordeals to be denied. As the destitute survivors of a centuries-old history, the sons of Abraham, Isaac and Jacob, they possessed nothing and aspired to everything. This duty to live in order to bear witness which Galewski offered them was a mission on the scale of their historic dimension. At the level to which they had sunk, only a total altruism could save them from despair, since they bought their lives with the lives of others. At Treblinka, during this period, an average of fifteen thousand Jews were gassed per day. The gang of Jewish workers at the camp might be estimated at one thousand. Therefore the price of "tenure" at Treblinka, calculated in Jewish heads, amounted to fifteen units per day. Of course, the work would have been done anyway. Others would have performed it. But such was the terrible arithmetic of a day's survival in Treblinka.

These exhausting nights established a great brotherhood among the three men. They decided that if Choken and Berliner brought off their escape, they would go into the ghettos to warn the Jews what Treblinka was.

On the first night without a suicide they talked about escape for a long time. Galewski was very moved. Berliner sensed it, and again asked him to come with them. After having refused for a long time, Galewski finally said that he would think about it. He was afraid of finding himself alone again. His life had recovered a certain meaning since he had met Berliner and Choken, and he told himself that he might be more useful in the ghettos than in Treblinka. But fate was to decide for him. A few days later, Kurt Franz gave the Jews one night to choose a leader. He decided it was his duty to stay.

His nomination would facilitate the escape. Having become a personality in the camp, he would easily procure gold from the *Goldjuden*. As it was unwise to keep gold on your person, Choken buried it in the sand floor of the barracks. The plan he proposed was relatively safe. The doors of the cars were not closed until a German had checked to make sure they were completely full. So the two fugitives were to slip into the car when it was three quarters full and block the door with a wall of clothing that would give the impression that it was full. When the wall was finished, Galewski would go and get a German and tell him that the door could be closed. Since the prisoners returned to the barracks only in the evening to sleep, they must anticipate the operation a day in advance, so that Berliner and Choken could dig up the gold and take it with them.

When Galewski had explained the plan they remained silent, as if hesitating. Since the prisoners were never safe from a search, the risk of spending a whole day with their pockets full of gold seemed to them too great. Galewski offered to keep the gold himself and pass it to them when they were already in the car.

Choken and Berliner did not want him to take this extra risk, but he insisted.

"Without gold, you won't last twenty-four hours. Besides, you have a mission to carry out. For me this is all that matters. In any case, I know I will never leave this place alive. Now I am sure of it: my life stopped the day I arrived at Treblinka. My agony may be longer or shorter, but I will never return to life."

He had spoken with great sadness but without bitterness or defiance. His two friends understood that it would have been useless, almost in bad taste, to offer him encouragement.

"Where do you find the courage to help us escape? How do you find the strength to spend your nights encouraging other men?" Berliner asked him.

"What is the source of that madness that has always driven the Jews to live and to remain Jews despite all the misery this name brings them?" replied Galewski. "Where did my father find the courage to condemn me to suffer, and where had his father found it and his father's father? It would have been enough for one of them to have the weakness or the strength to decide that his son would not be a Jew to break the chain of disaster, to assure his lineage a life of peace."

"Perhaps it was because then his lineage would not have had any meaning for him," Choken answered gently. "Tradition says that when a Jew leaves Judaism, all Jews are in mourning. For a father, a non-Jewish son is like a dead son, and a dead man cannot have children. With a converted son, the lineage dies."

"You are right," said Galewski pensively. "I think if I were still outside and had a son, I would have him circumcised."

"When I was brought from Warsaw," Choken told them, "a strange problem was being discussed; I remember it now. It seems that the Catholic Church had offered to hide five hundred Jewish children in convents, and that it had even promised not to try to convert them. I don't know whether the offer was finally accepted, but many people were against it. They said, 'If we turn the children over to them, they will convert them in spite of their fine promises. For a Catholic, to convert people is a duty. So whatever we do, our sons are lost. When they died at the stake, our fathers taught us that a dead Jew was better than a renegade Jew.' "

VIII

A FEW DAYS LATER Galewski learned that there would be a shipment of clothing the following day. He had been expecting this news for a long time, but at first he took no joy in it. He would be alone again. He wondered whether he would have the strength to resist despair. The goal that he had set himself of helping the other prisoners seemed too difficult. What could he hope to achieve in this solitude against such powerful enemies? How could he hope to fight singlehanded against the extermination of the Jewish people? With Choken and Berliner everything seemed possible; the few hours he spent with them in the evening helped him to forget the implacable reality of Camp Treblinka.

Galewski did not see Choken and Berliner again until that night in the barracks.

"You will leave tomorrow," he said, trying to hide his emotion.

Berliner seemed not to have heard. The other two men looked at him in surprise.

"By this time tomorrow we'll be free," Choken told him, putting a hand on his arm. "Only one more day, Meir, and we will be out of this hell."

"I don't dare believe it," Berliner replied. "All this time I have stood it only because I had hope of escape. Now that you tell me we are leaving," he continued, turning toward Galewski, "I feel as if I am dreaming. To return to a normal life, after all we have been through, seems impossible."

"You're not happy to be going?" Galewski asked him.

"Oh yes, I'm happy, more than happy; but I can't imagine myself as a free man. It's hard for me to believe there is still a world beyond this barbed wire, a world in which I can have a place."

"I know how you feel," said Galewski slowly. "Perhaps it takes more courage to escape than to remain, more to go on living than to die. Sometimes I feel like letting myself die. It would be so much easier."

"I think all this is beside the point," Choken broke in, to tone down the emotion. "We aren't living to enjoy ourselves but to fight."

"You're right," replied Galewski in a firmer voice. "We have other things to do on our last evening than feeling sorry for ourselves."

They spent the rest of the night perfecting the final details of the escape and their mission in the ghettos. They also decided to try to find a way to get information about Treblinka to London. When everything was settled, Berliner suggested that they agree upon a place in Palestine where they would meet after the war if they were still alive. They chose a *kibbutz* in Galilee where a cousin of Berliner's lived and went to sleep with their heads full of dreams.

Tragedy struck the next morning; it was to change not only Berliner's own destiny, but that of the whole camp.

The oral tradition of Treblinka has not preserved what Berliner did that morning. It is known that he dressed warmly in spite of the season and that he had his pockets full of gold. The last word he said to Choken in the morning, when they were driven out of the barracks under the customary hail of blows, was, "I still can't believe that anyone can get out of here. I won't believe it until the train begins to move." Did he have a premonition of what was going to happen? It is impossible to say. And yet when Galewski thought it over afterward he was struck by Berliner's ambivalent attitude from the moment Galewski had informed him that the escape would take place the next day. When Galewski told Berliner's story to Kurland, the *kapo* of the "hospital," who was to become the camp's chronicler, they discussed at length the possibility that Berliner had already been too broken in spirit to undertake anything, to have the will to return to life.

Galewski saw Berliner again for only a few minutes in the early afternoon. His face was distorted by a mixture of grief and hatred. Without looking at Galewski, he said, "It's all over, I'm not leaving. I knew I would never leave this place."

Thinking that Berliner's nerves had given way, Galewski tried to console him.

"You can't help me any more," Berliner replied. "No one can help me any more. My parents arrived a little while ago. I managed to hide and they didn't see me. I watched them for a few moments. They were separated: the women to the left, the men to the right. At the last minute my father wanted to kiss my mother, as if he suddenly understood that he would never see her again. He turned around to go to her, as she was already walking away. Just then Max Bielas appeared and he hit my father so hard that he fell down. Some people helped him to his feet and led him away running under the blows."

Berliner spoke in a jerky, altered, unrecognizable voice. Galewski had the feeling that he was about to commit an irreparable act. Putting as much conviction into his voice as he could, he said quickly:

"It is because your parents arrived today that you must escape. You cannot live one more day in Treblinka and you must live to get revenge."

"Revenge! How long I have dreamed of it!" Berliner replied before walking away.

Galewski wanted to follow him, but Kurt Franz sent for him just then. All afternoon Galewski looked for Berliner, but he did not find him. He did not see him again until that night at roll call. By that time it was too late.

The loading of the clothes was to take place in the afternoon. During the short break for lunch, Galewski found Choken and told him what had happened.

"Perhaps you should postpone your escape. If Berliner is caught with all the gold he has on him, the cars will be searched and the shipment supervised very closely."

"I can't stay another day in Treblinka," answered Choken. "I'll take my chances."

Galewski handed him a vial of poison. "Take this. No one can say how he will react under torture. Neither you nor I."

For some time, whenever a prisoner had been caught with gold on him, he had been tortured until he revealed who had given it to him, and this person was then tortured too.

"See you later," replied Choken, quickly slipping the vial into his pocket.

Galewski detained for a moment. "Do you think we'll see each other again?" he asked.

"Yes," said Choken with an inspired look. Then he added, quickly, "Later, at the station." And he disappeared into the crowd of prisoners.

Galewski was pacing up and down in front of the train when he saw Choken arrive at a run, half buried under an enormous bundle of clothing.

"Third car! Stay near the door. I'll let you know when to get in," he murmured as Choken went by.

He was nervous and jittery. He had not been able to find Berliner, and he was expecting a catastrophe to strike at any moment.

There had never been so many Germans and Ukrainians on the

platform. The directors must have taken measures following the recent attempts to escape. Galewski realized that he would never be able to get Choken into the car without being seen. The car was almost full. Choken turned around questioningly. Galewski decided to risk everything. Raising his whip, he rushed at Choken, shouting, "There's nobody in this car, get in, you lazy pig!"

Choken understood. He jumped into the car just as the prisoner in charge of arranging the bundles reappeared at the door. He knocked him to the ground. The whole thing took only a few seconds. The other man, before he understood what was happening, heard Galewski calling him.

"Take the bundles, good-for-nothing Jew, and pile them well."

No longer trying to understand, frightened by the shouting, terrorized by the blows, the prisoner seized the bundles that were beginning to pile up near the edge of the car and carried them to the back, which was still empty.

"Thanks, friend," murmured Choken. "Galewski will reward you for this."

By his next trip the other man had already pulled himself together. As he laid down his burden he murmured in the same subdued tone that Choken had used,

"I understand. Good luck, friend!"

"Put the bundles in front of the door. Leave me enough room to move."

Meanwhile Galewski had moved off and was abusing the prisoners at the next car to divert the attention of the S.S. and the Ukrainian guards. When he saw that the door of the car Choken was in was almost blocked, he returned, and pretending to be checking to make sure that the car was completely full, he murmured through the rags:

"Pile bundles behind so the wall won't fall down. In three minutes I'll call a German to have the car closed."

"Don't forget!" said Choken. "We shall meet in Israel."

Galewski was about to walk away when he met the eyes of the man who had been working in the car in which Choken was now hidden.

"Thanks!" he said under his breath.

"Well done!" answered the other, not pausing from his work.

"Come and see me tonight in the barracks."

They had exchanged these few remarks without moving their lips and without looking at each other. As he left, Galewski told himself that he had found a new recruit, and all at once the courage that was beginning to fail him returned. He looked at his watch and began to count the minutes. He decided to walk alongside the train for a minute and a half and then to retrace his steps. When he turned around he saw that the door of the car was completely blocked with bundles of clothing and that the workers were standing idle, which was dangerous for them: the rule was that a prisoner who stopped working for a second was a slacker. A guard was already approaching the group, his rifle leveled. Galewski looked at his watch: more than a minute. The guard was closer to the door than himself, but he was walking slowly. Once again Galewski dashed forward, raising his whip.

"Lazy pigs!" he shouted. "What are you waiting for?"

"The car is full!" shouted the man who had let Choken in.

Galewski was already in front of the door. He turned toward the guard who was still advancing. If the Ukrainian kept on coming, there was a chance that he would see the wall of bundles move from within. Galewski shouted over his head to a German who was standing behind him.

"The car is full, sir. It can be closed."

Surprised, the guard turned around. The German had heard. He arrived slowly.

Galewski glanced swiftly at his watch. Choken must be waiting motionless, holding his breath.

127

The S.S. man looked around quickly, pressed the bundles with one hand, and leaned forward to make sure there was no space between the bundles and the wall of the car. Then he turned to Galewski, who concealed his anxiety beneath a humble and cringing tone.

"Is everything all right, sir?" asked Galewski in a timid and respectful voice.

"Have it closed!" ordered the guard in a contemptuous voice.

Turning to the workers, Galewski shouted like a sergeant bullying his men:

"All right, close the door, you lazy pigs!"

Pushed hard, the door slammed shut with a final sound.

"Good luck," Galewski murmured to himself.

At the sight of the tightly sealed car he felt a great relief. The Committee of Resistance had just won its first victory.

It was only then that Galewski remembered Berliner. His last words re-echoed in his head: "Revenge! How long I have dreamed of it!" The tone in which his friend had uttered these words returned to his memory, and the vague fear he had felt filled him again. Galewski understood that Berliner had reached a point beyond which even the instinct of self-preservation no longer operated.

As he explained to Kurland afterward, he had not taken Berliner's threat seriously. At that time no one could even imagine the possibility of any act of rebellion. But Berliner, who had abandoned all hope and all will to live, might do something foolish. If he were arrested with all the gold that he was carrying on him, Berliner might reveal under torture not only Choken's escape, but the role Galewski had played in it. If this should happen before the train left, it would be a total catastrophe. Even after the train's departure the consequences might be dramatic. If the Germans learned that the Jewish commandant of the camp was heading a resistance movement, their distrust would become so great that nothing could ever be attempted again.

All this was going through Galewski's mind as he supervised the loading of the train. If Berliner were caught, should he himself swallow his vial of poison or should he remain alive to make a denial? Suicide was the easy way out. It spared him torture, but it represented an admission of guilt with which the Germans would not remain content. To stay alive in order to try to exonerate himself was a terrible gamble, for Galewski knew that he would be tortured to death and only a silent death under torture would dispel the Germans' suspicions. But would he hold out under torture? Although he was free to choose between killing himself and letting the S.S. kill him, he had no certainty that he would not talk. When he thought it over he realized what an extraordinary victory over the S.S. death system it would be to die under torture without admitting anything; and he decided not to commit suicide. So that this would be an irreversible commitment, he took his vial of poison out of his pocket unobtrusively, dropped it on the ground, put his foot on it, and slowly, firmly pressed down. There was a small sound of breaking glass. When he moved his foot, tiny fragments of glass glistened in the dust.

Having made his choice, Galewski spent the rest of the afternoon waiting for what now seemed to him inevitable. To prove to himself that he was not merely submitting to fatalism he began to look for Berliner. The departure of the train seemed the crucial point, for these last few days his whole life had been directed toward the escape of his two friends. It seemed to him that the prisoners had never taken so long to load a train. In his desperate impatience he spent the last moments of the loading harassing the Jews like a real sheep dog. Indeed, he showed so much ardor and conviction that Kurt Franz, seeing him at work, congratulated himself on his choice.

The German was making a mistake in his interpretation of the

Jew's zeal; Galewski was not thinking about Kurt Franz's opinion when with raised whip he threatened the prisoners who did not run fast enough to please him; and yet these few minutes were to have considerable influence on the future of the camp. When Kurt Franz explained to Galewski later that it was the ardor he had displayed at the time of the loading of the train that had saved the camp from extermination, once he had recovered from his surprise, Galewski realized all the advantages to be derived from such a misunderstanding. It is difficult to locate the precise moment when the Jews escaped from the all-powerful pressure of the Technicians, when, still preserving the appearance of perfect slaves, they began to prepare their revenge, when, in spite of appearances, the roles began to be reversed; but this misunderstanding on the part of the Technicians as to Galewski's real motive seems to be one of the Germans' very first serious errors of judgment. One need only remember their infallible control in the manipulation of the ghetto and their scrupulous desire for perfection in the selection of the commandos, and compare all this with the sudden blindness which caused them to congratulate a Jew for showing zeal in tricking them, to realize that at that moment a change took place in the relations between killers and victims: a change that seemed harmless enough, but one that allowed the possibility of a radical reversal at some future time.

During these minutes of extreme tension, however, Galewski was very far from these optimistic thoughts. Shouting, cursing, threatening, he looked for Berliner. Before him he saw a thousand Berliners running with their faces hidden, their shoulders hunched, torn between an overwhelming fatigue and a terrible fear, an excruciating desire to lie down and die and a fierce will to go on, to triumph over death; a thousand identical "forked sticks" who, in their effort to blend together and disappear, could no longer be distinguished even by size. Their clothing, which had once been part of their personalities, had found a common

denominator of color: dust gray. There was something frightening and stupefying about this ballet of forms whose speed increased with fatigue. When he thought that once, in another
world, they had all been men, fathers, husbands, sons, business-
men, rabbis, peddlers, lawyers pleading cases, doctors tending the
sick; that they had loved, suffered, hoped; that they had been
jealous at times, and impatient too; that they had been human
beings, Galewski was seized by contradictory emotions. Besides
the aching pity that he felt, a kind of pride overtook him in the
face of this superhuman resistance which was equal to the inhu-
manity of the ordeal. The Jews met the Technicians' will to exterminate them with an even greater will to live.

The afternoon was almost over by the time the door of the last
car was bolted. Galewski had not found Berliner, but neither had
the Germans. Slowly the train began to move and left the camp,
carrying Choken and his terrible message. Choken: the first victory of the Committee of Resistance.

As soon as the last car had been loaded, the commandos were
reassembled and led, as they were every evening, to Roll Call
Square, where the convoys undressed. The day had been very
hot, and the sky was red in the west. For the first time since he
had arrived in Treblinka, Galewski looked at the sky: red and
ragged at sunset, already dark blue at sunrise. He did not see it as
a sky of regret, the sky of the past. He did not think that the sky
was the same as the one he used to see in the other world, nor did
he think that at this hour free men looked at it the way he did. It
had become the sky of Treblinka.

On the roofs of the barracks on either side of the yard, as every
evening, Ukrainian guards were bringing machine guns into firing
position. Down below in the yard the whips of the guards corrected the alignment of the Jews. At this time, the ritual of the
roll call was still very rudimentary. The prisoners, an anonymous

mass, were not even counted. The roll call consisted of two parts. The first, which might last from a quarter of an hour to two hours, was devoted to cap drill. The cap was the only uniform of the prisoners of Treblinka.* At the command *"Mützen ab!"* they had to take off their caps with a rapid gesture and slap them against their right thighs in unison; at the command *"Mützen auf!"* they had to put them on again. A parody of weapons drill, this exercise was in theory supposed to last until the thousand caps made a single sound, sharp as a gunshot, as they struck the thousand thighs. In practice, the ceremony very frequently lasted much longer, for the purpose of the maneuver was not to teach the Jews to remove their caps in unison, but to break their spirits. When its perfection could not be doubted, the S.S. orchestra leader would slap his thigh violently, look at the prisoners, and say, "That was almost perfect, but you will begin the exercise again because of that Jewish pig who is always behind"; and the exercise would resume until once again fatigue broke down the perfection. At this point the blows began to fall again, and the Jews set off again in pursuit of a new perfection, beyond this new threshold of exhaustion. Sometimes, rarely, a few murmurs arose from the mass of the prisoners, and from the roofs would come the sound of the machine guns being cocked. Then the exercise would begin again.

The second part of the roll call, which was optional, generally consisted of a speech made up of curses. It was during this second part that changes in organization were announced to the prisoners.

That evening while Choken was living his first moments of freedom, Galewski, standing in front of the prisoners, who were lined up in five rows, saw Max Bielas himself arrive accompanied

---

* Unlike prisoners in most of the concentration camps, the Jews of Treblinka never wore the famous striped pajamas. The manufacture of these pajamas did not begin until a few days before the destruction of the camp.

by the handsome Kurt Franz. Etiquette required that he personally turn over the roll call to the S.S., so he turned toward the prisoners to give them the *Mützen ab!* It was then that he saw Berliner again—in the front row, right across from him. He was amazed that he had not noticed him sooner, and he tried to catch his eye. But Berliner, frozen at a stony attention, saw nothing, seemed to have lost all vision. The S.S. approached. Galewski, raising his voice, bawled, *"Mütze-e-e-en ep!"* A thousand caps were snatched from their heads and fell violently against a thousand thighs. Before executing the prescribed quarter turn toward the S.S., Galewski glanced swiftly at his friend. He was bareheaded now. Galewski turned toward the S.S., quickly removed his cap, and turned the roll call over to them.

When he saw Max Bielas walk over to review the ranks, he knew that the catastrophe was about to strike. Without knowing what form it would take, he sensed that the moment Bielas came opposite Berliner something would happen. It was inevitable.

Rigid, terrified, and helpless, Galewski stared at Bielas, who was moving rapidly down the rows. The thing happened at a moment when everything could have been avoided. A second before he arrived opposite Berliner, Bielas paused as if satisfied with what he had just seen, and turned his back to the prisoners. Galewski was beginning to breathe again when he saw a figure, as if catapulted from the ranks, dash toward Bielas, a big knife gleaming in its raised right hand. The hand fell with an extraordinary violence. Bielas' body seemed to hesitate, then slowly crumpled. Galewski saw the handle of the knife appear under the left shoulder blade. Then he looked at Berliner, who was standing motionless exactly where he had been when he had struck Bielas. Head bowed, arms dangling, he awaited death. It came in a volley of falling gun butts. He sank down and did not rise again. He had his revenge.

Kurt Franz had rushed over to Max Bielas and, supporting

him under the arms, was helping him to walk. When the first blast of machine-gun fire rang out Bielas was passing Galewski who, dumfounded, had not moved. He noticed that Bielas' mouth was red with blood; he thought that he was going to die. It was then that the second blast was heard: longer, deafening this time. A few seconds later the other machine guns began to fire in chorus. This scene, each of whose elements had occurred almost simultaneously, had lasted less than a minute: time enough for the prisoners to realize what had happened, for the machine gunners to begin firing at random, for the Jews to be seized by panic. "We'll all be killed," someone shouted, running forward. This was the signal.

Like horses stampeding in a corral, the prisoners rushed in all directions and began to run around the yard. S.S. and Ukrainians withdrew hastily to avoid the machine-gun fire and the blind charge of the prisoners. After a few minutes Kurt Franz realized that the Jews were going to be annihilated. He shouted to the gunners to stop firing, but his voice was drowned out by the noise of the machine guns and the cries of the prisoners. It was not some kind of sentimental attachment that made Franz fear the massacre of the Jews; it was rather the way in which it was taking place—in disorder, without the decision being made beforehand and the order being given in accordance with regulations. Once again the S.S. man shouted, but could not hear his own voice. It was then that he made the decision that was to earn him his officer's epaulettes. He ran through the wild, maddened herd of prisoners and the bursts of machine-gun fire to the center of the yard. There, he pulled himself up to his full height, drew his pistol, and fired at the machine guns on the left-hand barracks. Everything stopped suddenly, as if by magic. Galewski who had thrown himself to the ground, stood up. The Jews looked at each other, terrified. The Ukrainian guards and the S.S. troops reappeared.

"Fall in!" ordered Kurt Franz in a dry voice.

134

After the ranks were reformed with the few hundred survivors, thirty prisoners were chosen at random and led away to the "hospital." Then the others dragged the dead and wounded there at a run. In a quarter of an hour the yard had been cleared. Kurt Franz then gave the order to lock the prisoners in the barracks. Meanwhile an S.S. guard had gone to get a car to drive Bielas to the hospital in Lublin.

While the prisoners were being shoved into the barracks with the aid of gun butts and whips, Galewski saw four S.S. men pass in front of him, carefully carrying Bielas. His face was very pale and his eyes looked blind. Kurt Franz joined the group just as it was passing Galewski.

It was then that he heard the dying Max Bielas mutter in a feeble voice:

"Kill all the Jews!"

IX

He was a tall man with an enormous nose, blue-green eyes, and a weather-beaten face. His name was Adolf Friedman, and he had been arrested in Lodz with his father, his mother and two of his sisters. His father had been a well-to-do manufacturer, the owner of a candy factory. He had belonged to that minority of middle-class Jews who had believed that assimilation was possible at the time of the Constitution of 1919, which made the Jews almost full-fledged citizens for the first time in the history of Poland.

Although he continued to celebrate the Sabbath, to fast on Yom Kippur, and to commemorate the flight from Egypt, the elder Friedman called himself a "Pole of Mosaic persuasion." A cultured man and a democrat, he had decided to break out of the walls of the ghetto. After many insults he had succeeded in making a few friends among the Gentiles of the town. It was true that the Gentiles were more inclined to accept his invitations than they were to receive him in their own homes, and he was sometimes seized by doubts about the authenticity of his friends' feelings, but as a good humanist he had too much faith in man to give way to despair. Without denying his Jewish origins he was ready to understand all, accept all, forgive all. His hour of triumph had

136

also been his greatest hour of doubt. The eldest of his four children was a girl of extraordinary beauty. Her name was Hannah, but she was known as Anne at the boarding school for young girls of good family to which her father had managed to get her admitted. Hannah had always been a mystery to her father. Mr. Friedman's feelings toward her were ambivalent. She was too beautiful, too remote, too indifferent for him, the son of a ghetto Jew. Along with pride, she inspired a certain uneasiness in him. She was something of a stranger to her father. One day when she was entertaining some friends from her class, he heard them call her Anne, and he was deeply shocked. Calling her into his library that evening, he asked her the meaning of this. She replied that she had gotten tired of hearing herself called "the Jewess," and that, in view of her father's refusal to take her out of this school and put her into a Jewish, or at least mixed, school, she had decided to carry the adventure of assimilation one step further.

"But my child," said her father, "why didn't you tell me it was that bad?"

"I thought your fondest desire was to see us carry on your work."

"What work?"

"The renunciation of our Judaism. Even now, though you don't forbid us to see our grandparents, you do your best to keep us apart except at Yom Kippur and Passover."

"That's not true," said the father, crushed.

"And yet there is just as much difference between your parents and you as there is between you and me."

She was fifteen at the time. Mr. Friedman had felt tears fill his eyes. Then she had come over and kissed him in a burst of tenderness which had further increased her father's confusion.

"It's my fault," he had told her.

"No, Father, you can't spend your life in a ghetto."

Then confidence had returned. In the end Mr. Friedman had

chosen to believe her, for he found it convenient to have a daughter who was Jewish with the Jews and a Gentile with the Gentiles.

But one day exactly three years after this scene, Hannah had come to see her father in the library and announced that she wanted to get married. The man was handsome, vaguely titled, non-Jewish, and of modest means. She was beautiful, Jewish and rich. Although he doubted that he had really wanted this, Mr. Friedman sensed that he was reaching the goal of his life.

The occasion was no model of gaiety, but everything went off well enough. The in-laws had the tact to have a simple religious ceremony and not to invite relatives who were too violently anti-Semitic. Mr. Friedman, for his part, was wise enough not to be stingy with the dowry.

The rupture was completed the next day when Hannah came to say goodbye before leaving on her honeymoon. Only Adolf, who was sixteen at the time, did not cry. His despair was too great. Hannah had been his greatest love, and he knew that he had just lost her. Tomorrow Hannah, who had been his whole life, would be a stranger, and some day her children might call him a "dirty Jew." He lost his last shred of hope when, as he kissed her, he asked. "Why have you done this, Hannah?"

"But I love him!" she replied, in a voice from which all Yiddish accent had disappeared.

Although they spoke Polish perfectly they were accustomed, when they were together, to mingle their Polish with certain Yiddish intonations. For the first time Hannah had just spoken to him like a stranger. Adolf held back his tears.

"So long, dirty goy!" he said, trying to keep his voice steady, and left the room.

When his father, who had witnessed the scene, came to his room where he had taken refuge, Adolf said, "I hope you'll get to see her oftener than we see our grandparents."

"Is it a curse to be Jewish, then?" murmured his father, sinking into a chair.

"It's not for me to say, Father! But I think it is only for those who don't want to be."

"But if you feel like a Jew, Adolf, it is because I have taught you that you were."

"You have taught me only to go through the motions, which have never made sense to me. It isn't you who have taught me that I am Jewish, but the nice classmates you gave me in your fashionable school. And it wasn't with vague prayers that they taught it to me, but with their fists. I'm sorry you had to find out about it, but since I'm leaving, since I'm going to stop playing your phony game, it doesn't matter any more."

The father looked up, incredulous. He made an attempt to recover his authority.

"Adolf, I forbid you to leave."

"And how can you keep me from leaving when you have given your blessing to this Madame Anne What's-her-name, Countess so-and-so, heretofore the Yid daughter of Friedman the Jew?"

"But Adolf, Hannah is your sister!"

"Countess Anne Kowalski can't be the sister of Adolf Yitzak Friedman any more than she can be the daughter of Solomon Joseph Friedman. You could have figured that out by yourself."

Mr. Friedman was a decent man. Everything he had done, he had done for the good of his children. He had really believed that assimilation was merely a question of good will. "But they love each other," he said in a voice full of conviction.

"That may be true, but that doesn't change anything. Even if she loves something about him besides his title, and even if he can see her behind the big pile of gold she is bringing him, that doesn't keep our family from being broken!"

Whether out of genuine blindness or a need to lie to himself, Mr. Friedman protested. "But she will come to see us, and we will visit her."

"Well, when you go to see her, don't forget to leave your *pay-ess* and your nose at the door."

"Adolf!"

"Father!" replied the son, rising.

The two slaps he received were the first and last that his father ever gave him.

He worked his way across Europe and pretended to be eighteen when he enlisted in the French Foreign Legion.

At the Marseille station to which he was sent the recruiting officer asked no questions. He said only: "You're Jewish, I'm an agnostic, others stutter or have unfaithful wives. None of us has chosen to be what he is, but all have chosen to become Legionnaires."

"I don't know if you joined the Legion to forget you were a Protestant, but I am here to learn to be a Jew."

Until 1933 he was a model Legionnaire. His courage earned him the Médaille Militaire and his sense of discipline a corporal's stripes. Then one day he attacked and mutilated a German Legionnaire who had called him a "dirty Jew," and he was reduced to the ranks.

"I think you were right," his commanding officer told him, "but a corporal does not strike one of his men for personal reasons. It's a question of discipline."

The second brawl earned him the "hole," the celebrated Legion punishment.

The third time, he deserted when he realized that his opponent was dead.

After making a tour of the world and of every more or less respectable activity, he returned to Poland before the declaration of war to enlist in the Polish army.

At that time the Foreign Legion was one of the best military schools in the world. Adolf, although Jewish, was quickly appreciated. Having saved his company from total annihilation in the course of their first engagement, he was made a sergeant on the

battlefield. He had managed to work his way around the enemy
while carrying a heavy machine gun, thus creating a panic in the
German ranks and enabling his company to retreat. Then he held
out alone for three hours against the attacks of the Germans, and
managed to escape during the last attack. His exploit caused a
good deal of comment in the Polish army and this was how his
brother-in-law, who was an officer, heard about him.

They had seen each other only once, on the day of Hannah's
wedding, but Adolf recognized him immediately when he walked
into the field infirmary where he was being treated for a few
minor wounds. However, he pretended not to know him. When
his brother-in-law told him who he was, he answered coldly, "You
must be mistaken, sir. I am an only child."

But Kowalski had seen too many pictures of him among his
wife's belongings and on her dressing table not to recognize that
nose and that intense face, which neither sunburn nor the lines
etched there by fortune had changed.

Under other circumstances Kowalski would have left after
slapping this Jew whom he was doing the favor of visiting. But
Adolf was no longer a Jew, he was a hero. Besides Kowalski had
another reason for persisting, a reason which Adolf could not
know, since he had left Lodz the day after his sister's wedding
and had never corresponded with his family since. Her marriage
and her brother's departure had torn Hannah apart. She had died
a year later of exhaustion and grief while bringing a son into the
world, as if she could not bear to give birth to a Gentile. Hannah's
death had been a terrible shock to her husband, who loved her
passionately. Instead of diminishing with time, Kowalski's sorrow
had only increased. Hannah had taken on exaggerated proportions
in his memory. Everything that had belonged to her, everything
that she had touched, everything that had been dear to her had
become the object of his morbid love. When he went through his
wife's belongings after her death, Kowalski had learned that

Adolf had been the only person she had ever loved. Kowalski had found letters she had written to her brother—without ever mailing them, of course—in which she constantly asked for his forgiveness.

When Kowalski had read the name of Adolf Friedman he had been sure that this was Hannah's brother, and had hurried to see him, to hear him talk about her.

Before Adolf's indifferent face Kowalski hesitated for a moment and then he said very slowly, "Hannah is dead."

"And plenty more Hannahs are going to die! All the Hannahs are going to die!"

"But she was your sister and she loved you more than anything in the world."

"It's not true!" cried Adolf, trying to sit down. "Who told you that?"

He could not resist the evocation of all that Hannah had meant to him.

That night they talked at length of the woman whom they had both loved with a painful love. Kowalski told Adolf that his father had been severely upset by his departure and by the death of his daughter, and that he lived in his house in Lodz as a recluse. Adolf rediscovered a whole world of emotions which he thought he had lost forever.

Kowalski left in the morning. Adolf waited a few minutes and then, without making a sound, got up, dressed, and left the camp. A luminous dawn was rising over that Poland which one week later, for the hundredth time in her history, would suffer defeat, invasion and division.

Lodz was already occupied when he arrived, and the persecutions had begun. He tried to persuade his parents to flee into Russian territory, but his exhausted father would not listen to him. Since Hannah's death he had returned to his faith. Interpreting the teachings of Judaism in the light of his painful personal experience, he saw the ordeals to come as the punishment of God.

"If the Lord wants to punish me for trying to forsake Him I shall not flee His wrath, and if He is to forgive me, we shall survive these ordeals in whatever manner He is pleased to indicate."

Adolf felt that he had a share of responsibility in the tragedy of his family, and he did not want to come into direct conflict with his father. But since he was unable to remain inactive, he began to organize a resistance movement in the ghetto. He was its head and heart until the day of the first deportation, which surprised him at the home of his parents. He offered no resistance and let himself be taken away with them. His father died during the trip. As Adolf leaned over to receive his benediction, he made him swear to survive.

"Forgive me, my son, so the Lord will forgive me," he said, "and promise me to stay alive and to be a good Jew."

After he had closed his father's eyes, Adolf tried to remember the words of the prayer which his grandfather had taught him. But only the first two came into his mind:

"Yiskaddal veyiskaddash . . ."

He repeated them until the train arrived at Treblinka.

"Yiskaddal veyiskaddash, yiskaddal veyiskaddash . . ."

His mother and sisters prayed along with him, mechanically.

When they arrived at the camp they were separated without even being able to say goodbye, and Adolf plunged into that world of anguish with nothing but the memory of the oath he had made his father.

He had been studying the possibilities of escape when Choken had leaped into the car. And now in the barracks which was rapidly being claimed by darkness, he was wandering in search of Galewski.

The prisoners remained motionless as if stupefied. Not a cry, not a groan was heard. Everything had been too quick: the reel-

143

ing form of Max Bielas, the bursts of machine-gun fire, the panic and the mad race. Then suddenly, incomprehensibly, everything had stopped. When the running had resumed under the whips, they had left like automatons, dragging the dead as well as those who were merely dazed, understanding that their only security was to run faster, always faster, dragging something by one foot. Some of those who were only stunned recovered during the running. They managed to release themselves from the desperate grip of their companions and get to their feet again. They began to run with the rest. Others were thrown alive into the ditch of the "hospital." Now that the doors had been violently slammed and bolted, a heavy silence had replaced the sound and the fury.

When the machine guns had begun to fire, Adolf had recovered his soldier's instinct. He had thrown himself to the ground and crawled toward a corner of the barracks. Although it was absolutely forbidden to enter them in the daytime, the doors to the barracks where the prisoners slept were not locked during the day. When he had reached the corner Adolf had worked his way to the door in short dashes, as during the first phase of an attack. Then, watching the gunners on the roof of the other barracks, he seized a moment when they were looking the other way to slip through the door, which he closed immediately. For safety's sake he had not tried to follow what was going on through the narrow windows which let a little light and air into the barracks, but had hidden behind the door, ready to pounce on the first enemy who entered, disarm him, and die fighting. Choken's sudden appearance in the car today had been a revelation to him. He had recovered his reflexes and now, lurking in ambush, he waited, sure of himself, in control of his body, with a kind of serenity that came from the certainty that he would be able to kill the first German or Ukrainian who crossed the threshold and disarm him before anyone had time to intervene. He had planned his maneuver: he would leap from behind the door and knock the enemy to the ground. Then he told himself that if only one man came in, he could even take care of him without alerting the guards. He would only have to push back the door as he rushed in. He thought that in this case he could do much more damage by putting on his victim's uniform. Having prepared himself, he relaxed. Shortly afterward the shouting became clearer and louder. Adolf crouched down when he heard the door being pushed open. But instead of the guard he was expecting, it was a rush of prisoners who charged through the doorway. Slightly disappointed, Adolf made way for them. It was not that easy to die.

Galewski had come in a few moments after the mass of prisoners and had stayed by the door. Adolf recognized him and walked over.

"My name is Adolf," he said, standing squarely in front of him.

Galewski stared at him with a look of astonishment. Then, as if he were emerging from a deep sleep, his face, then his eyes, then his mouth gradually seemed to come back to life.

"Adolf? That name means nothing to me."

But his eyes, which were gazing at Adolf intensely, suddenly showed a gleam of recognition.

"And yet I know your face."

Adolf reminded him quietly of the train, Choken, the escape.

"Ah, yes, now I know," said Galewski in a tone that was relieved and infinitely weary, like that of a dying man who suddenly hunts for a memory, and even as he finds it, tells himself that it wasn't important. "That was a long time ago."

"A few hours!"

"A few hours which represent a whole life, our whole life. We were like condemned men waiting for their pardon. Now we have just learned that it has been refused."

This afternoon it was Adolf who had been downcast. The revelation of an organization among the prisoners had brought him back to life. Tonight the roles were reversed. Galewski seemed to

145

have reached the depths of despair, but Adolf had taken up the torch.

"Condemned men? We were that anyway," he said, in a voice that was deliberately indifferent.

He understood that it was his duty to restore to Galewski that courage which he had breathed into him, that some other day, perhaps, if they were to go on living, the roles would be reversed again, that the two of them would breathe this courage into a third who, in turn, might some day restore it, that all three would then inspire a fourth, and so on with an absurd passion until death, which seemed at that time the only ponderable certainty. Because life is a duty, and despair the gravest of sins.

"The only difference," he continued, "is that now we know the exact date of our death."

"That is why we no longer have any hope to cling to."

"But then since we have no more illusions, we are free to act," reasoned Adolf.

What Adolf was telling him Galewski had thought all along. It was by giving himself this argument that he had found the strength to go on living in order to prepare the prisoners to make the day of their death a day of glory. But events had overtaken him, this day of death was catching him too soon.

"You and I, yes," he replied; "but not the others. Look at them! Don't you think they are more prepared to die than to revolt?"

Emerging slowly from their stupor, the prisoners had begun to pray or talk in low voices, exchanging final memories. For some, the inescapable proximity of death restored a semblance of life, as sometimes the sky, before the night claims it, is suddenly filled with a strange brightness.

Adolf ran his eyes slowly over the barracks, which was almost entirely consumed by darkness.

"You think they won't follow us if we revolt when the Germans come for us?"

146

"I am sure of it," replied Galewski with recovered assurance. "Something has been broken in them which it would have taken a very long time to put back together. They are alive only by virtue of an old ancestral reflex, but unconsciously they are ashamed not to have died with their families. That is the extraordinary power of the Nazi system. Like certain spiders, it puts its victims to sleep before killing them. It is a death in two stages: you put men to sleep, then you kill the sleepers. This may seem very complicated, but actually it was the only way. Suppose that the S.S. had arrived announcing that they were going to kill us all, swearing it, starting to prove it. There is no doubt at all that the three million Polish Jews would have revolted. They would have done it with their backs to the wall, with the courage of despair. And it wouldn't have taken a few thousand men to beat us, but the whole Wehrmacht—and even then it isn't certain that all the soldiers would have obeyed! Then look at *us!* Not only do the Jews let themselves be killed without a gesture of revolt, but they even help their killers with their work of extermination. We, the accomplices, the employees of death, live in a world beyond life and death; compromised so profoundly that we can only be ashamed to be alive."

"Monsters, in short?"

"Yes, a new species of men in keeping with this new world."

"But monsters who do revolt sometimes, like that one just now?"

"Berliner was a friend. He was supposed to leave with Choken, the man who ran into you in the car. Actually he did not revolt, he went mad. Mad for us, that is to say; normal for other men. When he saw his parents arrive, he immediately became a man of the other world again, and a man of the other world can't stand the life we live; so he went mad, or became "normal" again, as you please. Why did he kill Max Bielas? No doubt it wasn't planned. If he had planned his act he would have killed Kurt Franz, who is much more dangerous. Either he killed at random, or else he was carrying out some plan which we don't know, and never will know. It isn't Berliners that we need, but fighters of a new dimension: soldiers of death, as there are soldiers of faith."

"Like you and me?"

"Perhaps, but we aren't going to take the camp by storm between the two of us; especially since there is still something missing: a reason for doing it."

"What do you mean?"

"When I spent my nights taking down men who had tried to hang themselves, I told them they had to survive in order to testify. But I don't really believe it. Some day the graves will be opened. The people who find them will be able to imagine what our suffering was like."

"I'm not sure," Adolf said pensively. "My bones will tell that I died, but they won't tell how I died. They won't say that first I was put to sleep, or that I became a killer myself, a victim-killer. The ditches will tell that so many million Jews were killed, but that's only statistics." He spoke haltingly. "What the ditches won't tell is why and how we died. How this could have been possible—on either side: for the victims as well as the killers—how we let ourselves be killed, and how they succeeded in killing us."

Galewski looked at Adolf with gratitude. Once again he had recovered the absurd courage to continue the struggle.

The night was almost over and still the Technicians had not reacted to the murder of Max Bielas. Since death was slow in coming and since for a long time now among the Jews hope had merely been a question of faith, the prisoners were slowly coming back to life. The change had been imperceptible until a voice from the back of the barracks said, "After all, they need us. Why would they kill us. They would be forced to replace us and it would be the same thing."

This statement of hope climaxed a discussion that had gone on almost all night. It rang through the barracks like a message.

Yes, these men could still hope. After a night of agony, in the first glimmer of dawn that heralded the return of day and the new victory of light over darkness, once again the Jews began to believe in the miracle. There is a mystery here whose explanation can be found only in another and greater mystery, which is the survival of the Jewish people. Reason can enumerate a certain number of causes for this phenomenon—devotion to a faith, sense of solidarity, familial fanaticism, and so on—but other nations in which these same conditions applied have disappeared, at best leaving behind only a few fragments of stone. Heirs of this age-old mystery, the Jews of Treblinka revived it once again. And yet this time all the conditions seemed to point to its not being renewed. Perhaps it is in this individual denial of death, this congenital inability to imagine it, that one can find the underlying cause of this miracle or survival. The Jew, more than another man, realizes himself within his national community; as a Jew he can exist only insofar as he belongs to it. As soon as he leaves it he loses himself in the broader species of man. If the individual Jew remains mortal in spite of himself, his will to deny death renders the community immortal. This immortality of the community in turn reflects back on its members, who participate in its immortality.

Did the Technicians understand this complex process? Probably not, as the rest of this story seems to prove. But there is something they did understand: that "to rid the earth of its Jews," intimidation, slavery and decimation were not enough, that it was necessary to kill them all, down to the last man, that it was necessary not only to kill them, but to uproot their very memory from the earth. This, too, they tried to do; it was then that the Jews felt the breath of oblivion pass over them and decided to do something.

The blue of the windows paled in the rising sun. The spirit of the discussions rose. Many remained pessimists, to be sure, but a great many of these would have become optimists if the optimists had been pessimists. They say that Jews do not react like other men, and it is true, or at least it was this morning of Rosh Hashana. These same Jews who, the day before, before the assassination of Max Bielas, were mere automatons, existing in a no man's land between life and death, these same Jews who had imagined themselves dead a few hours before, because they believed that they had just escaped death, were now suddenly seized with an insane hope. They had discovered that even in Treblinka one can always be more miserable.

Since the wearing of a watch was punishable by death, only Galewski possessed one, so he was the first to know that something was wrong. It was a quarter past five. The Ukrainian guards should have driven the Jews out of the barracks fifteen minutes ago. So as not to frighten the others, he leaned toward Adolf and murmured, "I think we're nearing the end after all. We should have been taken out a quarter of an hour ago."

"It was too good to be true," Adolf whispered back.

"I'd like to see what's going on in the yard," said Galewski in the same tone.

"If you stand up to look out a window you might scare the others." Adolf was using the familiar *"du"* for the first time. "After all, we don't know. Maybe your watch is fast, or maybe they've decided to let us sleep late this morning."

"I doubt it, but with these people who knows? Listen, this obviously isn't the moment to talk about it, but if we aren't all killed now, we must organize so we'll be able to try something the next time."

Adolf looked up.

"Count on me," he said, laying his hand on Galewski's arm.

They gazed at each other for a few moments. Then the whistle of a locomotive rent the air.

X

THE BARRACKS seemed spellbound. The first convoy was arriving, and they had not been taken outside yet. Everyone had under-stood. Stupefied, they looked at each other. The dream had ended, the agony was beginning again. For several moments no one moved. The train slowly passed the camp. The silence was so profound that you could hear the bump of the mufflers and the jostle of the cars at each rail joining. Like the inhabitants of Pompeii who were found preserved in lava in the attitudes in which death had surprised them, the prisoners remained frozen in the positions in which the whistle of the locomotive had caught them. Suddenly one of the prisoners dashed to a window. He looked out quickly and dropped down again.

"The barracks are surrounded," he said in a flat voice.

Galewski was about to get up and try to calm the prisoners when the uproar broke out. Stupor gave way to panic. Many wept, others blasphemed, still others prayed. The prayers were more like savage incantations, desperate appeals that rose and drowned each other out. The Jews swayed back and forth as they prayed, but so violently that their heads nodded in all directions as if they were about to come off their bodies. God, the great absentee, was simultaneously cursed with rage and praised with ecstasy. The rage of some was such that they looked for the filthiest words that have ever been used for the lowest prostitutes with which to revile Him. Others called Him the sweetest and most glorious names. They thanked Him for these ordeals and asked Him to multiply them infinitely. Adolf, dumfounded, contemplated this spectacle.

"This is real faith," Galewski told him, raising his voice to make himself heard. "A perpetual and passionate dialogue with God, a succession of radical doubts and blind thanks."

Adolf's answer was lost in the uproar.

Little by little the shouting subsided.

"What will they do with us?" asked some.

"They'll throw grenades!"

"They're going to burn the barracks!"

"They'll take us to the gas chambers!"

The answers rang out from all directions, increasing the panic even more.

Soon the sun was high in the sky and the heat became stifling. The smell of the latrines, which had not been emptied, was suffocating, and many—although they were inured to filth—could not keep from vomiting.

Around the barracks the Ukrainians and the S.S. stood motionless, with guns aimed.

The torment lasted all morning.

At noon, one of the prisoners, who was perched on the shoulders of another and keeping watch, cried, "Here they come!"

It touched off a stampede. The prisoners rushed toward the back of the barracks, where they crowded together in an inextricable human mound. Each tried to melt into the mass of the others, the ones in front tried to slip between those in the second row and the latecomers, panic-stricken, scaled the tangle of bodies in order to hide in the very back. But those who were underneath and who could not breathe, pushed, and in trying to get out from under, swayed the human pyramid.

When they opened the door the Ukrainian guards drew back, appalled by the spectacle and suffocated by the smell. The S.S. drove them forward with their whips.

Adolf and a few *kapos* had stayed near the door with Galewski.

The Ukrainians, maddened by the whips, began to beat the pile of bodies furiously. The whips hissed and the clubs made a strange noise as they struck flesh, but the mass, instead of disintegrating, seemed to fuse together more closely than before. Galewski looked on, terrified.

"Do something," Adolf told him in a flat voice, "or they will kill them all."

"They will anyway," replied one of the *kapos*.

"Not like this," cried Adolf, turning quickly to the *kapo*.

"You're right," said Galewski. "Either you fight back or you die like a man, but this butchery is pointless."

Kurt Franz was in front of the door. Galewski walked over to him and asked his permission to speak to the prisoners. Franz agreed and called off the Ukrainians.

"You have two minutes to make them come out of their hole," he said.

Two minutes. It was not enough time to make a fancy speech, to explain to the prisoners that if they had to die there was nothing they could do about it—the Germans had only to machine-gun the barracks—and that therefore the best thing to do was pull themselves together so they would have an easier death. Galewski even doubted that the Jews were still accessible to reason. They were petrified with terror, in a state of trance. As he walked to the middle of the barracks, he had made his decision.

"My brothers," he said, "I understand your fear. But the commandant of the camp has just assured me that you will remain alive, that no harm will be done to you. I believe him, because he has nothing to gain by telling me this. However, he also said that if you were not all outside in one minute, he would give the order to burn the barracks."

The pyramid collapsed, changing into a human tide that rushed toward the door.

Once outside, the prisoners were divided into three columns and led to the platform where the trains arrived. The left-hand column was led away to the "hospital" without offering the least resistance, without a cry or a murmur. When they heard the fusillade, the other prisoners knew that for the time being they had been saved. They looked at each other, astonished to have survived again. When they were lined up on the platform, Kurt Franz sent for Galewski.

"There are criminals among you and you did not inform me of the fact." He slapped him with all his might. "This is the last time I will slap you. The next time I am displeased with you, you will be executed."

Next a short, fat S.S. officer made the Jews an insane speech, which he politely begged Galewski to translate into Yiddish. He began by telling them that the gold and clothing that had been collected were to serve in the creation of Jewish "reservations." Six states would be created, of which Treblinka would be one. Next the S.S. officer announced that they would move into new barracks, where they would sleep on wooden bunks and would receive two blankets apiece. He promised more water to wash with and ended with a threat. Curiously, it was the threat that reassured the Jews the most. The promises were too wonderful to believe; but when the officer concluded, "Those who do not work will be eliminated," they understood that it was not out of humanity that they were being treated this way, but out of need.

This threat of death, by counterbalancing the promises, gave them value.

The prisoners were slowly recovering from their surprise when Kurt Franz began speaking again. It was at this moment that he received the nickname that was to follow him throughout his career: *Lalka* (the "doll"). Tall, very blond, graceful and muscular, his round fallen-angel face gave him an aspect that was fascinating and disturbing at the same time. When he planted himself in front of them, his arms crossed in front of his chest, his feet slightly apart, and his chest thrown out, all the prisoners found him very handsome.

"He has the face of a doll," someone whispered.

The expression stuck.

His speech, which was worthy of a general's address to his troops, is a collector's item. Only his very shrill voice sounded a discordant note.

"I promise," he began, pausing dramatically, "I promise each of you personally that no worker will suffer any harm whatsoever."

He had emphasized the word "worker," to the astonishment of the prisoners. They did not understand this sudden metamorphosis of the Jews into workers. As they came to realize later, the world of death was also to become a world of lies in which the gas chambers were known as the "factory," and bodies *figuren*, the prisoners "workers," and so on.

"I promise," Franz went on even more convincingly, "that each of you will leave the camp in the condition in which he arrived. I give you my solemn oath on my honor as an S.S."

Lalka liked to talk. On that day he took pleasure in explaining pompously what it meant for an S.S. to give his word of honor and how valuable it was. To hear him talk, Treblinka was to become an earthly paradise. He promised to organize plays and athletic events, to provide plentiful nourishment, and even to build an infirmary. In return for this, what did he ask? Discipline and efficiency.

While Lalka was talking, Galewski was trying to guess what had happened during the night among the Technicians. He sensed that Franz had played a decisive role. This manner of addressing the prisoners must be the result of a deliberate technique. He was looking at him, intrigued, when he noticed that in place of the insignia of a noncommissioned officer which he had still been wearing the day before, his impeccable black uniform now bore the silver epaulettes and flashes of a second lieutenant, an *Untersturmführer* in the S.S. Galewski learned the details only through bribes and much later.

Realizing that he ran the risk of being blamed for this breach of discipline, the commandant of the camp had wanted to hush up the Bielas case. When he called his staff together, he proposed to execute all the prisoners and to replace them the next day with new arrivals. It was at this point that he came into conflict with Kurt Franz. Although Franz was only a noncommissioned officer, he was a member of the secret police, and the commandant, in spite of their mutual antipathy, could do nothing without his approval. Franz, an ambitious young officer, was determined to make him purchase this approval at a very high price. In his opinion, Berliner's act merely demonstrated the absurdity of the present policy toward the Jews. Therefore the important thing was not to kill the Jews, but to reform the system. He offered to do it himself, but demanded carte blanche.

"The actual running of the camp, in short?" the commandant asked.

Without answering directly, Franz went on: "However, I am ready to make a concession although it costs me a great deal, since everything that has been accomplished so far is my work: if you agree, I'll leave you the Jews."

156

The commandant was ready to give in when the telephone rang. It was the officer who had accompanied Bielas to the hospital in Lublin. Bielas had died when he reached the hospital, the town authorities had already been informed, and there was some danger of an inquest. At once the commandant was ready to agree to anything, but Franz, who had followed the telephone conversation, saw in the unexpected turn of events a way to get rid of his superior once and for all and at the same time to relieve himself of responsibility for what had happened.

A few minutes later another telephone call summoned them all to Lublin, where, at Franz's request, they were questioned separately.

The commandant was the first to be heard. Since he did not know what his subordinate had decided and since he was afraid that he would betray him, he decided to relate the facts as they had happened. But he was only a poor minister gone astray, more sadistic than clever. For him, crime was only a fatal temptation and not a supreme good. He did not commit evil, he submitted to it with delight. He was an immoral, rather than an amoral, man. The Technicians realized that his appointment had been a mistake.

Kurt Franz, on the other hand, was one of them, a real Technician. He knew how to talk to them. The picture he painted of the camp was not very charitable toward his former superiors, the commandant and his assistant Max Bielas.

"A sadist and a pederast," he said.

The last detail keenly interested the leading Technicians. Franz satisfied their curiosity. He omitted no detail. His account was enlightening.

The handsome Max Bielas had had a harem of little Jewish boys. He liked them young, no older than seventeen. In a kind of parody of the shepherds of Arcadia, their role was to take care of the camp flock of geese. They were dressed like princes and possessed several suits of clothes, but they had to wear the same thing at the same time, so that they would still be in uniform. Bielas had had a little barracks built for them that looked like a doll's house. It was located in a small pine wood on the western boundary of the camp. Around it was a miniature park and around this park was a barbed-wire enclosure. The house was made of roughhewn logs which gave it an improbable rustic quality. There was a little roof over the door and multicolored curtains adorned the windows. Except for a small hallway, the interior of the cabin consisted of one large dormitory. On either side of a central aisle there were two rows of identical beds separated by little bedside tables on which candlesticks were placed. Every evening the boys stood at attention at the foot of their beds when Bielas came to wish them good night. During the day they walked in the park. Sometimes Bielas took them for a walk in the neighboring woods, but usually he kept them within the camp limits. Every day he spent several hours in their company, watching them at the rustic table which was set in front of the cabin when weather permitted and amusing them by organizing games or telling them fabulous stories of deep forests, charming princes and bloodthirsty dragons. The boys were very happy. They called him Max and seemed very fond of him. Whenever he came to see them they rushed to meet him with cries of joy.

Max had explained to them that their parents had gone to work in the Ukraine. Sometimes he waited two days without going to see them and when he returned he told them that he had gone to the Ukraine, where he had seen their parents. "They asked me whether you are being good, whether you are working hard, and whether you miss them. You must not forget your parents, my little ones, your parents who are working for the Reich."

Carried away by his tale in spite of himself, Kurt Franz added admiringly, "And not for a single moment did the children suspect a thing!"

Then Franz went on to the commandant. He described him as a sadistic intellectual incapable of directing an undertaking like Treblinka. "For him," he explained, "the extermination of the Jews is evil, and this is what attracts him. But he has understood nothing of the grandeur of our work of purification. He is not just a bad Nazi, he is the opposite of a Nazi. Just as Bielas sought in Treblinka only the satisfaction of his homosexual instincts, the commandant wanted only to appease his sadism. Hence the enterprise was conducted in the most complete disorder."

Then Kurt Franz launched into a criticism of the system, taking credit, of course, for the only positive achievements, in which, for that matter, he was not altogether unjustified. In the tests for screening the prisoners he found nothing to criticize, but here the directors had merely followed the manuals to the letter. Their mistake, according to him, had been not to lessen the pressure at the time of the first great reorganization.

"We had at our disposal an extraordinary material, perfect subhumans. This success, which was interesting from a theoretical point of view, presented a certain number of practical disadvantages, for the mass had become virtually unusable. We decided, therefore, to organize and specialize it, and I chose *kapos*. The maneuver was delicate. In effect we were about to recreate more normal living conditions among individuals utterly devoid of hope. I suggested that we resume our old policy, which consists of always leaving a little margin of hope to which the victims can cling. I explained that hope is to the Jews what fuel is to a motor, that you can starve them, as long as you leave them a minimum of hope. But nobody would listen to me.

"This was when the suicides began. I returned to the attack. I saw them as the confirmation of my theories and a serious manifestation of lack of discipline. In vain I explained that by allowing the Jews the freedom to die, we were letting them get away from us, we were permitting them a degree of independence. I was told that since in any case all the Jews were to die, the suicides meant that much less work to do.

"Finally the suicides ceased, why I don't really know, but it was then that the escape attempts began. It was impossible to combat them effectively as long as prisoners could not be identified. Therefore I proposed giving them numbers.

" 'Numbers!' they retorted again. 'And why not names, private rooms, and the right to strike? And we'll call them Mister, too, and we'll organize elections.'

"So, you see, a man can be a good anti-Semite and a bad technician," Kurt Franz concluded.

His superiors asked him what he thought should be done. He explained succinctly and in exchange was promoted to second lieutenant and given carte blanche for Treblinka.

Max Bielas was buried with military honors; and the commandant was transferred to a Waffen S.S. unit on the eastern front.

When he returned to camp, before lying down for a few hours, Kurt Franz had his epaulettes sewn on and Max Bielas' little boys executed. The S.S. man who was assigned this task came back sick. His name was Menda. Until that day he had been a model executioner.

Before Hitler's accession to power Kurt Franz had been a waiter in a little town in Bavaria. He had had his revelation in the very early days of the Nazi regime. It had been one of those extraordinary encounters between an individual and his destiny. From a waiter in a second-rate café, Lalka was to become a technician of death of very high rank.

Formerly everything about him had been mediocre. At school a real lack of talent reinforced by a certain natural indifference kept him perpetually near the bottom of the class. Colorless in his nonentity, little Kurt was too lacking in courage and too fearful of authority to dare spend class periods on the banks of the river which ran through the town. Later his love affairs languished under the same sign of indecision and failure, in spite of his good looks. After a few unsuccessful professional experiences, he became a waiter.

It was then that he began to have ambitions. He threw himself into boxing, but lost more fights than he won, received more punches than he gave. Although he was mortified by his defeats, a certain pride was already developing in him. He claimed that the fights were rigged and renounced the noble sport. Meanwhile his looks had brought him to the attention of the owner of the leading café in town, who hired him. For young Franz this was a promotion. He was aware of it and took great pride in it. An orchestra came to play every afternoon. Franz, who had a good ear, dreamed of becoming a musician and devoted his savings to this new ambition. He studied with the leader of the orchestra and spent his nights trying to wring a few coherent sounds out of an old worn-out violin. More a victim of the will power of his pupil than of the spirit of gain, the poor orchestra leader did not dare discourage him, although he had realized from the start that Franz would never be capable even of being an extra in the municipal choral society. To the future misfortune of several hundred thousand of his coreligionists, the orchestra leader was Jewish.

The Reichstag fire caught Franz on the brink of a despair to which he had been led by the belated but sudden realization that in music as in everything else he was a failure. He was on the point of recognizing his own nothingness when he attended his first Nazi meeting. At last, he had discovered his path.

When he returned from Lublin that morning, the head of S.S. Untersturmführer Kurt Franz was seething with ideas. At last his value had been recognized. He was going to show his superiors how right they had been to have confidence in him. The first task was to take the Jews in hand again, to begin the training all over at zero. Next he would have to reorganize the work in order to arrive at maximum output. Then and only then would come the crowning achievement. Treblinka would not be just an extermination camp, but a complete world with a life of its own, plays, entertainments, sports, weddings and parties.

XI

THE TRANSFER OF the prisoners to new quarters had been anticipated for some time; Max Bielas had been killed just as he was
about to announce the news of their change of residence.

The new barracks, which had been constructed as an extension
of the headquarters of the *Hofjuden*, formed a U-shaped unit.
The decision to relocate the Jews had been one of several measures taken to prevent escapes. The new enclosure was surrounded by a barbed-wire fence around which there was a guard
path. To the right of the barracks a large open space was to become the new Roll Call Square. The kitchen, which until then
had been a simple portable field affair, was installed at one end of
the barracks of the *Hofjuden*. A sort of slot was cut into the partition here, and through it the prisoners, filing by one at a time,
received their food three times a day. On the other side of Roll
Call Square trees were planted. Finally, a well had been dug opposite the kitchen. The area formed by the barracks and yard,
which the Jews left only to go to work and to which they returned
as soon as work was over, was called the Ghetto.

Everything was ready to welcome the prisoners. They were led
to the Ghetto immediately after Lalka's speech.

When they entered their new barracks the prisoners knew that they had just won their first victory. A new feeling seized them. It was not joy or even relief, but a vague emotion born of the hope that some day something might be attempted. They had just ceased to be merely objects in the hands of the Germans. A Jew had killed a German and the Germans, instead of killing all the Jews, had made speeches, had tried to restore their hope. It may all have been lies, but the fact that someone was taking the trouble to lie to them was seen as a sign. Something had just changed in their relations with their killers.

Suddenly the game was becoming more complex. The killers had retained the right to kill, but they felt the need to give explanations. The death of the Jews ceased to be a gratuitous phenomenon governed by a blind force; it became part of a logical system: "Work and your life will be spared." Naturally, the prisoners suspected that this promise was only a lure and that in the final analysis, when the Technicians no longer had need of them, they would execute them in their turn. But they also knew that in the meantime a kind of contract had just been made with them, a contract valid for the duration of the extermination of the Jewish people and nonrenewable.

Such were the limits of the new life expectancy of the Jews of Treblinka. They knew this and they were determined, unconsciously as yet, to take advantage of it.

When he assumed the actual direction of the camp (an officer who was his superior in rank would be appointed afterward, but that officer would be concerned only with administrative work), Lalka realized that the task would be a heavy one. The mass of the prisoners represented the result of a kind of natural selection. Those physically or psychologically weak had not survived the multiple ordeals. Only the "tough ones" remained. It was inherent in the logic of the system. Kurt Franz could, of course, have killed everyone and started again from scratch, but the situation would quickly have returned to the same point, and meanwhile the output would have suffered. He decided that it was not worth the trouble and that it was preferable to create conditions of oppression calculated to keep the prisoners in a state of absolute servitude. It was then that the "Lalka system" was born. It consisted of a certain number of oppressive measures each of which was sufficient to lead a man of normal temperament to despair.

First there was the technique of the Sword of Damocles, or "pigeon shooting." This technique, which was merely a new version of the technique of the black eye, presented a certain number of advantages over the latter. During work hours Lalka, who was an excellent shot, would mount one of the piles of clothing (they easily reached the height of a two- or three-story house). The prisoners who were working below were not allowed to look up. A few Ukrainians watched to see that they did not. Lalka's pistol was suspended over the workers' heads like a Damocles' sword; with it he immediately killed those whom he caught doing nothing. Of course the system was far from being infallible, for Lalka could not personally keep an eye on the six hundred workers in the different sorting commandos, and his influence was more psychological than real, but it did succeed in mythifying authority, while at the same time sparing the workers. The worker could always take the risk of stopping work and watching Lalka and the Ukrainians out of the corner of his eye, but the effect imposed by such a choice was more costly in the end than the one required by the work. Therefore the prisoners deliberately chose to work. But while they were working, with lowered eyes, they felt weighing on them a permanent menace which assumed exaggerated proportions in their minds because of its invisibility. With an extraordinary economy of means—a gun and a few Ukrainians— Lalka succeeded in creating a psychosis of fear, which was all the more powerful because it was not objectively justified. This irrational fear could only lead to the mythification of the power of Lalka, a mythification that would last to the very end.

Later Lalka had a dog, Barry, whom he used in the same spirit. When he was not perched on the pile of clothing, he would walk silently among the workers. As soon as he saw one who seemed to lack ardor, he would set Barry on him with the command, "Look, man, that dog isn't working!" (*Sieh mal, Mensch, dieser Hund arbeitet nicht!*) and the dog, which was trained to attack a man's private parts, would rush at the Jew, whom Lalka was usually humane enough to put out of his misery. It was a crude idea to call the dog "man" and the Jew "dog," but by dint of daily repetition the Jews almost accepted it, at least in the special world that Treblinka had become. Every society has its scale of social values: in Treblinka, the dogs took precedence over the Jews.

To keep the Jews in a condition of slavery, Lalka began with the principle that it was necessary to repeat to them, and to make them repeat until they were convinced of it, that they were inferior beings. His presence on a pile of rags was designed to do this. Barry also contributed to the same result. But these two measures required no participation from the prisoners. He devised a third, which would fill this gap. He had a song written, which, when sung to some military air, became the anthem of Treblinka. The Jews had to sing this anthem a dozen times a day: when they went to work and when they returned, during roll call, whenever they moved from one place to another. It became automatic and their wills ceased to resist the repetition of the brutal meaning of the words:

> The tramp of the workers is heard
> Their faces are set and grave
> Their columns leave for work
> Always faithful and brave.

166

Refrain: This is why we are in Treblinka
Whatever fate may send,
This is why we are in Treblinka
Always ready for the end.

When the voice of our master thunders
And when he seems to look our way
We form columns and stand waiting
Always ready to obey.

Work is our existence
We must obey or die.
We do not want to leave . . .
. . . 'Til destiny winks its eye.

The first time they heard it, the prisoners could not help smiling in spite of themselves at the inanity of the words. They learned them with the help of whips, and stopped smiling.

After a day's work, they had to repeat it tirelessly for hours on end while standing at attention on the new Roll Call Square; word by word, line by line, stanza by stanza, they droned it until they no longer knew what the words meant. Any attempt at resistance was as impossible as it was absurd. The Ukrainians strolled through the ranks like sheep dogs, looking for those who were only pretending to sing. When the Jews knew the words and music of the anthem, they learned to sing it as they marched: arms stiff, legs straight, necks rigid, hour after hour, beyond repugnance, beyond all will. Marching on and on until they abandoned themselves entirely to the dulling rhythm of the cadenced step, until the words came out of their mouths in an unchecked stream, until they began to believe what they were bawling.

You cannot invent sincerity, you cannot manufacture belief. But Lalka had warned them, "You will stop marching when I feel that it is not from your mouths that you are singing, but from your hearts, from the bottoms of your hearts." And then they had begun to march. It was five o'clock in the evening. The attack had been indirect. At first the guards had spent an hour making them stretch their arms, straighten their necks, hold up their heads. The singing was pure cacophony, but nobody seemed to notice. The prisoners concentrated all their efforts on their posture and forgot the anthem. Steady marching, with the effort of fusion it requires, annihilates individual wills. It plunges men into a euphoria of pain, a kind of second state which makes them lose their individuality, reduces their power to resist. Lalka attacked the song only when he felt that they had reached this state. By eleven o'clock at night when they returned, dazed, to the barracks, the prisoners were humming the anthem without knowing it. The next day the exercise resumed, and the day after that. The treatment went on this way for two weeks.

If there was a constant in the Technician's methods at the different levels of operation Final Solution, it was meticulousness. With a doggedness that would have been ridiculous in any other circumstance, he returned his work to the work table two hundred times, polishing and repolishing it with the conscientiousness of a Tibetan monk. Nothing discouraged him, nothing ever satisfied him. Driven by an inexhaustible energy, his mind perpetually in search of further improvement, he went on, never losing confidence, inaccessible to doubt, impervious to weariness or boredom.

Lalka could have been satisfied with this set of measures, which formed a respectable whole. To think so would be to misunderstand his professional conscience. In the early days of Treblinka he had dreamed of creating a system that would run itself, "without our even having to press a button when we get up in the morning," as he had put it. This first attempt had resulted in failure. A Prometheus of extermination, he was off again in quest of this idyllic goal: a camp in which everything would run itself, or almost.

The first measures were designed for the psychological conditioning of the prisoners. They were intended to make them into slaves without any mental reservations, slaves ready to devote all their energy to carrying out the work that was demanded of them. In this respect they represented considerable progress over the disorderly methods of the previous administration. From another standpoint, however, because they spared lives, they no longer assured the elimination of elements that were physically or psychologically unfit. In the early days of Treblinka the working force of the prisoners was renewed in its totality about once a week, which meant that approximately one seventh of the working force was killed every day in one way or another. This rapid rotation assured the camp a constant turnover, new blood. The new system, on the other hand, no longer insured this turnover, and for this reason it ran the risk of letting the camp become congested with unproductive elements.

It was to combat this danger of asphyxiation that Lalka developed the "rule of the quarter." Applicable to the prisoners as a whole or only to groups, it was designed to reduce the body in question by one fourth. Its principle was simple: you took a group of prisoners or all the prisoners and subjected them to a certain number of exercises until one quarter of the treated force was eliminated. This procedure, which at first glance closely resembles the second aptitude test, nevertheless differs radically from it: the point was no longer to hold out a certain length of time but to hold out longer than one quarter of your comrades. The double advantage it presents can be seen immediately: in the first place, it makes it possible to determine precisely the percentage of survivors, and in the second place, it pits the subjects against each other, since the survival of some depends on the death of others.

This rule of the quarter was rarely applied to the prisoners as a whole, because the exercises, which were very taxing, fatigued the survivors enormously and consequently reduced the efficiency of their work. On the other hand, it was applied to limited groups practically every evening. These groups were composed either of entire commandos whose work had not given satisfaction, or of individuals chosen during roll call or in the course of the day. When roll call was over all the prisoners were arranged in a circle around the space in which the exercise was to proceed. The exercise itself is very well known. Although prohibited, it is commonly used in all the armies of the world. It consists in making men run and then ordering them successively to lie down, walk on all fours, crawl, lie on their backs, lie on their bellies, get up, sit down, run again, and so on. Very exhausting, it is designed to break stubborn individuals. But its military use cannot be compared with the application that was made of it in Treblinka, for there those who were exhausted did not go and lie down, they were immediately led to the "hospital."

Although the Jews of Treblinka had reached a point of saturation where death had lost much of its emotive power, they called this exercise the "race of the dead."

At the beginning of the exercise, in a last gesture of solidarity, the condemned men would stay in a compact group, but soon the whips went into action, falling on the last members of the pack. The latter then accelerated in order to melt into the mass, but the next-to-the-last also accelerated to keep from becoming the last, and little by little the panic caught up with the whole group, which from this moment on began to fall apart. Then a drama began which would last as long as the will to live of the weakest.

One of the most tragic of these "races of the dead" was the one in which Professor Mehring died. When he had arrived in Treblinka one of his former students had managed to save him and, with a few other friends, had taken care of him. Professor Mehring was an old man and there was no room for old people at Treblinka.

Professor Mehring had been one of the great personalities in the Lodz ghetto. Christian friends had invited him to take refuge in their homes, but he had refused. He had just learned that the convoys of Jews who were leaving Lodz were not going to clear the uncultivated lands of the east, but were going to Treblinka, and that Treblinka meant death. Every day he saw the Jews leave without offering the least resistance. They must learn the truth, they must organize, they must resist. He was deported before he was able to convince a single Jew. In ancient Rome people cut off the heads of messengers who brought bad news; in Lodz and in Vilna, as in Bialystok and in Warsaw, they simply refused to listen.

Professor Mehring had understood that the Jewish people was undergoing one of its greatest crises, and at night in the barracks he would gather a few prisoners around him to explain his vision of the world and to beg them to stay alive. "That the people with whom our relations were most fruitful can wish to destroy us," he said, "means something that we must try to understand! There is a mystery which will illuminate all of history, beyond our martyrdom. I would have understood such a desire for extermination on the part of Poles or Russians, but Germans . . ." At this point his voice would trail off. This question obsessed him. In this world of death there was in him neither bitterness, nor anger, nor desire for vengeance; only this desire to understand.

Despite the precautions of his friends, one day at roll call he was taken out of the ranks. When the group had begun to string out, a sudden and extraordinary will to live had seized him, and he had begun to run like a madman. Lalka had noticed him and after the quarter had fallen, he prolonged the exercise to see how long the old man, who was running several yards behind the others, could hold out.

"If you catch up with them, your life will be spared," he shouted.

And he gave the order to whip the group of survivors.

171

They hesitated and slowed down to help the professor, but the blows redoubled, making them reel, tearing their clothes, covering their faces with blood. Blinded with blood, drunk with pain, they accelerated again. When the professor, who had gained ground, saw them move off again, he threw out his arms as if to catch them, or as if in supplication. He stumbled once, then again; his tormented body seemed to come apart; he tried once more to recover his balance and then suddenly stiffened and collapsed in the dust. When the Germans came over to him they saw a thin trickle of blood coming out of his mouth. Professor Mehring was dead.

But poor Lalka was not yet at the end of his troubles. When he discovered this he wondered whether he would ever see the last of them, whether he would ever find any peace with his Jews.

He made this discovery in two stages, the first of which was the result of chance. The Jews had already been installed in the Ghetto for almost two months when one morning he happened to enter the barracks that they had occupied before the move. Since he believed all Jews to be carriers of contagious germs, Lalka had never set foot in this barracks. But for some time now the severe Continental winter had descended upon Treblinka, and Lalka thought the cold must have killed all the microbes. He was passing the door with nothing to do when this idea occurred to him. He hesitated for a moment, and then decided to go and see the place where his Jews had lived. As he came nearer, he heard whispering and muffled scratching noises. He immediately thought of a tunnel, the jailer's obsession. Without making a sound, he crept over to the door. He could not understand how the prisoners could enter the barracks without being seen, and already he was imagining a whole network of accomplices among the Ukrainian guards. He drew his pistol and pointing it in front of him, violently pushed open the door. Amazement paralyzed the two Ukrainian guards who saw him enter. Lalka was not the least astonished of the three men, who stared at each other for a few moments, mute with stupefaction. The Ukrainians were each holding an agricultural implement that resembled a hoe. The ground was dug up around them as if it had just been plowed. Lalka did not understand what this meant, but the fear that he read on the faces of the Ukrainians told him that he had just caught them red-handed at something.

Recovering the use of speech before the guards, he shouted, "What are you doing here?"

Terrified and incapable of uttering a word, one of the Ukrainians slowly opened his left hand and held it in front of him. In the half-light of the barracks it shone with the yellow glitter of gold and the sparkle of a few diamonds.

"God in heaven!" murmured Lalka, slowly realizing what it meant. "The swine! The gold of the Reich!"

He was genuinely disturbed to discover that in the very heart of Treblinka the Jews had been capable of trying once again to steal the Germans' gold. The idea that this gold belonged to them never occurred to him, not only because they were dead (and those who were not might as well be), but because in any case Jewish gold could only be stolen gold. At least he was profoundly convinced that this was so.

For a moment he was tempted to kill the two Ukrainians, but he wanted to know how long they had been coming here and digging up the gold which the Jews had hidden.

"Two months," they replied, trembling.

"Since the day after the Jews were moved?"

"The same day," murmured one.

Such candor disarmed Lalka, and he put away his pistol. The Ukrainians relaxed and showed him that the whole dirt floor of the barracks was full of gold, currency and jewels.

The results of the search which he immediately had made were impressive: ninety pounds of gold and precious stones and several hundred thousand dollars and zlotys.

The matter might have stopped there, but suddenly he got the idea of having the prisoners searched. Work had just resumed after the noon break. Only one convoy had arrived that morning. Nothing was left of it but a pile of bodies which the prisoners of Camp Number Two were carrying to the big ditches. Camp Number One had recovered its innocent appearance of a market for secondhand goods. The men of the red and blue commandos, having completed their specialized work of greeting and undressing the convoys, had been absorbed into the sorting commandos. The immense sorting square looked like a bustling market with its huge orderly piles of clothing and various belongings and the smaller piles formed by the articles of that morning's arrivals. These new piles seemed to be at the mercy of an army of ants who were in the act of taking them to pieces. Each commando came to look for the objects for which it was responsible and take them to another place where they would be "conditioned" before being finally stored in the great heaps that rose in the back. S.S. men, Ukrainians and booted *kapos* reigned over the bazaar, each trying to steal without the other's knowledge—some gold, some clothing, some food. It was an ordinary day, the kind of which there were seven every week and thirty or thirty-one every month. A fine mist, which the pale winter sun failed to dispel, softened the distant contours of the barracks and the gas chambers. The surrounding countryside was still, as if the world of Treblinka were separated from the other world by a no man's land of sound and light. And here, on the square, in the middle of this cold opacity, there moved with weary gestures a special breed of men who lived only to serve these two brick buildings which, in their private idiom, were known as the "factory."

The whistles of the Ukrainian guards rent the droning silence. The prisoners froze like statues of salt. Anxiety slowly banished the sweet numbness. For them any event that broke the monotonous void of work could only mean bad news. Their "happiness" depended on nothing happening; they had even come to hate the cries of the tormented. Why cry? Why resist? It could only result in an increase of pain.

"Fall in! Fall in!"

The order had come like an echo that was gradually taken up by all the guards and *kapos*.

The mass began to move slowly. The whips cracked, the movement accelerated to the rhythm of the whips, the pitch of the shouting rose, further hastening the flow of the formless mass.

When the thousand prisoners had formed five rows, Lalka appeared. He was not smiling, but this was not necessarily a good sign. Without a word he walked over to the first man in the first line and ordered him to empty his pockets. Chance decreed that this man had no gold on him, and Lalka began to walk down the rows, staring at the prisoners. But already, without a word being uttered, news of the search had spread throughout the ranks. No gold was found on the second man, nor the third, nor the fourth. By the tenth Lalka began to have doubts, first about his suspicions and then about the effectiveness of the search. At the twentieth he gave up. He was about to dismiss the ranks when he got the idea of making them step back a few yards.

"Five steps backward, march!" he commanded, and the mass moved in jerks. The area it had occupied the moment before looked like an athletic field after a school picnic, but the greasy papers were bank notes, and the yellow gleams were not buttercups, nor were the iridescent flashes drops of dew.

It was that night that for the first time the rule of the quarter was applied to all of the prisoners. In the mind of Lalka this punishment was merely a way of marking the event. It did not solve the problem of the escapes which this incident had revealed, or at least recalled more vividly than before.

What bothered Kurt Franz about the escapes was not so much the fact that Jews were eluding their destiny, since he knew that some day they would be recaptured anyway. As he told the prisoners after the punishment in a good-natured and reasonable tone:

"Why run away? Why take risks? Why cause so much trouble, when in any case you will be recaptured some day? No matter where you go, no matter how far you may flee, you will always come back to Treblinka, for the earth will be purged of its Jews. For you, Jews, Treblinka is like the bottom of an immense funnel whose edges are the ends of the earth. You are the nearest to the bottom, for you were the first to arrive. But the others are already falling, they will join you soon."

He spoke in a soft voice like a teacher gently scolding pupils who aren't paying attention.

"It's for your sake that I say this; it is all the same to me. Every day thousands of Jews arrive, and I can easily make up your ranks; but you who are privileged, you will remain alive after all the others to bear witness to a vanished race, you want to run away when it is outside, and not here, that death threatens you. Of course you must work in Treblinka, and I am well aware that you are not used to it, but he who works here is entitled to bread and clothing. Only the unfit are eliminated; but this is not our law, it is the law of nature. Do you think she lets blind wolves and sick lions stay alive? Believe me! Work, work hard, do not try to flee your responsibilities, and Treblinka will become for you a world of joy. I swear it again on my honor as an S.S."

There was some truth in what Lalka had just said. The life expectancy of the Jews at this time was hardly any greater outside the camp than it was inside. But the problems raised by the escapes were different. What the Technicians feared was that the escapees would eventually convince the Jews who were still in the ghettos of the reality of the extermination. Certainly, they had taken precautions; certainly, they knew that the situation of the Jews in the ghettos was controlled in such a way that they preferred to find solace in lies rather than heed the revelations of their own people, but the situation threatened to reverse itself if too many witnesses told the same story. Then there was danger that the whole world would learn the truth and that history would condemn the Third Reich.

One fact played into the hands of the Technicians: the monstrousness of the truth. The extermination of a whole people was so unimaginable that the human mind could not accept it. Everyone knows the famous Nazi principle which holds that the more incredible a lie is the more readily it will be believed. But inversely, the more incredible a truth is, the less it will be believed. Such is the human mind, which seems to prefer lies to the truth: the very monstrousness of the undertaking was a guarantee of its secrecy.

The Technicians knew that it was impossible not to let anything leak out, but they also knew that only a large accumulation of testimony would succeed in convincing the Jews in the ghettos, let alone the entire world and history. What had to be avoided, therefore, was the prisoners getting into the habit of escaping, the practice of escape becoming general. It was for this reason that Lalka decided to attack the problem when he discovered its full extent.

The desire to escape was born in the Jews at the moment when pain had reappeared, when the camp had been reorganized for the first time. At this period some had chosen to die, but others, a few at first, had immediately thought of escape. To all, life in Treblinka had seemed impossible. There existed only two methods of avoiding it: death and escape. But suicide is repugnant to the Jew, not because the religion forbids it, but because to a Jew life, any life, is sacred. Galewski had not had much trouble in putting a stop to the suicides; they were merely an immediate reaction, a kind of vertigo in response to the horror of the situation. But when death had ceased to be a solution, everyone had thought of escape and, while waiting to find a way, had begun to prepare a little nest egg. This was how the floor of the barracks had been transformed into the Cave of Ali Baba.

After the terrible night of anxiety the prisoners had begun making plans again, but this time on a much larger scale. Those hours of agony had forced them to emerge from that still vegetative life into which their arrival in Treblinka had plunged them to enter another life, a new life as different from normal life as the world of Treblinka was different from the ordinary world. In this life the supreme reason was flight. They wanted to escape the way other men in other circumstances crave money, power or pleasure. It was not so much a conscious desire as an instinct, like the one that impels migratory birds to leave. After this day nothing else mattered to them. Once again the Jews had become the "stiff-necked people."

A certain number of escape routes had been developed: the train, the "hospital" and the piles of clothing. The train, which had been the first method of escape, was the most complicated, for it required the complicity of several comrades.

The "hospital" route offered the advantage that it could be utilized without any help. But it required considerable luck, great cleverness, and a courage rarely found. What the S.S. called the "hospital" was no more a hospital than the gas chambers were a factory. It consisted of a little barracks on which a red cross was painted and a big ditch where the bodies of executed prisoners were burned along with all the documents, papers, and photographs belonging to the Jews of the convoys. The cremation in the ditch was done with sulphur. But since Lalka had decided to reduce the slaughter of the prisoners and, on an average, only a dozen were killed each day, sulphur was no longer poured on every day and the fire no longer burned continually. When prisoners who wanted to escape came to throw papers and photographs into the ditch, they could wait until the Ukrainian guards looked the other way, jump into the hole themselves, and hide under the bodies. Once there, they had to wait for night before they could try to cross the barbed wire.

If it was easy to get to the ditch, it was much more difficult to escape the attention of the Ukrainian guards. Indeed, instances of success were rare until *kapo* Kurland, noticing the maneuver, began helping the prisoners. At this time his position as foreman of the "hospital" made him suspect, and this was why Galewski, who had personally perfected this method of escape, had not wanted to ask for his help. But one day Kurland had seen a prisoner jump into the ditch. Instinctively he had called the Ukrainians to divert their attention, and since then he had formed the habit of staying near the ditch at the end of the day in order to help potential escapees. Thanks to him, the problem raised by the vigilance of the Ukrainians was practically solved.

Once in the ditch, all was not yet won—far from it. Indeed, the smell of rotting and burned flesh was so strong that many passed out. Another even more terrible danger was that of falling in on the day when the Ukrainians poured the sulphur. This day was unpredictable, since it depended on the number of men killed at roll call. Those who had the bad luck to try to escape on a sulphur day were burned to death or died of asphyxiation.

Finally, when night fell, the escapee still had to creep out of the hole. This was not the most difficult part, for the Ukrainians were usually drunk and the barbed wire was not electrified. Once he had left Treblinka, the prisoner faced the final ordeal, which was perhaps the most murderous of all: the ordeal of "freedom." His only weapon was the gold he had managed to bring out of Treblinka.

The third route was less dangerous, but it required the help of several comrades and very careful preparation. It consisted in hiding, again at the end of the day, in a large pile of clothing. But it was difficult to do this. The piles were like pyramids composed of large bundles of clothing arranged in parallel fashion. The bundles were so closely stacked that it was impossible to slip between them without changing the shape of the whole pile and risking landslide. So during the day while the bundles were being stacked, it was necessary to arrange inside the edifice a hiding place which was large enough for a man and could be plugged with one bundle so that nothing would show. This required a certain skill, and in no case could it be accomplished by a single man. But if the prisoner who wanted to escape succeeded in obtaining the help of a few comrades and the discretion of the rest, once imprisoned in his hole he had a good chance of succeeding. This route, too, was practically abandoned when the informers began to prevail.

The escapes raised great problems for Galewski and monopolized all his energy. He incited the prisoners to flee by tirelessly repeating the same order: "Tell! Tell! Tell what you have seen!" But he also had to hide the escapes from the Germans. To do this he filled out the gangs with the next day's arrivals. Every day the Germans selected a certain number of men from the convoys destined for the gas chambers to replace those who had died the day before during the "race of the dead." But Galewski, with the help of Adolf, whom he had appointed foreman, was organizing his own selection. This clandestine selection raised few problems until the day each prisoner was assigned a number. The escapes took place in the evening before roll call and Galewski could not complete the gangs until the next day after morning roll call. So there remained roll calls during which he had to juggle the figures to fool the Germans. As long as the Germans only pretended to count, it was merely a question of gymnastics. He knew the number of escapees, and all he had to do was make a mistake when he counted out loud. But when the Germans began to count, each roll call became for Galewski an exhausting exercise in prestidigitation.

For one month Galewski, without showing his hand for a single moment, held Lalka in check; one month during which the Jews, transcending their condition of slaves, found the courage to revolt. For one month every measure Lalka took produced a countermeasure on the part of the Jews. He made each prisoner sew a number on his jacket; the Jews who escaped left their jackets behind for the replacements. He organized the prisoners into groups of three in which each man was responsible for the other two; the prisoners escaped in threes Nothing worked—neither promises, nor threats, nor spectacular executions. This will to escape that drove the prisoners was stronger than their fear of dying, even in excruciating pain.

Then a certain Küttner arrived. The prisoners thought he looked like a Jew and called him Kiwe. He established a network of informers that became the terror of the prisoners, but they continued to try to escape. Although the percentage of successes dropped from one day to the next, there were still a few who were willing to risk their lives for freedom. They knew that this freedom was not worth much more than life in Treblinka, but their desire to flee was not rational. They went as if driven by an imperious instinct, the same instinct, perhaps, as the one that has driven the Jews to keep on being Jews for such a long time.

Even so, one day the escapes ceased. Lalka and Kiwe thought that they had finally destroyed the resilience of their prisoners. They felt a great satisfaction which was unconsciously mingled with a kind of vague fear in the presence of men who, in the depths of despair, had suddenly found the strength to resist after submitting for so long.

This satisfaction was their second mistake. The Jews had transferred all their energy and all their hope to an undertaking that was insane, grandiose, and almost unique in the history of the camps of Nazi Europe: an armed revolt.

XII

THE CHANCES OF success of an escape had become practically nil when Langner decided to try his luck. Son of the owner of a shoe store in Czestochowa, he had arrived in Treblinka like hundreds of thousands of other Jews. Like the others, he had not wanted to believe the rumors that were rife, the tales of terror that were told in whispers. But if he did not put enough faith in these stories to agree to wage a desperate combat, he was sufficiently afraid of the danger represented by deportation to hide during each raid.

And then one day, like millions of other Jews, he had been flushed out of his hiding place. In the train that took him to Treblinka he had preferred to cling to the promises of the Germans rather than finally accept the truth. They were one hundred in his car, one hundred praying, weeping, discussing *ad infinitum* the exact purpose of their voyage. When one of them had stood up and said, "Let us revolt!" the others had given him the eternal argument: "If we revolt we will all be killed on the spot, whereas if we wait we may be killed too, but maybe not, and maybe not right away." And the discussions had resumed. When there had been no more water in the car, the children had begun licking the sweat on their mothers' faces, and the adults had withdrawn into themselves. Then the man who wanted to revolt had announced, "I'm getting out of here. Who wants to come with me?" As he asked this question, his eye had fallen on Langner, who without thinking replied, "Me!" A few men had tried to prevent them from tearing off the grating that covered the window, but they were too exhausted, and a few punches had sent them sprawling among the prostrate bodies. Langner and the other man had drawn straws to determine who would jump first, and fate had chosen the other man. Langner had seen him disappear with a sudden wrenching noise. He had seen him roll over, get up, and run zigzagging toward a clump of trees. At this moment shots had rung out and Langner had lost his desire to jump. He had collapsed at the foot of the window, weeping. Several times he had tried to stand up again in order to jump, but his legs, which were trembling, had refused to support him, and fear had descended upon him, sovereign, paralyzing.

When he arrived in Treblinka he had been saved by an old friend from Czestochowa who had recognized him. The fear had never left him, but another emotion had joined it: the sense of having acted like a coward in refusing to jump He remembered the face of the man who had fled and saw him again, suddenly getting up amid the dying and saying, "Let us revolt!" simply, as if it were a natural thing. He had said, "Let us revolt!" as others would have said, "Let us pray, my brothers." At the time, this idea of revolt had seemed absurd to Langner. What could you do with your bare hands against tanks, what could women and old men do against these strong young soldiers, well trained and well armed? It was madness. But now Langner lived in a world of madness, and the voice of the other man re-echoed in his heart. He still did not know how to revolt, but the idea filled him more each day, and little by little he forgot both his fear and his cowardice.

He got caught stupidly, slipping a wad of bank notes into his pocket while he was sorting clothes. Lalka concluded that he was preparing to escape and decided to make an example of him. For the first time he had a living culprit, and he wanted to take advantage of it. A gallows was erected in the middle of the yard, and Langner, who was already battered from the lashes he had just received, was hanged by the feet. It was morning; a convoy was moving slowly toward the gas chambers; the sorting commandos, who had stopped working, received the order to continue. Only a Ukrainian guard stayed by the gallows, making Langner swing with his whip.

In the middle of the afternoon, when the last Jew of the convoy, duly undressed and searched, had taken the "road to heaven," all the prisoners were assembled on the sorting square and arranged in columns. Down there in the middle of the yard, Langner was swaying and moaning, begging the guard to finish him off. After a quarter of an hour of cap drill, when the ranks were impeccably straight, Lalka, who always planned his effects carefully, appeared.

"Jews," he began, pointing to Langner, "this Jew is going to die! For a Jew to die is not rare in Treblinka. I would even say that, generally speaking, that's why they come here. But this one who is hanging down there will not die like the rest. You have been in a position to notice the care we take to make our Jews die as nicely as possible. Well, we are going to take the same care to make this one die as slowly as possible."

Lalka spoke slowly, leaving long silences after each sentence. During these silences Langner's moans reached the prisoners who had to listen while standing motionless at attention.

"Jews," Lalka continued, "that you are afraid to die is a fact which is well known and which, personally, has always astonished me. I will confess frankly that I have never really understood this fanatical attachment to life." (Another pause, more

184

groans rising and falling, interspersed with entreaties whose words carried with extraordinary clarity to the prisoners, who could only pray in their hearts for their brother who was about to die.) 'I have never understood it, especially since it is often more difficult, more arduous, more painful to live than to die.

"Him, for example," he said, waving his arm toward Langner. "Listen to him! What does he ask? To die. What does he beg his guard to do? To kill him. At last he has discovered wisdom. Unfortunately it is too late for him. But may his example serve as a lesson to you. You will have the rest of the afternoon to meditate on the disadvantages of trying to get away from us, for I doubt that he will die before evening."

When Lalka had finished his speech, he made the prisoners march by Langner single file, singing the Treblinka anthem. Then he sent them back to work.

The afternoon lasted an eternity. No one said a word. The silence was so profound that Langner's groans could be heard from every corner of the immense yard. When he called for his mother, every man thought of his own. When he begged to be killed, every man wanted to die. Langner's agony was the agony of all of them, his cries were their cries, his pain their pain. They would have liked to run away so they would no longer hear, to stop their ears, to become deaf, if only they could stop hearing him, if only they could stop seeing the torn body of their brother which still quivered at each blow of the whip. In spite of themselves they looked at him secretly where he hung, bloody, mutilated, shapeless. They saw the blood trickle slowly from his hair as from a flayed animal, they saw large shreds of skin that hung down, revealing raw flesh of a brilliant red. Suddenly he uttered a great cry that chilled the prisoners and the guards, and everyone thought that he was finally going to die. But immediately the prisoners heard him calling them in Yiddish:

"*Yiden! Yiden!* Jews, Jews my brothers!" (A silence, and once again the voice that seemed to come out of nowhere.) "Revolt! Revolt! Don't listen to their promises. You will all be killed. They can't let you leave this place after what you have seen. Even if they wanted to spare your lives they would be forced to kill you, for the world will never forgive them for what they are doing and they know it. Revolt! Avenge your fathers and your brothers, avenge yourselves. Save the honor of Israel! Since you are going to die, die fighting! Long live Israel, long live the Jewish people!"

At first the guards and the Germans, stupefied, had listened without understanding, but when Langner had said, "Long live Israel!" they had realized that it must be an appeal to resistance. Lalka had rushed over, grabbing a gun from a guard on the way. When he reached Langner he saw that his body was jerking violently. Enraged by this speech, which he had not understood but whose meaning he suspected, he seized the rifle by the barrel and clubbed Langner's head until the skull was shattered.

That night the barracks buzzed for a long time with passionate whispers. Everyone felt that Langner was right and that the only solution was revolt. The idea had suddenly appeared like a revelation. It was true that they were doomed, it was true that they had nothing to lose. No matter what happened, they knew, they were going to die. But how could they revolt? How could they find so much as a stick? Who could organize them so they would throw themselves on their killers as one man? In little groups the prisoners, who were on their guard against informers, discussed the possibilities of an uprising. No one believed that it could succeed, but many were ready to die, even if there was not a chance.

Since the German invasion, they had fallen from one renunciation to the next, until they had reached a state of physical and moral slavery which may have been unknown in the history of social relations. In the course of this vertiginous descent it seemed as if nothing would ever stop them. It was as if a spell had

186

been cast over them which prevented them from recovering their balance. A kind of fatality made them fall into all the traps that the Technicians had set for them. The supreme masters of their destiny, the Technicians reigned over them like some other-worldly power.

Physically weakened and morally broken, the Jews had let themselves be led to death like a flock of animals to the slaughterhouse, had let themselves be transformed into accomplices in the extermination of their people. And these accomplices were not criminals but good Jews, sometimes even great Jews. And then, suddenly, came the miracle. Just when their abdication was total, when all values had ceased to exist, when their humanity had almost left them, the Jews, rousing themselves at the bottom of the abyss, began a slow ascent which death alone would stop.

A few months earlier these men had won back the right to die by committing suicide; now they were discussing the right to die by fighting. It was that night, in that buzzing barracks, in that insane world of Treblinka, that the miracle occurred at last: "the miracle in abdication."

XIII

GALEWSKI HAD NOT waited for Langner's death to think about a revolt. Old and sick, psychologically broken by the execution of his family and by all he had gone through as Jewish commandant of the camp, Galewski now lived only for this idea. At first an act of faith, a mad hope, revolt had become a workable plan in his eyes on the morning when the S.S. had not massacred all the Jews. When Lalka had slapped him he had lowered his eyes and thought, "You are big and you are strong, but you have just made an error in judgment which may cost you much!"

In the Ghetto he was no longer lodged with the rest of the prisoners, but in the barracks of the *Hofjuden* where, all things considered, living conditions were much more tolerable. The barracks was smaller and very clean, pleasant in comparison to what he was leaving. He had a wooden bunk of his own and even a crate that served as cupboard and night table. The *Hofjuden* had access to a well, where they washed sketchily every morning. And since they worked under almost normal conditions, they managed to be quite clean and smelled only faintly.

The *Hofjuden* gave him a very cool reception, and it took Galewski some time to establish contact with one of them. He was the doctor of the Germans. His name was Chorongitski, and he had been one of the most celebrated physicians in Warsaw. Of his former splendor he retained, besides his good manners, only the elegant though frayed suit of clothes which he wore under his white tunic. Galewski had chosen him as his first objective because he spoke to no one. Tall, gray-haired, his face as immobile as if he were dead, he never answered questions and never addressed a word to anyone. In the barracks he spent long hours lying with his eyes open, seeming to see and hear nothing of what was going on around him. There was something pathetic in his muteness that aroused curiosity. Even after they became friends, Dr. Chorongitski never talked about himself, his family, or the circumstances of his arrival in Treblinka. It was as if on that day he had begun a new life which had completely wiped out the old one.

Galewski had observed him for a long time before he decided to speak to him. The privileged position that Dr. Chorongitski enjoyed with the Germans decided him in the end. The doctor could make an effective contribution to the revolt.

While he was looking for a way to approach Chorongitski, Galewski, seeing the rather self-centered way the *Hofjuden* lived, had an intuition that the doctor's silence was a way of showing disapproval. Taking the risk of revealing his plans to an informer, he decided to confront the doctor directly.

"Don't you think," he said to him one day point-blank, "that we could organize something instead of letting ourselves be massacred like this?"

Chorongitski looked up and for the first time Galewski saw his eyes brighten.

"What do you mean?" he asked in a neutral tone as if to hide his feelings.

Galewski sensed a tinge of mistrust in the doctor's attitude. He thought he understood: he had lost all belief in man, and everything had become suspect to him. He himself mistrusted the doctor, as he mistrusted the whole world *a priori* and above all the

Hofjuden; but he also felt that if he did not show his hand first, the doctor would reveal nothing of his thoughts. Still hesitant, he studied Chorongitski, who calmly returned his look. Paralyzed by the coldness of those eyes, he was about to give up, when he thought he caught an imperceptible encouragement in the doctor's look. It may have been only an illusion, and even as he opened his mouth to start to speak he had the feeling he was making a mistake. His mouth stayed open, but no sound came out of it.

"You are afraid to speak," the doctor said. "You don't trust me. Here everyone mistrusts everyone else."

"Not with us!" replied Galewski bluntly, suddenly feeling his solidarity with the other prisoners.

"Wait until they recover hope, wait until the first one begins to believe the Germans' promises, and you'll see if everyone does not start to mistrust everyone else."

Both men knew where this discussion would lead them, but tacitly they decided to size each other up by talking about something else at first.

"Do you believe that so little can be expected of men?" asked Galewski, playing the game of diversion.

"I believe that every man wants to save his skin and that he is ready to do anything to do it."

"But suppose it becomes obvious that there isn't a chance left?"

"The art of the Germans is precisely to keep it from ever becoming obvious. A German told me that Hitler ended one of his speeches on the extermination of the Jews by stating that, of all the Jews in Europe, there would remain just enough to fill a car which would be driven through the streets of Berlin. Well, every Jew believes that he will be in that car. It's what might be called the car complex."

"In short, the Jews are cowards?"

"On the contrary, it is not cowardice to believe in the impossible. When a Jew is born in America, his parents believe that he will become a millionaire, in France that he will enter the Institute, in Rome that he will be pope. To the Jews nothing seems impossible, above all if it seems to partake of the miraculous. This has been their extraordinary strength, and it is now their terrible weakness. Why we are like this, I don't know. Perhaps because we have never had a country, and because it never seemed necessary for there to be Jewish road laborers. But now all this is over. I even doubt whether there will be enough Jews left to fill the car."

Galewski listened absent-mindedly; he had long since passed this stage of discouragement. He decided to attack.

"Since nothing is impossible for the Jews," he said slowly, as if advancing cautiously, "why would it be impossible for them to revolt?"

Since Chorongitski made no reply, Galewski went on. "Don't you trust me?" he asked in a different tone.

"You are the head collaborator," the doctor replied.

"And you are their private doctor," retorted Galewski.

Chorongitski looked at him for a moment. Then, suddenly, his face relaxed and his eyes shone faintly.

"Do you have a plan?" he asked in a changed voice.

"No, but one can be found."

Pensively, as if he were concluding out loud a silent argument, Chorongitski added, "After all, you may be right: it may even work. With the Jews, anything can happen."

And his eyes became warm. He held out his hand to Galewski who shook it with feeling, thinking that he had just made a good recruit.

The next day they discussed the *Hofjuden* to decide who among them would be likely to join the Committee.

"They have much more freedom than the others and their aid

will be decisive," said Chorongitski, "but I am not sure that they will agree. They have a soft life, you know. Some of them even seem not to know what goes on 'down there.' "

Galewski looked at him, astonished.

"Yes, yes, it's true. At least they never talk about it. They have adopted the attitude of the Germans."

"But the smell? Now, with winter, it's more bearable, but what about last summer, when the smell of rotting flesh bothered even the Germans?"

"Not a word. The smells have become a forbidden subject, nobody refers to them. I think no one even dares scratch his nose. I remember one evening when the wind was coming directly from down there, it was unbreathable. I said, 'It smells!' I had just arrived. Everyone looked at me reproachfully and no one answered. That was when we stopped speaking to each other. The fact is that no one knows what goes on in Camp Number Two, not you nor I either. The others must know, or at least suspect, that the Jews are killed there, but it does not interest them, they refuse to learn any more about it. Intuitively they sense that the Germans will never allow a witness to leave this place, so they play ignorant. 'The gas chambers? What gas chambers? The smell? What smell? The cries? You certainly have a lot of imagination!' It is a miserable comedy which fools only the actors."

"Aren't you being a little unfair?" Galewski asked him.

"Yes, of course," replied the doctor calmly. "Yes, silence is a complex phenomenon. For the Germans, the explanation is simple. Stupid and disciplined, they obey—orders are orders, secrets are secrets. But with the Jews it is much more complicated. I hasten to add that the second explanation does not exclude the first."

It had been so long since Dr. Chorongitski had retreated into his silence that now that he had emerged from it he could not stop talking. He felt a compelling need to tell what he had seen, to explain what he had understood. And yet it was not a battle of words, it was the same need that seized so many Jews: the need to bear witness. Dr. Ginsberg had felt it in Vilna. In Warsaw, Dr. Ringelblum had devoted his time, throughout the existence of the ghetto, to noting the least little facts that were reported to him. When the final liquidation became imminent, with the help of his collaborators he sealed his notes into iron boxes and buried them in the ground so that some day future generations would find them. Mordecai Tenenbaum who, after Vilna, had reached Warsaw and then had been sent to Bialystok to organize the resistance there, had also kept a journal in which he had jotted down everything helter-skelter, his impressions, the program of the Committee of Resistance, anecdotes, the dates of deportations, the reactions of different personalities, everything he saw, learned or felt, so future generations would know what had happened and would understand how it had happened. Like Ringelblum, he entrusted his notes to the earth a few days before the liquidation. This journal, which was discovered after the war, begins with these words: "Greetings, unknown seeker who discovers these pages." A pathetic cry which might be the first sentence of a message placed in a bottle at the time of a dramatic shipwreck. Indeed, Judaism seemed to be suffering shipwreck. Mordecai told Tema, his fiancée, a few days before the uprising in the Warsaw ghetto in which she was to die: "In any case, all is lost; so live, live at any price. You will tell the story, you are so good at that." In the early days of Treblinka this need to bear witness had been, for many, a reason to survive. Galewski had discovered it as an argument to dissuade would-be suicides; it was to become the underlying reason for the revolt.

It was this same need that impelled Chorongitski to talk at such length.

"And what is the second explanation for the comedy the Jews are playing?" asked Galewski.

"Is it possible, in your opinion, to live with death?" the doctor asked first.

"I think not, and this is why all the prisoners in the work gangs try to escape after first wanting to commit suicide, which amounts to the same thing."

"Well, the *Hofjuden* have invented a third solution. They do not commit suicide and they do not escape. They know nothing, they act as if death does not exist. On Friday night they light the candles, they go to work in the morning, they take their meals at fixed hours, talk about the weather, gossip about each other: they have re-created the living conditions of their native towns. They lack two elements: the future and space, but they never talk about these two subjects for fear of destroying the illusion. Outside of these three taboos—the future, space, and what goes on here—everything else is an exact replica of their previous lives. Some even live with their families, wives and children. They live in private rooms and give their children some education."

"All this isn't very encouraging," said Galewski.

"On the contrary, my friend. This extraordinary ability to adapt should be helpful to you."

"Not in preparing a revolt."

"Ah well, I'm afraid that in that respect they're not good for much. They can't, at least for the moment. First they will have to come to terms with death. But there is one who might agree: my colleague in the 'hospital.' "

Galewski did not immediately understand to whom the doctor was alluding. At first he thought the doctor had misspoken and that he had meant the German infirmary, but he did not know any other doctor working in the infirmary. Seeing his confusion, Chorongitski added, "The *kapo* Kurland, the 'doctor.' "

"But he isn't . . ." began Galewski, who, suddenly understanding the joke, found it in bad taste. He was about to tell Chorongitski so, when the latter quickly added:

"You see, we even make jokes in our world. Here, everyone calls him Doctor. But for them it may not be humor," he continued after a moment's reflection. "It is part of their world of lies."

Galewski had recovered his composure. "Kurland, do you think?" he asked skeptically.

Galewski had never understood how a man could agree to do what Kurland did. His position as head of the "hospital" often required him to give fatal injections to persons in the convoys who could not be taken to the gas chamber because they were crippled or wounded. Clad in a white tunic, he received them in the little barracks whose back door opened directly onto the ditch and, pretending to give them an injection of digitalis, he administered a poison which killed them almost instantaneously.

Galewski did not blame him; he mistrusted him. He did not feel he had the right to blame him for anything, since all their activities, his own included, contributed to the same end: the death of their people. But he could not help feeling a kind of uneasiness in the presence of this man who had the courage to look his victims in the face and insert the needle while smiling and murmuring, "There, that didn't hurt! You feel better already, don't you?" All day in his little barracks decorated with red velvet benches he repeated these same words with the same smile: "There, that didn't hurt! You feel better already, don't you?" After a few moments he would beckon to his aides, who would carry the body behind the curtain that covered the door. While the body was falling directly into the ditch, Kurland was bending over the next patient, patting his hand, inserting his needle, smiling, and repeating, "There . . ."

"You're wrong!" Chorongitski told him, seeing the look on his face. "He's a very good man."

"I'm not judging him, but I think that in spite of everything I have seen here, I could never do that."

"Would you have imagined that you could become head *kapo* when you were in your apartment in Warsaw, sitting in your favorite armchair and reading your regular paper while the children played on the living-room rug?"

Because they evoked happy memories, his words stabbed Galewski who was too overcome to speak.

Chorongitski had not wanted to hurt him. Seeing his reaction, he quickly added, "Forgive me, I didn't mean—"

But Galewski had recovered. "You are right. No one, least of all we, has the right to judge in these matters. No man can say, 'I will never do that.' "

"Even so," added Chorongitski, "Kurland could have been a rat."

The next day the three men met together for the first time.

More than any other man in Treblinka, Kurland was a witness. He had been through so much that sometimes he even reached a point where he no longer felt directly concerned by what he endured, saw and did. He did not suffer from what he endured or did *personally*, but from what he endured and did as a Jew— from what all the Jews endured and did. Kurland had arrived at an extraordinarily heightened sense of the collective destiny of the Jewish people. And he lived this destiny not as an individual, but as one element of an invisible whole, an element endowed with a special function, that of witness.

His personal fate was totally immaterial to him. "My destiny," he used to say, "is only one man's destiny. All I can feel in the face of it is only human emotion. My personal suffering is only the suffering of a man, the tears I have shed taste the same as the tears of all men. Even my death will be the death of a man, and even if its circumstances are particularly dramatic, afterward my body will be indistinguishable from that of a man run over by a train. All this is simple, almost ordinary, and not to be compared with the disappearance of a people chosen by God and already three thousand years old." He also said, "God is not concerned about my death or that of any other single Jew, but he is concerned about our collective disappearance." He saw these events as the fulfillment of the divine will. For if God exists—and He did exist for Kurland—nothing can happen that He has not willed. But since God is not an arbitrary being, all this had to have a meaning. The holocaust that God was bringing on His people could not be gratuitous. It must represent a terrible warning. It was on this point that Kurland's thinking differed from that of most religious Jews. Whereas the religious saw the extermination of the Jews as a warning to the Jews alone, Kurland thought that it was a warning to the world, that God was using His people to say something to the world.

Unfortunately there remains nothing of all that Kurland wrote, and it is difficult to follow his underlying thought through second-hand reports of conversations, but it is certain that this Messianic conception of the adventure of the Jewish people was central to his preoccupations. He had become the camp historian and day by day he wrote the chronicle of the fulfillment of God's will so future generations could discern the hidden meaning.

His encounter with Galewski was an event for him. Kurland was a somewhat mystical dreamer and Galewski a man of action of rationalist education, but they had something in common: they were both Jews. Instead of opposing each other, they complemented each other. The possibility of a revolt gave Kurland hope that he might get his chronicle out of Treblinka. Kurland's mystical conception brought a new dimension to the revolt: the idea of redemption.

It was at this meeting that a rudimentary plan was worked out. Combat units would be recruited among prisoners who were reliable and knew how to handle a weapon. They would attack the Germans and the Ukrainians, destroy the camp installations, and organize the collective escape of all the prisoners. It was decided that Adolf, who did not attend the meeting because he slept in the big barracks with all the prisoners, would be in charge of the training and part of the recruiting of the men who would make up these combat units. The plan also called for seeking contact with the *Hofjuden,* who, since they worked for the Germans, had greater freedom of action. The problem of weapons was also brought up, but no one found a solution. Finally, they talked about the escapes. For themselves the question did not arise; they had a mission to fulfill, and flight would have represented a kind of betrayal.

"If we do leave this place some day," said Galewski in a voice that lacked conviction, "we will be the last."

Chorongitski attacked the escape policy followed by Galewski. He found it dangerous and futile.

"If we decide to prepare a revolt, we must devote all our energies to its organization. The risks you are taking," he said, turning to Galewski, "are out of proportion with the result. You are constantly at the mercy of a voluntary or forced confession. If you are discovered, you deprive the Committee of your aid, and you run the risk of jeopardizing the lives of all the prisoners."

"I have already considered this problem and I know it is serious, but we cannot refuse to help those who want to escape!"

Kurland agreed with Galewski. "We must seize every opportunity to get as many Jews out of here as possible."

"Not if it is going to jeopardize our plan. The escapes will interfere with our work. They are becoming more and more difficult and are keeping the Germans in a constant state of alert. We must lull the Germans, make them relax their surveillance. We must make them think they have broken us, make them believe us to be perfect slaves."

"But have we the right to prevent the men from running away in the name of a hypothetical revolt?" asked Galewski. "This is a very heavy responsibility for us. Escape is their only hope. Can we take it away from them?"

"Yes, if in exchange we offer them a revolt."

"But then we will be obliged to let many people in on the secret."

They ended with a compromise: the Committee would stop encouraging and aiding escapes once the date of the revolt was set. This decision was to have grave consequences.

In Treblinka it was not possible to have the smallest weakness. Galewski's scruples were a weakness.

Despite all the efforts of the members of the Committee, it was impossible to establish contact with the *Hofjuden*. They lived isolated in their world of lies, in a kind of anguished stillness from which it seemed that nothing could draw them. They had not suffered the calvary of the other prisoners and did not feel they had anything in common with them except the fact that they were all Jews. On a different level, of course, their behavior recalled that of the Jews in the ghettos who could not bring themselves to recognize the inevitable end. They had not yet touched the bottom; therefore they could not yet begin to rise again.

Kiwe was a good Nazi and a fierce anti-Semite. A jailer by profession, he claimed, not without pride, that no prisoner in his charge had ever escaped. This past record earned him the mission that had been entrusted to him: to stop the escapes. He had attacked it with passion and had lost no time in obtaining excellent results. He was never still for a moment; nothing seemed to escape his little close-set eyes. He claimed that he could not eat breakfast until he had killed at least two Jews. Immediately after reveille he began to prowl in search of his victims. His appearance unleashed panic among the prisoners for whom, even more than Lalka, he had become a cause of terror. As his appearance always resulted in the death of someone, they had nicknamed him the Angel of Death. Short, bull-necked, limping slightly, he would appear unexpectedly and pounce on his victim like a bird of prey. Although he usually walked with a certain difficulty, at these times he attained astonishing speed. When he reached his victim he would smile and say solicitously, "Don't you feel well? Come to the hospital." This was his expression, the prisoners knew. They did not even try to tell him that they were in excellent health. Lalka did not like him and did not always approve of his methods, but recognizing his effectiveness, he left him alone.

One day Kiwe went too far. It was only a remark, without apparent importance in this camp where all were to die; but this remark, which did not mean anything to Kiwe, opened the door to a new phase of the organization of the revolt.

To a good anti-Semite of rather limited intelligence like Kiwe, all Jews were the same, and the privileged status of the *Hofjuden* seemed an outrage. Lalka had explained to him something about this, but Kiwe found these subtleties useless and out of place in Treblinka. One day, in some perfectly harmless context, Kiwe said, in the presence of several *Hofjuden,* that for him there were no differences, that Jews were Jews, that is, a race on the road to rapid disappearance. For the *Hofjuden* this little remark was the magic formula that broke the spell. Suddenly the veil was torn away and the reality of their situation appeared to them in all its clarity: even if their lot was better for the moment, their end would be the same as that of the *Platzjuden,* and of all the Jews in Europe.

On the evening of that day two of the *Hofjuden* came to see Galewski, who was talking with Kurland and Chorongitski. Salzberg was a middle-aged man who lived in Treblinka with his two children and who represented a certain moral authority. Moniek was a young man of twenty-two who was their *kapo.* There was a moment of profound silence in the barracks as if to give more weight to what Salzberg was saying:

"We ask you to forgive us for our attitude up to now. Death no longer frightens us. We are all ready to do our duty to save the honor of Israel. We know that you have formed a committee and that you are preparing a revolt. We ask you to let us join you."

The tone was a little pompous, but Galewski felt that he could count on them.

"Thank you," he replied. "We knew that you were good Jews and that you would help us. I must tell you, however, that the chances of success are very slim. First we must overcome the camp guards, who are rather numerous—forty Germans and two hundred Ukrainians. Next, we will have to defend ourselves against the reinforcements who will certainly arrive. As witnesses we are too compromising for the Germans not to do everything they can to recapture us. Finally, those who are still alive will have to fight in the forests against cold, hunger, peasants, Facist bands and deserters. . . ."

Adolf, for his part, worked without respite. Thrown into a life of adventure by despair at the age of seventeen, action had become second nature to him. But while he had fought his other battles on foreign soil, this revolt was his revolt, his life's mission. For the first and no doubt for the last time as well, he would be able to fight under the Jewish flag, to fight as a Jew, for Jews. And his love of fighting was as strong as his sense of Jewish identity. Besides, he had a precise task to carry out. He was not operating on the conceptual level where so many problems foreign to action arise. He had been told: "Recruit and organize five combat units." It was not easy. In the first place, he had to maintain secrecy; he had to find prisoners who were determined to fight—not in order to escape themselves, but to allow others to escape and to destroy the camp. But the sole thought of almost all the prisoners was escape, individual escape. In addition to these two difficulties, there was a third: few Jews knew how to use a weapon. Treated as second-class citizens, massacred from time to time during pogroms, openly despised by all "good Poles," most Jews had tried, often successfully, to avoid military service. The majority had no military training.

But Adolf needed men he could rely on. He began by looking for all those who had been in the Polish army, especially those who had fought in the short campaign of June 1939. "Even they don't know very much," he told Galewski one day. "But the best soldiers are men who fight knowing they are going to die and anyway," he added with a smile, "we don't have any choice." When someone pointed out to him a Jew who had been in the army, he went over to him and began by talking vaguely to feel him out. If he sensed that the other man was not getting the point, he said no more; if the other responded to his hints, he would ask him point-blank, "Do you think we can do something?" The answer served as his definitive test.

Adolf appointed the first five men who answered yes group leaders; then, on Galewski's advice, he commissioned them to recruit the men in their own groups. To guarantee perfect secrecy, he forbade them to tell their men a single name, either the name of a leader or even the names of the other members of the group. Each man was to know only the name of his immediate superior. The five group leaders each received a vial of poison provided by Kurland. Only Adolf knew all the men recruited. He refused certain choices made by his group leaders. "It is when they are being beaten that you must judge them," he explained. "There are some who panic and others who remain calm, there are some who lower their heads and charge, others who protect themselves but try to see where the blows are coming from. These are the good soldiers, the ones who look."

Preparations for the revolt had reached this stage when the Langner incident occurred. Had he heard about the revolt? Probably not. His pathetic appeal was more likely an extraordinary coincidence. Following his solitary path, Langner had arrived at the same conclusion as the members of the Committee: after the time of death and humiliation comes the time of revolt. His appeal acted as a catalyst.

The Committee met that very evening, while the prisoners' barracks buzzed with impassioned conversation.

Galewski began by telling the story of Langner's death to the *Hofjuden*.

"This appeal is a sign," he concluded, "a sign that the time has come. Langner is our first victim, our first hero."

The Committee then proceeded to practical questions.

First, the date. The first snow would fall any day now, and it was impossible to launch the revolt before that. Therefore they must choose a day when snow would fall so that the traces would be quickly obliterated.

It was then that Dr. Chorongitski made a last attempt to persuade the Committee to make the decision to forbid escapes.

"Since the Committee includes two new members, I propose to submit the problem of escapes to them. Must we, to lull the suspicion of the Germans, take the responsibility of halting the escapes? Or can we allow them to continue, even without encouraging or aiding them? That is to say, must we consider that henceforth there is only one course for the Jews of Treblinka: *revolt!*"

This time Kurland agreed with Chorongitski.

"Individual destinies do not concern us. This revolt is not only intended to save lives; it is to be an event of historic importance. It must appear as a symbol of the destiny of the Jewish people, whom no earthly power has ever been able to defeat. This revolt must show the world that at the very bottom of the abyss we have not despaired. It must throw new light on our martyrdom, show that our submission was not cowardice, and that when we found profound reasons to fight, nothing could stop us. For this reason I believe we must rule out anything that represents the slightest risk to the success of our undertaking. Not to forbid the escapes, not to do all we can to stop them out of sentimental considerations is an error, a weakness, a betrayal."

But Salzberg and Moniek did not see the problem from this angle and in the end the first compromise was again upheld.

Then they went on to the next problem: weapons. Galewski had thought about it at length and had arrived at the conclusion that the only way to procure them was to have them bought on the outside by Ukrainian guards.

"What makes you think they would take such big risks for us?" asked Salzberg.

"Because they love gold."

"But they have all they want, all they have to do is help themselves."

The idea seemed insane to the other members of the Committee. Galewski revealed what he had just learned.

"After Lalka discovered the two Ukrainians in the old barracks, he took measures to prevent the guards from procuring gold. I learned this through the *Goldjuden*. The Ukrainians no longer have the right to enter their barracks and at each sorting station they are watched by a German. The *Goldjuden* also told me that sometimes the Ukrainians bring them a little food in exchange for money. I think we can try to procure weapons by the same means. The problem is to find the least fierce or the most corruptible."

The other members of the Committee felt that the risks were too great, but it was the only solution and in the end everyone agreed to it. The only problem was to decide who would be entrusted with this perilous mission. Galewski, as Jewish commandant of the camp, could not do it. If he were accused, the whole camp would be in danger. Salzberg and Moniek had no contact with the Ukrainians, who did not like them because they were not allowed to hit them. That left Kurland and Chorongitski. Kurland offered to try, but he had little chance of succeeding: the three Ukrainians in the "hospital" were mere animals, interested in nothing outside of their jobs as killers. At this point everyone turned to Chorongitski, who worked with two Ukrainian orderlies at the German infirmary. He remained silent for a few seconds, then looked up.

"I'll do it," he said. "I think I may have some chance of succeeding. At any rate, I am in the best position of anyone."

Then turning to Galewski, he added, "Prepare money, lots of money. I'll let you know when I'm ready."

The five men on the Committee slept little that night. There were many problems still to be solved, but they felt that the moment was near when they would be avenged for all they had suffered, when they would avenge the Jewish people as a whole and show the world that the Jews can be killed but not conquered.

XIV

MEANWHILE, Treblinka had become the great center of extermination. Convoys arrived from all the towns in Poland, from Greece, Bulgaria, and even from Germany.

To stimulate Lalka's zeal his superiors promised him that all of Europe would pour into Treblinka. When he heard the good news Kurt Franz decided to make the camp worthy of its mission. Kiwe's activities were beginning to bear fruit, and since the execution of Langner the number of escapes had diminished even more. The day when they would stop altogether was near. Lalka shifted responsibility for matters of discipline onto the faithful Kiwe and attacked the second part of his program: a reorganization of the work which would give Treblinka the means to carry out its mission.

Ten new gas chambers had already been built to answer the ever-growing needs of extermination, bringing the total number of gas chambers to thirteen. By packing carefully you could get in about two hundred Jews, which theoretically gave a maximum yield of two thousand six hundred Jews every half hour. Of course, this figure was theoretical; it represented the maximum capacity. The actual figure was much lower, for the organization was far from perfect. The preparation of the Jews, which had always taken too long, had been slowed down even more by the new requirement of cutting the hair of the women. So it was not the capacity of the camp that was at issue but the organization of the work.

Lalka attacked the problem at its root.

The sixty-car convoys stopped a few hundred yards from Treblinka, where they were divided into three strings of twenty cars each. Obviously, it would have been simpler to send the whole convoy into the camp, but the platform was not long enough, and if the six thousand deportees (about one hundred per cent) got off at the same time, it would cause a confusion, a disorder that might give rise to regrettable incidents. For this reason the Technicians had not deemed it necessary to lengthen the platform, which would not have presented great difficulties, and had preferred the system of rotation. This system avoided a mob, but it slowed down production considerably; each poorly organized debarkation gave rise to unpleasant scenes—uncertainties and confusion for the deportees, who did not know where they were going and were sometimes seized with panic.

So, the first problem was to restore a minimum of hope. Lalka had many faults, but he did not lack a certain creative imagination. After a few days of reflection he hit upon the idea of transforming the platform where the convoys arrived into a false station. He had the ground filled in to the level of the doors of the cars in order to give the appearance of a train platform and to make it easier to get off the trains. Opposite the cars the platform was flanked by a row of barracks where bundles destined for immediate shipping were piled. These barracks, which opened onto the sorting square, faced the platform with a long wooden wall. On this wall Lalka had *trompe-l'oeil* doors and windows painted in gay and pleasing colors. The windows were decorated with cheerful curtains and framed by green blinds which were just as false as the rest. Each door was given a special name, stenciled at eye level: "Stationmaster," "Toilet," "Infirmary" (a red cross was painted on this door). Lalka carried his concern for detail so far as to have his men paint two doors leading to the waiting rooms, first and second class. The ticket window, which was barred with a horizontal sign reading "Closed," was a little masterpiece with its ledge in false perspective and its grill, painted line for line. Next to the ticket window a large timetable announced the departure times of trains for Warsaw, Bialystok, Wolkowysk, etc. To the left of the barracks two doors were cut into the barbed wire. The first led to the "hospital," bearing a wooden arrow on which "Wolkowysk" was painted. The second led to the place where the Jews were undressed; that arrow said "Bialystok." Lalka also had some flowerbeds designed, which gave the whole area a neat and cheery look.

When all was completed, Lalka came to inspect. The windows were more real than real windows; from ten yards away you could not tell the difference. The arrows were conspicuous and reassuring. The flowers, which were real, made the whole scene resemble a pretty station in a little provincial town. Everything was perfect, and yet something was still lacking: nothing much, a detail, a little touch that would give that stamp of authenticity which cannot be invented. Lalka felt that something was still missing, but he could not decide what. He spent the whole morning on the platform, and at noon when he went to the mess for lunch he was troubled, pensive and preoccupied. Inspiration came with coffee.

"The clock!" he said suddenly, slapping his brow. "Of course, that's it! A station without a clock is not a station."

In front of the other Germans, who were stupefied, he sent for the carpenters. He explained to them what he wanted: a clock face with hands, painted on a wooden cylinder twenty-eight inches in diameter and eight inches thick. Just as he was getting ready to dismiss them one of the carpenters asked,

"And what time will it be in Treblinka?"

Lalka did not understand immediately and the carpenter explained. "What time will the hands point to?"

Lalka hesitated and then suddenly looked at his watch. It was three o'clock in the afternoon.

"Three o'clock," he said.

Untersturmführer S.S. Kurt Franz had just stopped time in Treblinka.

Hope is fine, but discipline is better. Lalka took a number of other measures designed to accelerate the debarkation of the passengers of death. The blue commando was divided into twenty groups, one to a car; their job was to politely but firmly get the Jews out of the cars and sweep the car floors in exactly five minutes.

When everything was ready Lalka returned and saw that it was good.

The oral tradition of Treblinka has preserved the memory of an episode which is no doubt one of the most terrible and one of the most revealing of what this world of lies and death was like. During the winter of 1943 there arrived in Treblinka the last German Jews, all great war heroes or holders of the highest order of the Iron Cross, from the First World War. Even more than the Polish Jews, they had still refused to accept the reality of extermination. On this subject Ringelblum noted in his journal that the first deportees from the Warsaw ghetto referred to Hitler as *unser Führer*. This terrible blindness lasted to the very threshold of the gas chambers. It was as if the Nazis, in a last gesture of gratitude, wanted to make the circumstances of their death different from that of the other Jews. So, the German Jews were brought to Treblinka not in cattle cars, but in passenger trains with sleeping and

dining cars. Everyone died in the same way, but some were conducted to death like animals and others like middle-class citizens,
with a final consideration which points up the madness of the system. The train rolled for a long time through fields and forests,
over main lines at first, then over smaller ones. Gradually, grass
began to grow between the tracks. But no one was worried; the
Führer had said that they were going to colonize the great plains
of the East. But the train rolled more and more slowly until,
grinding from one end to the other, it entered that strange station
where the tracks disappeared into a pile of sand. Through the
window of the car the passengers saw a charming little station. A
few S.S. and Ukrainian guards in uniforms seemed to be on duty.
Nothing disturbing so far. The Jews got off, confident. Well, not
completely: the men of the blue commando who took their baggage as they got off the train had a peculiar look about them, very
hangdog expressions for porters. Fortunately, each one had a
number. So in a last reflex of civilized men, the travelers unobtrusively took out scraps of paper and quickly jotted down the numbers of their "porters."

Lalka also decided that better organization could save much
time in the operations of undressing and recovery of the baggage.
To do this you had only to rationalize the different operations,
that is, to organize the undressing like an assembly line. But the
rhythm of this assembly line was at the mercy of the sick, the old
and the wounded, who, since they were unable to keep the pace,
threatened to bog down the operation and make it proceed even
more slowly than before. This problem appeared to Lalka just as
he conceived the idea of these rationalized stations of the cross.
So it was that he came to calibrate the victims. Individuals of
both sexes over the age of ten, and children under ten, at a maximum rate of two children per adult, were judged fit to follow the
complete circuit, as long as they did not show serious wounds or
marked disability. Victims who did not correspond to the norms
were to be conducted to the "hospital" by members of the blue

commando and turned over to the Ukrainians for special treatment. A bench was built all around the ditch of the "hospital" so that the victims would fall of their own weight after receiving the bullet in the back of the head. This bench was to be used only when Kurland was swamped with work. On the platform, the door which these victims took was surmounted by the Wolkowysk arrow. In the Sibylline language of Treblinka, "Wolkowysk" meant the bullet in the back of the neck or the injection. "Bialystok" meant the gas chamber.

Beside the "Bialystok" door stood a tall Jew whose role was to shout endlessly, "Large bundles here, large bundles here" He had been nicknamed "Gröysse Päck." As soon as the victims had gone through, Gröysse Päck and his men from the red commando carried the bundles at a run to the sorting square, where the sorting commandos immediately took possession of them. As soon as they had gone through the door came the order, "Women to the left, men to the right." This moment generally gave rise to painful scenes; to cut short the goodbyes, Lalka doubled the number of Ukrainian guards in this spot.

While the women were being led to the left-hand barracks to undress and go to the hairdresser, the men, who were lined up double file, slowly entered the production line. This production line included five stations. At each of these a group of "reds" shouted at the top of their lungs the name of the piece of clothing that it was in charge of receiving. At the first station the victim handed over his coat and hat. At the second, his jacket. (In exchange, he received a piece of string.) At the third he sat down, took off his shoes, and tied them together with the string he had just received. (Until then the shoes were not tied together in pairs, and since the yield was at least fifteen thousand pairs of shoes per day, they were all lost, since they could not be matched up again.) At the fourth station the victim left his trousers, and at the fifth his shirt and underwear.

After they had been stripped, the victims were conducted, as they came off the assembly line, to the right-hand barracks and penned in until the women had finished: ladies first. However, a small number chosen from among the most able-bodied, were singled out at the door to carry the clothing to the sorting square. They did this while running naked between two rows of Ukrainian guards. Without stopping once they threw their bundles onto the pile, turned around, and went back for another.

Meanwhile the women had been conducted to the barracks on the left. This barracks was divided into two parts: a dressing room and a beauty salon. "Put your clothes in a pile so you will be able to find them after the shower," they were ordered in the first room. The "beauty salon" was a room furnished with six benches, each of which could seat twenty women at a time. Behind each bench twenty prisoners of the red commando, wearing white tunics and armed with scissors, waited at attention until all the women were seated. Between hair-cutting sessions they sat down on the benches and, under the direction of a *kapo* who was transformed into a conductor, they had to sing old Yiddish melodies.

Lalka, who had insisted on taking personal responsibility for every detail, had perfected the technique of what he called the "Treblinka cut." With five well-placed slashes the whole head of hair was transferred to a sack placed beside each hairdresser for this purpose. It was simple and efficient. How many dramas did this "beauty salon" see? From the very beautiful young woman who wept when her hair was cut off, because she would be ugly, to the mother who grabbed a pair of scissors from one of the "hairdressers" and literally severed a Ukrainian's arm; from the sister who recognized one of the "hairdressers" as her brother to the young girl, Ruth Dorfman, who, suddenly understanding and fighting back her tears, asked whether it was difficult to die and admitted in a small brave voice that she was a little afraid and wished it were all over.

When they had been shorn the women left the "beauty salon" double file. Outside the door, they had to squat in a particular way also specified by Lalka, in order to be intimately searched. Up to this point, doubt had been carefully maintained. Of course, a discriminating eye might have observed that the clock was made of wood and that the smell was the smell of rotting bodies. A thousand details proved that Treblinka was not a transient camp, and some realized this, but the majority had believed in the impossible for too long to begin to doubt at the last moment. The door of the barracks, which opened directly onto the "road to heaven," represented the turning point. Up to here the prisoners had been given a minimum of hope; from here on this policy was abandoned.

This was one of Lalka's great innovations. After what point was it no longer necessary to delude the victims? This detail had been the subject of rather heated controversy among the Technicians. At the Nuremberg trials, Rudolf Höss, Commandant of Auschwitz, criticized Treblinka where, according to him, the victims knew that they were going to be killed. Höss was an advocate of the towel distributed at the door to the gas chamber. He claimed that his system not only avoided disorder, but was more humane, and he was proud of it. But Höss did not invent this "towel technique"; it was in all the manuals, and it was utilized at Treblinka until Lalka's great reform.

Lalka's studies had led to what might be called the "principle of the cutoff." His reasoning was simple since sooner or later the victims must realize that they were going to be killed, to postpone this moment was only false humanity. The principle "the later the better" did not apply here. Lalka had been led to make an intensive study of this problem upon observing one day completely by chance, that winded victims died much more rapidly than the rest. This discovery had led him to make a clean sweep of accepted principles. Let us follow his industrialist's logic, keeping well in mind that his great preoccupation was the saving of time. A winded victim dies faster. Hence, a saving of time. The best way to wind a man is to make him run—another saving of time. Thus Lalka arrived at the conclusion that you must make the victims run. A new question had then arisen: at what point must you make the victims run and thus create panic (a further aid to breathlessness)? The question had answered itself: as soon as you have nothing more to make them do. Franz located the exact point, the point of no return: the door of the barracks.

The rest was merely a matter of working out the details. Along the "road to heaven" and in front of the gas chambers he stationed a cordon of guards armed with whips, whose function was to make the victims run, to make them rush into the gas chambers of their own accord in search of refuge. One can see that this system is more daring than the classic system, but one can also see the danger it represents. Suddenly abandoned to their despair, realizing that they no longer had anything to lose, the victims might attack the guards. Lalka was aware of this risk, but he maintained that everything depended on the pace. "It's close work," he said, "but if you maintain a very rapid pace and do not allow a single moment of hesitation, the method is absolutely without danger." There were still further elaborations later on, but from the first day, Lalka had only to pride himself on his innovation: it took no more than three quarters of an hour, by the clock, to put the victims through their last voyage, from the moment the doors of the cattle cars were unbolted to the moment the great trap doors of the gas chambers were opened to take out the bodies. Three quarters of an hour, door to door, compared to an hour and a quarter and sometimes even as much as two hours with the old system; it was a record.

One of these details is interesting to note because it clearly reveals the desire for perfection that drove Lalka. Sometimes you could not fit all the victims in the same string of cars into a single batch. Although the cars usually contained one hundred heads, they sometimes contained as many as one hundred and fifty, and one hundred and fifty Jews times twenty cars equals three thousand victims for thirteen gas chambers with two hundred places each. Thirteen gas chambers with two hundred places equals two thousand six hundred places: four hundred left over. Under the old system, since the turnover was slow, there was time to make a special batch of this "overflow" of four hundred heads. The extraordinary precision of the machinery introduced by the Lalka reforms had accelerated the turnover to the point where as soon as the gas chambers were emptied and whitewashed with lime, they were filled again, the "overflow" thus joined the following convoy. But the victims "in question," having caught their breath, died less quickly than the others which made it necessary either to keep everyone in longer, or to "rekill" them as they came out. In both cases this represented a loss of time. To offset this disadvantage, which considerably lowered output, Lalka developed a number of gymnastic exercises—dancing, jumping, and so on—which were to be performed by all the victims who were waiting for the next ovenload.

But let us return to the men. The timing was worked out so that by the time the last woman had emerged from the left-hand barracks, all the clothes had been transported to the sorting square. The men were immediately taken out of the right-hand barracks and driven after the women into the "road to heaven," which they reached by way of a special side path. By the time they arrived at the gas chambers the toughest, who had begun to run before the others to carry the bundles, were just as winded as the weakest. Everyone died in perfect unison for the greater satisfaction of that great Technician Kurt Franz, the Stakhanovite of extermination.

Since a string of twenty cars arrived at the platform every half hour, the Lalka system made it possible to fully process twelve trains of twenty cars each—or four convoys, or twenty-four thousand persons—between seven o'clock in the morning and one-fifteen in the afternoon.

The rest of the day was devoted to the sorting of the clothing in Camp Number One and the disposal of the bodies in Camp Number Two.

Transported by two prisoners on litterlike affairs, the bodies, after they were removed from the gas chambers, were carefully stacked, to save room, in immense ditches in horizontal layers, which alternated with layers of sand. In this realm, too, Lalka introduced a number of improvements.

Until the great reform, the "dentists" had extracted gold teeth and bridges from the corpses by rummaging through the big piles that accumulated during the morning in front of the trap doors of the gas chambers. It was not very efficient, as Lalka realized. Thus he got the idea of stationing a line of dentists between the gas chambers and the ditches, a veritable gold filter. As they came abreast of the dentists, the carriers of the bodies, without setting down their litters, would pause long enough for the "dentists" to examine the mouths of the corpses and extract what needed extracting. For a trained "dentist" the operation never required more than a minute. He placed his booty in a basin which another "dentist" came to empty from time to time. After the take had been washed in the well, it was brought to a barracks where other "dentists" sorted, cleaned and classified it.

Meanwhile, the carriers of the bodies resumed their race— all moving from one place to another was done on the double— to the ditch. Here Lalka had made another improvement: previously the body carriers had gone down and stacked their bodies themselves. Lalka, that maniac for specialization, created a commando of body stackers which never left the bottom of the ditch. When they arrived, the carriers heaved their burdens with a practiced movement, the role of personal initiative being reduced to the minimum, and returned to the trap doors of the gas chambers by a lower route, as on a gymnastic platform, so as not to disturb the upward movement. When all the corpses had been removed from the gas chambers, which was generally between noon and one o'clock, the ramp commando, in charge of removal of the bodies, joined the carrier commando. The burial rites lasted all afternoon and continued even into the night. Lalka had made it a rule that nobody was to go to bed until the last corpse had been stacked in its place.

In Camp Number One the afternoon was devoted to sorting. Here again, there was a new technique: all clothing and all belongings had to be inspected, and any indication that they had belonged to Jews had to be removed. Lalka, still taking his inspiration from the example of industry, decreed that each worker write his registration number on the bundles he made. This measure was designed to make it possible to discover the author of an irregular bundle immediately. The next day, on the advice of Kiwe, the "king of discipline," Kurt Franz opened a bundle at random, pretended to find a Star of David, summoned the culprit, gathered all the prisoners, and had the unfortunate man hanged. The whole incident took a quarter of an hour and put a final touch on the reorganization of the work.

Lalka then returned to problems of discipline. One point preoccupied him: the escapes, although they had diminished considerably, still had not stopped.

"They're still leaking a little," Kiwe had told him.

This was intolerable. It was necessary to put a stop to this scandal at once. But neither promises nor threats had any effect. Lalka found himself faced with a cruel choice: to kill all the prisoners and thus destroy his marvelous organization, or to reinforce the surveillance, to institute systematic searches, to create such a climate of insecurity that the prisoners would no longer dare even to dream of escaping. The choice was merely theoretical, Lalka had already made it on the first day: he decided to take all necessary measures to make the camp airtight.

It was on the day after this that Dr. Chorongitski told Galewski that he had finally succeeded in making contact with one of the Ukrainian orderlies, and that the man had agreed to procure weapons for the rebels.

The Committee met at once.

XV

THE *Hofjuden* HAD sensed the exceptional nature of the meeting, and no one was talking in the barracks. Everyone was lying in his bunk with his eyes open, staring at a point beyond the wooden walls, a point outside the camp, outside time itself; a point of felicity where all memory was effaced; a point beyond life and death, beyond personality. It was a point whose contours shifted, becoming successively a house, a feast, a face, a winter day, the sun. The Jews were looking at hope—the hope of living, the hope of dying, the hope of leaving, beginning again, forgetting. Hope for these dead men? But for them everything had become absurd from the day they had arrived in Treblinka. And yet it had begun quite normally: One day trucks had arrived. They had been driven out of their homes, which had been the homes of their parents and grandparents. They knew them well, those homes, they knew every nook and cranny of them, they had crossed their thresholds thousands of times. This time they had crossed them for the last time, but as they did not know it, they had not paid any more attention to them than usual. In the village street a row of trucks waited. The street was deserted and the doors of the houses shut. The Jews were being taken away; it did not concern anyone. When night had fallen they had no longer recognized the road. It was at this moment, no doubt, that they had ceased to belong to the world. They had disappeared. Dead or alive, they were in another world—a world which resembled the real one, but in which all the values were inverted, in which death had taken the place of life.

Structured, organized, stratified, disciplined in the image of the other, this world was its negative, its shadow, its reflection, its projection. "I was at the edge of a well," a survivor tells, "and the sky was at the bottom."

But in the darkest corner of the barracks, four men were listening to a fifth.

"It's curious," Chorongitski was saying. "At first the Ukrainian didn't trust me! Yes, in some way he was afraid of me. He must have thought I was a 'sheep.' Every time I approached him I saw his face close as if he were afraid of something. But at last we began to chat, and little by little I came to realize that he was not cut out for the job of killer. He is an anti-Semite, of course, but he does not understand why the Germans are killing the Jews. In his eyes we are part of the Manichaean balance of the world. One day he told me, 'It's like someone wanting to fill in the valleys because he doesn't like mountains.' I did not see what he meant. 'Well?' I asked him. 'But then there would be no more mountains.'

"Another day when we had become more intimate, he explained how, in his opinion, it was going to end. It was *Had Gaddia,* the old Passover legend in which the ox drains the water that put out the fire that burned the stick that beat the cat that—you know. Well, according to him, and I think he is right, when we have finished helping them kill the Jews, the Ukrainians will kill us, then they will be killed by the camp S.S. who will themselves be executed by super-S.S. Thus, not a single witness will remain."

"And the bodies?" Galewski asked suddenly.

"I asked him about that. He replied that they were well buried and that no one would ever find them."

Kurland looked up as if to say something, and everyone turned to him.

"Do you know how many bodies there are?" he asked.

No one knew.

"According to my calculations there are already more than five hundred thousand. You can't get rid of five hundred thousand corpses just like that."

The figure had impressed everyone.

"It's not possible," murmured Salzberg. "Five hundred thousand down there in that little plot of ground. It's frightening."

"The common grave of the Jewish people," said Kurland.

There was a moment of silence, as if to honor the memory of the dead.

Galewski was the first to emerge from his painful reverie.

"We must succeed at any price," he said slowly. Then, turning to Chorongitski, he asked him to continue.

"It was when the Ukrainian gave me his ideas about the end of the camp that I decided to put my cards on the table. I told him that a revolt was being prepared in Treblinka. He was more surprised than if he had just learned Hitler was dead. Through the astonishment that could be read on his face there shone a gleam of admiration. He immediately replied that we had absolutely no chance, that it was madness, and that he did not want to be involved in this business. His astonishment had given way to fear, and for a moment I was afraid he would rush to the Germans and tell them everything. I think the Ukrainians are even more afraid of them than we are. It was pointless to talk to him about money. His fear was so great that all the gold in the world would not have made him change his mind.

"I decided to try to convince him that we had a good chance of succeeding. I told him about Adolf and his shock troops. I described the determination of all the prisoners. I invented a perfect plan. I talked on and on confidently, as if for me there was no doubt about the outcome. When I saw that he was beginning to listen with interest, I told him suddenly that anyway we had other ways of procuring weapons and that if he refused it would be too bad for him. Not only would he have no money, but he would also run the risk of getting killed during the revolt, for he would not have the advantage of our protection. If I had been the devil himself the poor man would not have looked at me differently. Before his eyes he saw the slave turn into the master, the great dispenser of life and death. Me, a poor Jew, I was going to decide who would die and who would survive. Although my life seemed worthless, I indulged in the luxury of threatening him to withdraw my protection. It was so unimaginable that suddenly he began to waver. You know that the anti-Semites attribute miraculous powers to us."

"Ah, if only they were right," Galewski interrupted.

"Who knows?" said Salzberg. "If we succeed, it will be something of a miracle."

Everyone stopped talking, to let Chorongitski finish his story.

"Since he had never understood how the Jews let themselves be killed, the Ukrainian was fully prepared to believe, without understanding it any better, that we were about to go from the role of victim to that of killer. All that remained was to discuss the price. It was the only point that presented no problems, but I bargained to play the game. We agreed on a price of five hundred gold dollars for the pistols and grenades and two thousand for the guns, but he is not sure he can get the guns into the camp."

"Five hundred gold dollars for a pistol," murmured Kurland thoughtfully. "This really is a world of madmen."

"That's what I said to myself as I was bargaining with him. We are richer than the Bank of Poland. Well we went through with it as if he were trying to sell me a can of leeks for two zlotys and I only wanted to pay one and a half. I must give him three payments of five thousand dollars. He will start bringing the weapons after the first payment. I insisted that he get us as many grenades as possible."

Chorongitski stopped. He had pronounced the last sentence in a tone that implied, "Mission accomplished." The other four men looked at him with a mixture of gratitude and admiration.

"That's good, that's very good, thank you," said Galewski slowly.

The combat units were ready, the weapons would soon be here, the revolt was going to take place.

"Yes, we will soon be free," said Moriek.

Even while they were actively preparing the revolt, there had remained deep in their hearts a doubt, the vague sense of an impossibility, the impression that they had passed the point of no return and that anything they might attempt would be doomed to failure, as if a curse were hanging over them. And now, suddenly, the revolt was here, before their eyes. In a few days they would begin to receive the weapons; in two weeks, a month at most, they would launch the attack against the camp, they would kill their tormenters and flee into the forests. In a month life would begin again, the hands of the clocks would begin to move again, once again time would be divided into hours, weeks, months, years. Once again they would grow old, hope, build, once again they would live, driving before them an army of plans to conquer the future, and leaving a trail of memories in their wake.

"Good," said Galewski suddenly, as if coming out of a dream. "You will have the money tomorrow morning. I will see Adolf during the day to work out the details of the attack. He has told me that it was not his business, but I think he has some ideas."

Galewski had already warned the *Goldjuden* that he would be needing money for a big project. So when he asked the banker, Alexander, for the five thousand gold dollars brought to Dr. Chorongitski, he was not surprised.

Alexander had been one of those influential bankers of pre-war Warsaw. He was what is commonly called a money Jew. He had all the mannerisms, down to the tastes of a Maecenas. A luxurious existence, travel, entertaining—life had brought him everything. In a few generations his family had gone from the misery of the ghetto to the pinnacle of fortune. They were a family of Hasidim, completely immersed in the study of the Torah. It had seemed that nothing would ever interrupt the age-old pattern of this mystical poverty. The goods of the world were illusory to them beside the munificence of the princess Sabbath. "When the Sabbath comes," said a revered rabbi, "every Jew is king in Israel," and for centuries and centuries the Alexander family had preferred this weekly royalty to the adventure of the world. Who minded the blows, the gibes, the muddy streets, the winter cold, or the hunger, when on Friday evening, as the first star appeared in the sky, every thatched cottage in the ghetto was transformed into a palace, as in a fairy tale. To welcome the princess the single room had been scrubbed all day, even in its darkest crevices. The table was covered with an immaculate cloth, so white that it seemed to reflect the joyous flame of the candles which the mother, in observance of the tradition, had just lighted. The silver candlesticks, the family's only earthly possession, gleamed with all the love that the mother, the guardian of the hearth, had put into cleaning and polishing them and polishing them again in honor of the royal guest. When day had begun to wane, the whole family had bathed with care and put on their holiday clothes: shirts as white as the tablecloth, kaftans of black silk. All the honors in the world could not have brought as much joy as they felt when the father began to read the first benediction. At this precise moment the kingdom of God descended to earth. There were no more poor, no more weak, no more oppressed; each Jew was a king.

But one day an Alexander went bad; whether for lack of education or of character, he had transferred the love of God that he had been taught to money. Since this love was very strong in the Alexander family, the prodigal son had made a fortune.

The wealth of the Alexander family had lasted for one century; then, when the Germans entered Warsaw, the mistake of destiny had been corrected. First there had been the ghetto and then the death camp. As if this century of wealth had not existed, the banker Alexander became once again Alexander the Jew, a "forked stick," then because of his qualifications, a *Goldjude*. It was he who had already provided money for the escapes of Choken and Berliner. Since then he had made contact with Kurland, who had asked him for an estimate of the sums forwarded to Berlin, for his chronicle. Thus he had automatically become one of the members of the organization with the twin role of treasurer of the Committee and Kurland's financial adviser.

It was ten o'clock in the morning when Wildenstein, one of Adolf's men, came to get the money at the appointed place. He did not know the *Goldjude* who was supposed to deliver it to him, but the other man knew him by sight. For this extraordinary mission he had received, in addition to his instructions, a small bottle of poison, and he had realized that it must be very important. He was to take no risks and to swallow the poison at the slightest alarm. Although Galewski was still hampered by a few moral considerations, like the refusal to prohibit escapes, he had understood the necessity for burning your bridges behind you. All men to whom the Committee entrusted a special mission received a dose of poison in order to cut short any attempt at investigation.

Wildenstein slipped the sack containing the gold pieces into his shirt and glanced rapidly around him. The *Goldjude* had already disappeared. The infirmary was a hundred yards away on the other side of the central path of the camp, at the edge of the German quarter. The path was deserted and Wildenstein would have preferred to wait until a few *Hofjuden* came along to start down it, but he was even more afraid of keeping the sack of gold on him. Theoretically, the area around the infirmary was not off limits, but it was always dangerous to remain idle. He hesitated for a few more moments. Then suddenly, like a man throwing himself into the water, he advanced toward the path. Head bowed as a sign of humility, with rapid steps to give the impression that he was hurrying toward some work, he began to walk down the path in the direction of the infirmary. He was walking without turning around and with his eyes riveted on the corner of the infirmary, when he noticed a broom made of branches a few yards in front of him. Without stopping, he grabbed it and went on with more assurance.

Dr. Chorongitski started when he heard him come in. He was alone and seemed nervous. He took the sack from Wildenstein's hand and said, "Leave quickly, I think I am being watched." Wildenstein replied that he had noticed nothing out of the ordinary. "You're probably right, I'm imagining things," murmured the doctor in a shaky voice. He glanced around for a place to hide the sack. Seeing him hesitate, Wildenstein pointed to his overcoat, which was hanging from a nail on the wall. "Yes, you're right, that's a good idea." The doctor spoke unsteadily as if he could not control his nerves. Wildenstein had to tell him several times to go and open the door and see if anyone was coming when he was ready to leave. As he walked by, he looked at Chorongitski closely.

"Don't be afraid," said the doctor, who knew what Wildenstein was thinking, "you can depend on me."

Wildenstein saw Lalka just as he was getting ready to enter the path. The German had not noticed him yet and Wildenstein began to sweep the path in front of the infirmary furiously.

Impeccable in his black uniform, his cap placed very slightly to one side, his boots flashing, Lalka advanced with the slightly loping gait of a sportsman in top form, slashing the air from time to time with his eternal stick. Each man has his element, in which he feels at ease, in which he takes on a new dimension. Kurt Franz's element was Treblinka. When he put on his civilian suit to go on leave in his nice German town, he was suddenly transformed into an ordinary German—one among millions. Tall, blond, washed out, his glance dull, his eye empty, wearing a green hat and a suit made of some kind of synthetic fabric, Herr Franz was unimpressive. Drab and unobtrusive, he again took his place in ordinary life. But when Untersturmführer Kurt Franz returned to Treblinka, to his kingdom on the outposts of the Reich, once again he became Lalka, the Prince of Death. His kingdom was small, about fifty acres inside the barbed wire; but his subjects were so numerous that he did not mind. Over them he had an absolute power whose only limit was life, as is normal for a Prince of Death. And when he walked down the paths of his domain, his cap at an angle, his boots polished, his uniform faultless, something snapped in the hearts of the prisoners.

Lalka passed Wildenstein without noticing him and entered the infirmary before Wildenstein had time to warn Dr. Chorongitski. Through the window of the barracks Wildenstein saw the doctor jump when the door opened. The window was closed because of the cold, and Wildenstein saw the two men face each other, but was not able to hear what they were saying. At one point the doctor turned toward the window and seemed to bend over the table which was under it while Lalka moved toward the back of the room and disappeared from view. Wildenstein, intuitively fearing a calamity, stayed where he was and saw the German suddenly reappear right beside the overcoat. Lalka was turned sideways and he was smiling. The doctor was not moving and his eyes were fixed on a spot to the left of the window, where

Wildenstein remembered having seen a mirror.

Suddenly Lalka raised his right hand toward the coat; at the same moment Dr. Chorongitski turned and literally leaped in the German's direction. Wildenstein saw them both sink to the floor, and a dull thud echoed through the barracks. He wanted to run away, but a kind of terror mingled with curiosity kept him rooted to the spot. Lalka, who was physically much stronger than the doctor, must have immobilized him, thus preventing him from taking his poison. Galewski would have to be warned. Everyone must know that the doctor had been captured alive. Everyone would have to be ready to take poison if they were to save what could be saved.

While these thoughts were going through his mind Wildenstein felt in his pocket and squeezed the little bottle that Galewski had given him. The touch of the glass suddenly reassured him. Everything was over: the hope and the struggle and the horror. He felt very calm. Death did not frighten him; on the contrary, this death which he held in the palm of his hand had something soothing in it. He had only one gesture to make, and after that no one could do anything to him. When the door of the barracks opened violently, as if blown by an explosion, Wildenstein hurriedly took out his bottle.

The doctor appeared first. Lalka, bareheaded, his jacket torn, rushed out a second later. He took out his pistol and aimed. "My God, make Lalka kill him," thought Wildenstein. But Chorongitski had already taken his vial of poison out of his pocket and was trying to open it as he ran. Wildenstein heard a shot, the doctor staggered, seemed to hesitate, and fell. Lalka rushed to him. But the doctor had already gotten his hand to his mouth. His body tensed in a last effort and he fell over on his back. Just as Lalka reached him, Wildenstein saw his bloodstained mouth with bits of glass still on the lips.

Lalka had kept his nerve when Dr. Chorongitski had suddenly dashed out of the barracks. He had immediately dec ded that the doctor had gone crazy and had drawn his revolver to kill him, as one finishes off a wounded horse or a mad dog. But when he had seen the doctor's gesture, he suddenly realized that the matter might be more complicated than it had seemed at first. A man who kills himself under such circumstances is a man who has something to hide. When the doctor, unable to open the vial of poison, had brought it to his mouth and broken it with his teeth, Lalka had had an intuition that he was trying to take some secret with him to the grave. The German had good reflexes and he had lost no time calling other S.S. men to the rescue The doctor, who was still breathing, was carried to the infirmary. Wildenstein took advantage of the moment of confusion to slip quietly away and report to Adolf what had just happened.

While the two Ukrainian orderlies were trying to revive Dr. Chorongitski with the aid of a stomach pump, Kurt Franz had dumped the contents of the sack onto the table and was inspecting them. The first thing that struck him was that all the money was in gold dollars. His impression that the doctor had a secret was confirmed. His intuition became certainty when he had counted the sum: five thousand gold dollars, exactly. "What would a man be doing with five thousand dollars in gold pieces?" Lalka wondered. His first idea had been that the doctor was preparing an escape and that he had accumulated this hoard to survive in the forest. The doctor's suicide did not completely invalidate this hypothesis. Indeed, after the exemplary punishments inflicted upon unfortunate candidates for escape it was understandable that the doctor might have preferred to commit suicide. But if the doctor had wanted only to escape, why did he need exactly five thousand dollars, and in gold pieces? There was something here that did not make sense. Why hadn't he taken precious stones, jewels, rubles, or any other kind of money? Why had he taken the trouble to select? And why a round number? While he was revolving these ideas, Lalka was threatening the orderlies, telling them that they would answer for the doctor's life with their own. Lalka was convinced that the doctor had not been trying to escape.

If the hypothesis of flight was dismissed, only two solutions remained. Either the doctor was planning to bribe someone or he had gone mad. Although absurd on the face of it, the second hypothesis seemed more likely to Kurt Franz than the first. How are we to explain this sudden blindness on the part of the Technicians? Having introduced the hypothesis of a bribe, any objective investigator would at least have considered the possibility of the acquisition of weapons. Lalka, however, preferred to imagine that the doctor had gone mad, that it was merely a reflection of the proverbial Jewish passion for gold. This error in judgment, this failure to understand the mentality of the victims may seem strange. Actually, it is the necessary conclusion of the assumption which underlies the whole policy of extermination, the anti-Semite's belief that the Jew is an inferior being whose cowardice is equaled only by his love of money. To be sure, Lalka, that master Technician, was mistaken, but the reasons for his mistake are the same as the reasons for his successes and for those of his colleagues in Vilna and elsewhere. Indeed, it was this absolute certainty of the inferiority of the Jews that enabled the Technicians not only to succeed but even to undertake their policy of extermination in the first place.

Even as he developed his hypotheses, Lalka did not renounce his attempt to verify them. He hurried the orderlies, commanding them to revive the doctor. There was in Lalka the obstinacy of the tyrant who cannot accept the fact that something is resisting him. Death was his business. He distributed it with sufficient art to believe that he had become its master. The immobility of this corpse was an intolerable personal insult to him, a crime of high treason.

He hung over the body of Dr. Chorongitski until evening, unable to accept this defeat. When time for roll call arrived, in a last gesture of spite and impotence, an absurd demonstration that he remained the master, he had the body carried before the prisoners and tied to the punishment stand, and ordered a guard to give it fifty lashes. It was then that the prisoners understood that he too was mad.

The members of the Committee who, since morning, had been ready to die, began to hope again. Perhaps, after all, the organization could be saved.

But Kiwe, like the good professional jailer he was, knew how to conduct an investigation. Lalka's hypothesis had not seemed very convincing to him; he was persuaded that this gold had been intended for something, probably to bribe a Ukrainian. But for what purpose? He had interrogated the two orderlies, but not having enough evidence, he had not been allowed to torture them and had got nothing out of them. Then he had decided to continue the investigation at the other end: the origin of the gold. The size of the amount, the round number, and the fact that it was in dollars suggested that it could only have been collected by the *Goldjuden*. To make them confess, Kiwe had a plan.

When the "punishment" was over, he called all the *Goldjuden* aside and told them that before he died Chorongitski had admitted that it was they who had given him the gold. He promised a reward to anyone who would put him on the trail of the "thieves." Alexander had needed a maximum of complicity to raise the money, and all the *Goldjuden* were at least partly informed about the matter, because they had either helped to get the gold together, or seen it, or heard about it. There was considerable risk that one of the *Goldjuden* would break down under torture. Alexander realized the danger when he saw Kiwe take eight men out of the ranks, and imperceptibly he took his vial of poison out of his pocket. The *Goldjuden* all knew him, and he knew Galewski.

Kiwe took the first man to the "hospital," where he had had the fire stirred up. When they reached the edge of the ditch, he made him an offer: the ditch or a name. The first man chose the ditch without hesitating. As he fell into the fire he gave a terrible cry, which was heard distinctly in Roll Call Square. All the prisoners gathered there had understood, and they looked at the seven others who waited motionless. The second made the same answer, as did the third. Then the last five were led away together. When their five howls of horror rang out, Alexander realized that he would never survive Treblinka, for he would never be able to forget the cries of these forsaken men, these men who had died for him, for the revolt, these men whom he could have saved at the cost of his own life. He need only have said, "It was I!" then taken the poison at once. But he had a role to play. He had ceased to belong to himself since the revolt had given him back a reason to live.

If he still had a reason to fight, Alexander had just lost his reason to survive the victory. Although by a different path, he had arrived at the same conclusion as Galewski: there was no longer a place for them in the other world.

That evening the Committee met. At first no one spoke. Without daring to say so, everyone realized that Chorongitski's death was not merely the result of chance, that they might have been able to avoid it by taking more precautions to lull the suspicions of the Germans. The doctor's insistence on prohibiting escape now had a tragic dimension: it was by trying to combat escapes that Lalka had almost discovered the revolt. The secret was safe, but Chorongitski was dead.

Galewski, above all, could not forget Chorongitski's request that the Committee forbid the escapes. He felt personally responsible for the death of the first nine victims and for the failure of this attempt. During the agony of the *Goldjuden* he had been tempted to give himself up, but the sense of his responsibility to the movement had prevented him. Now, he wondered whether he would have the strength to go on. These long months of struggle had exhausted him, and this failure just as he thought they were reaching their goal shook his resolve.

"We should have forbidden escapes as he asked us to do," said Moniek slowly.

It was not a reproach, only a logical conclusion, that he was drawing from the event, but Galewski, psychologically shattered, lost control.

"Forgive me!" he stammered, and he began to weep softly.

On the night of its first battle the Committee had lost eight men, one member, and its leader.

XVI

THE PRISONERS WERE slowly recovering from this first failure when the epidemic of typhus broke out.

It was winter, and the thermometer never rose above freezing. The convoys, which represented an important source of food supplies, were becoming less and less numerous. Finally, the Technicians had reinforced the discipline even more since the Chorongitski incident. The Jews blamed the attempt. Only Adolf had lost none of his faith and did what he could to keep up the morale of his combat units, but everyone felt that the revolt had been postponed to a distant date which was not even determined. It was not despair that they felt, but a kind of lethargy, an immense lassitude in the heart of this interminable continental winter, under the blows, with hunger in their bellies, in this world of death, at the mercy of this implacable machine which exterminated with frightening regularity.

The news of the epidemic spread instantaneously. In one week half the prisoners had been stricken. What happened then had a miraculous quality: the miracle in abdication, the miracle of life. For this new threat, instead of snuffing out whatever life was left in the prisoners, revived their fierce will to live. Suddenly all passivity appeared to them as cowardice. Typhus, a fatal illness in their situation, was the ally of the Germans. Therefore they had to resist it with the same determination they used against them. In the face of this new danger, the "stiff-necked people" raised their heads again. Against the illness they channeled that energy which they had not been able to use against the killers. Doctors may call this story impossible, but all the evidence gathered attests to its authenticity. Barely eating, sleeping little more, ill clad, beaten constantly, the sick went to work with fevers of 105 degrees. Not only did they work, but they even managed to elude the Germans, who, now more than ever, tracked down the weak. The fever lasted from two to three weeks and left the men panting with weakness, anemic, exhausted, with only a fierce will to survive, that terrible three-thousand-year-old will which is stronger than illness, stronger than death. Ninety-five per cent of the prisoners had typhus; only fifty per cent were judged unfit and were executed by the Germans.

In its first stage the Jews tried to conceal the epidemic from the Germans, realizing that if they learned of it they would further reinforce their system of "natural selection." The doctors had no medicine, of course, and they could only advise the sick to eat as much as possible. But at this period the convoys had become rare, and the daily diet was as frugal as ever. It was then that there arose what the Germans called "speculation."

Speculation had begun the moment the Germans had prevented the Ukrainians from helping themselves. Since they did not perform their duties out of idealism, like certain of their masters, the Ukrainian guards had established contact with the *Goldjuden* in order to buy gold in exchange for alcohol and *Delikatessen*. But since the risks outweighed the advantages, business had remained on a small scale.

When typhus broke out after the failure of the revolt, the situation changed completely. The necessity of procuring food became vital. Since everyone had money and since the epidemic had spread with great rapidity, a vast quantity of gold was thrown on the market, resulting in a terrible rise in prices. This was the second phase of speculation, the phase of inflation. An orange, which had cost ten gold dollars, rose to one hundred dollars and more, a herring rose to eighty dollars. Only alcohol did not rise— a pint of vodka stayed in the neighborhood of fifty dollars. The trading took place in the latrines of the Ghetto at the end of Roll Call Square, along the barbed wire. One Ukrainian serviced several Jews. They agreed on a place where the money would be left and where the Ukrainian would leave the food in exchange. After they had settled on the price, the Jew left the money in the chosen place in the evening and theoretically found the food the next morning. Only theoretically, because, due to the rush of requests, the Ukrainians were more and more inclined to cheat. The sudden transition from a buyer's to a seller's market (until then it had been they who had asked the Jews for money in exchange for food and alcohol) encouraged them in this. But there was another reason for this phenomenon: the original Ukrainian dealers, who had acquired a certain professional conscience, were not numerous enough to supply the whole camp and the sick prisoners applied to anyone at all.

The inflation lasted until the Jews realized that soon they would no longer be able to obtain anything; observing the impunity of their dishonest colleagues, even the honest Ukrainians began to cheat.

The only way to make the Ukrainians more reasonable, to curb inflation, and to regulate the market was to artificially lower the demand. But to lower the demand it was necessary to find another method of procuring food, that is, to break the monopoly of the Ukrainians. Such a method existed, but it was not without risk. The camouflage commando went out into the forest almost every day to gather the branches which were used to conceal the barbed wire and to give the camp an innocent appearance. The two Ukrainians who accompanied it would not be very difficult to bribe, but it was necessary to find a way to buy the merchandise outside the camp and then to bring it back inside. This last point presented considerable risk. Adolf commissioned Kleinmann, who was both the *kapo* of the camouflage commando and the head of one of his combat units, to study what could be done.

Kleinmann immediately accepted the job with enthusiasm. He was twenty-one and had been formed in the hard school of the Hashomer Hatzaïr, one of the toughest Zionist youth movements. Young and well trained, he had had a chance to flee into the forests but had chosen to remain in the ghetto of Radom, thinking he would be more useful there than he would be waging a solitary battle. His strength had caused him to be selected after disembarking, and then he had passed several days before understanding. When he had realized what was happening in Treblinka, he had wept for the first and last time in his life. It had been the only concession he had ever made to a feeling of sadness, confusion, or sentimentality. He was a *sabra* before the fact, who, like members of the Legion, had only one country: the Hashomer Hatzaïr. Adolf had understood him on sight and had entrusted him with the command of a group in spite of his youthfulness. Kleinmann had become Adolf's brother.

With the help of the men in his unit, he quickly succeeded in establishing contact with Polish peasants in the forest. The latter, who rivaled the Ukrainians in love of money, readily agreed to cooperate. The first findings were encouraging: the Ukrainian guards had been multiplying the price that the food cost them by twenty. Kleinmann conceived toward them a hatred even stronger than that he felt for the S.S. The S.S. were criminal madmen who were not even human, but the guards, who also killed on occasion and not without pleasure, were pigs. Pigs can be bribed, and the two guards of the commando soon were. All

237

that remained was to get the money out and the food in. For a small extra charge the Ukrainians agreed to handle the money. Since they were never searched, they took very little risk. The food was to be brought in by hiding it in the branches. When everything was ready, Kleinmann started making deliveries. He was given the money in the morning and he brought back the food in the evening. Since the *Goldjuden* were kept under constant surveillance and could no longer take money out of the barracks where they worked, everyone had to pay for what he received. Adolf would have liked to set up a kind of treasury, but this was not possible, since the only available money was that which everyone procured from the clothing of the victims.

The system functioned this way for some time, until informers heard of it. But since they received nothing but frozen potatoes in payment for their activities, they preferred to say nothing in exchange for a part of the take.

After this it prospered so long and so well that one day Lalka got wind of it. He threatened and punished, but nothing worked. Then he decided to have the commando escorted by a German. He was more expensive than the Ukrainians, but he was finally bribed in his turn. The machine was running. The killers were already becoming the prisoners of their victims.

Meanwhile the campaign to reform prices had borne fruit. An apple had become stabilized at thirty dollars, a small loaf of bread at twenty dollars or one thousand zlotys or ten rubles, a sausage at sixty dollars, a pint of vodka at forty, a kilo of ham at eighty, a small can of sardines at twenty and a large one at forty, a bottle of liquor—which was in little demand—at one hundred, and a herring at twenty. These prices were not much higher than those set by the camouflage commando, whose costs were raised considerably by the bribing of the Ukrainians, the informers, and the German guard. However, the system of the box lunch containing an orange, a small loaf of bread, a piece of

chocolate and a pint of vodka, sold for one hundred dollars instead of one hundred forty retail, began to spread, considerably
simplifying operations. Finally—a last point which showed the
distance they had covered since the first sign of social life among
the Jews in Treblinka—not only had dishonest guards been eliminated from the economy, but many of those who continued to do
business agreed to extend credit.

In spite of the precautions that were taken, the Germans eventually became aware that an epidemic of typhus had spread
through the camp.

Three months earlier, Lalka would have had everyone executed in the name of the blessed output. Now he was content to
let Kiwe eliminate the weakest. He had already become the prisoner of his handiwork. He had grown fond of this world which he
had created out of nothing and for which he still had many plans.
The Jews of Treblinka were no longer Jews but his subjects, and
the worst tyrant cannot help occasionally feeling some fondness
for his subjects. After all, they had done this work together. Its
execution had united them the way age and rust eventually unite
pieces of iron. For some time now Lalka had even been recognizing a few faces, remembering a few names.

So, Kurt Franz authorized the doctors to open an infirmary.
Obviously it was inadequate for the several hundred sick men in
the camp, but since the doctors had no medicine anyway, this did
not make very much difference. The "happy elect" entered it on
the sixth day of fever and left, theoretically, as soon as the fever
had dropped. The infirmary had one advantage and quite a few
disadvantages. The advantage was rest, the disadvantages were
death.

As there were always more than twenty sick men in the little
barracks, Kiwe came there almost daily to clear out the surplus.
Except for a few rare privileged persons, one never knew who

was entitled to be there and who was crashing, and Kiwe selected at random when he did not take everyone. The sick lived in continual fear of the arrival of the "angel of death." He would suddenly appear in the doorway, without anyone hearing his step, and smile, pleased with the effect he made. For the occasion he had perfected a new dialectic, which delighted him. Approaching each prisoner, he would ask him whether he was sick. If the prisoner answered no, Kiwe would pretend to fly into a rage at the "malingerer" who was lying on his back in the infirmary and letting his comrades do his work, and he would take him away for exemplary punishment. But if the prisoner answered yes, Kiwe would look at him, wag his head with an air of commiseration and end by telling him to come to the "hospital" to undergo radical treatment. There was nothing you could do but play the game, for "hard heads" were beaten before they were executed. The conditions of "hospitalization" were such that many preferred not go to the infirmary. Indeed, the only ones who did were the privileged, *kapos*, and informers who had nothing to fear, and the desperate, who had nothing to look forward to.

The others organized. For some time there had been a small shed on the sorting square that served as a latrine. The prisoners transformed it into a "house of rest." Until then the shed had served as a social center. In the course of the day the prisoners came there to munch a crust of bread found in the clothing, to take a few drags on a cigarette, or simply to chat, to exchange the latest news or to trade a good pair of boots for cigarettes. Although the premises were very cramped, the social function filled by the latrine was very important psychologically. Indeed, the odor was such that even Kiwe avoided its vicinity, and this innocent spot had become a patch of neutral territory within the camp. Here the Jews were at home, here they experienced a feeling of confidence which was all the more intense because it was precarious.

With the onset of typhus the role of the latrines changed once

again. When the infirmary created by the Germans proved to be
nothing but a trap—not because they planned it as such, but
rather because of a certain dynamic of perversion, an ingrained
habit—it was the latrines that became an underground infirmary.

Granted, this is only a detail, but it has its importance, for it
reveals the change that had taken place in Treblinka. The more
the time passed, the clearer the future became: the prisoners of
Treblinka would be executed when they were no longer needed.
But Lalka wanted to hide this truth, for he knew that it might lead
the prisoners to some desperate gesture. The prisoners, on the other
hand, were not yet thinking about the end. Their daily lives remained too full of dangers to allow them to imagine a future,
however near at hand. Illness, beatings, hunger and exhaustion
were destroying them. How could they think about that distant
day when "destiny would wink its eye," as in the last line of the
camp anthem? They were like exhausted marchers who concentrate all their effort on the step they are taking without thinking
about the one that is to follow, let alone the one after that. Every
day represented a battle, every evening that drew to a close a
victory. There was even an expression, a kind of communiqué of
victory. "Another day that they didn't get!" the prisoners would
say as they crossed the threshold of their barracks in the evening
after roll call. The enemies were sickness, beatings, hunger and
exhaustion. To combat them there were two weapons: food and
rest.

Speculation partly assured provisioning; the latrines became
the "house of rest." With the agreement and often the aid of the
kapos, the most exhausted slipped in in the morning and did not
leave until evening. A kind of tacit solidarity had created an
order of preference which everyone respected. Designed for five
persons, the shed generally contained more than twenty. It functioned for a long time until the system had become too smooth
and the discipline perfect, and whole days went by without anyone going there to take care of his natural needs. The shed was

full from morning on, no one either came or went all day. Kiwe was long in noticing the stratagem or rather the absence of a stratagem. Then one afternoon, intrigued, he approached. The sick were taken to the "hospital."

The incident greatly amused Lalka, who got the idea of creating the position of *Scheissmeister* ("shit master"). The creation of this new post was the subject of conversation that evening in the German mess.

"He will be dressed like a rabbi," said one.

"He will wear a Russian cap," said another.

"No, a top hat," outbid a third.

"Yes, yes, a hat," shouted the listeners.

"And we'll give him a whip."

"We'll make him grow a goatee."

"And we'll tie an alarm clock around his neck."

The *Scheissmeister* assumed his duties the next day. After rummaging through the pile of clothing, Lalka came upon the habit of the cantor of a synagogue, which he found more becoming than the sober rabbi's habit.

"Cantor or rabbi, either way it's the same shit."

The "shit master" had instructions to let only five prisoners enter at once and to make them leave after three minutes. To make himself obeyed he could use the whip or write down the numbers. He was not required to do any work, and the prisoners who came to the latrines had to salute him. At each evening roll call Lalka would ask him:

"Rabbi, how goes the shit?"

"Very well, it stinks," he had to reply, invariably giving rise to general hilarity.

He was a rich merchant from Lodz, a man who was already elderly, calm and dignified. He had a round face and very gentle, almost innocent, blue eyes. He was one of those men you know are good the first time you see them. He had arrived in Treblinka with his whole family.

XVII

Since the death of Chorongitski and the eight *Goldjuden*, Galewski had changed profoundly. No matter what his friends told him, he felt responsible for these deaths and this failure.

"Once again, I do not believe I will have the courage to forbid the escapes," he told Kurland one day. "I am afraid this fight is beyond my strength."

Then he added, "Take the command! You may be the leader we need for such a situation."

But Kurland did not feel he had the strength to assume such a responsibility either.

It was the middle of January, during the last and most terrible outbreak of typhus. The cold was intense and the snow that covered everything added to the unreal quality of this world which was sinking deeper and deeper into madness.

The Committee met to study the situation. The report that it made was like a certificate of helplessness: three quarters of Adolf's men were sick, the discipline was tougher than ever, informers were omnipresent, and the problem of weapons was apparently insoluble.

It was on that day that Galewski tried to hand in his resignation.

"I struggled as long as I had the strength. I began at a time when the camp was no more than a chaos of dead men, an abyss of shadows, when half the prisoners were killed every day, when we said to each other every morning, 'See you tonight, maybe.' I refused to run away. I stayed because a mysterious force told me that my duty was here, because I believed I could do something."

The others listened to him, unmoving. Beyond the words, they watched their leader abandoning the combat for which he had brought them together. There was no hostility in their attitude, but no acquiescence either. Galewski felt this coldness.

"It was not you who elected me leader. It was I who chose you as my lieutenants. You have no right over me. Without me there would have been no Committee, for at first it was against you that I had to fight."

He had turned toward the *Hofjuden*.

"History will hand out the medals," said Moniek suddenly. "Our problem is to win the battle."

"Well, take the command yourself," Galewski retorted. There was a long silence.

Moniek was an ambitious young man whose privileged relations with Lalka made him an object of suspicion to many. Not that he was suspected of being an informer, but it was feared that he sometimes put his personal interest ahead of that of the community. For example, he did not hesitate to strike a prisoner when Lalka said, "Tell me, little Moniek, don't you think that one is shirking?" Moniek had already explained his position: "If I do not give him two lashes, Lalka will have him given twenty-five that night after roll call." This argument was logical, it had half convinced the others, and nothing further had been said on the subject; but from there to trust him with the command of the Committee was a big step which they hesitated to take. However, even if they did not want Moniek as commandant, his presence on the Committee was necessary, for as *kapo* of the *Hofjuden* he

244

controlled the strategic points of the camp.

Salzberg broke the silence before Moniek could agree.

"We know how much we owe you, but we ask you to think it over for a few more days before making your decision."

Once again, Galewski gave in.

The Committee adjourned on this compromise which did not involve the future, did not solve any problem. The fact was that the revolt was canceled. This lassitude that Galewski felt, this sense of hopelessness, of the vanity of any attempt, was felt by every member of the Committee with more or less intensity. These were tired, defeated men who had lived too long with the idea of death. Beside death, all else suddenly seemed only empty arguments. The convoys, which were more and more rare, were coming from farther and farther away, from Czechoslovakia, Germany, Bulgaria, Greece. It was as if the Technicians, nearing the end of their work, were reduced to scraping the bottom of the barrel of Europe. What meaning could the honor of the Jewish people have when soon there would be no more Jews, when the miracle of survival would soon come to an end? Over the camp, day after day, it snowed, and the whole landscape disappeared under this white layer, this virginal carpet which seemed to want to hide the last traces of the massacre. The snow, the cold, and this vast night of the world were going to engulf them all. The snow would never melt, spring would never come again. The whole world was disappearing under a fatal spell. So why struggle? Why not let oneself drift off very gently in this immense cemetery which served as the common grave of the Jewish people?

An event, commonplace in itself, was to reinforce this impression a few days after the last meeting of the Committee.

One morning shortly after work had begun, a young couple presented themselves at the entrance to the camp. The request that they made seemed so strange to the Ukrainians on duty that at first they were reluctant to let them enter. The young man must have insisted that they go and get a German. Thinking that he had mad persons or troublemakers on his hands and afraid he would be punished, the head guard could not make up his mind. Finally, when the young man and the young woman had lain down in the snow right in the middle of the path, after over an hour of hesitation he decided to send for Kiwe. The latter's stupefaction equaled the Ukrainians' and, suddenly at a loss, he begged the pair to go back to wherever they had come from, assuring them that it was impossible to comply with their request. The determination of the young people finally got the better of Kiwe, and letting them enter, he had them taken to the "hospital." But he could not have them executed without first referring the matter to Lalka, who was not due back from Warsaw until some time that afternoon.

The witness who reported this adventure to us no longer remembers the names of the young man and woman, but he knows that they were married. He thinks he remembers that they came from a little Jewish village in the vicinity of Bialystok. Of the fifteen hundred inhabitants of the village over one thousand were Jews. At the beginning of the German occupation no one had been worried, and if it had not been for the obligation to wear a yellow star on the chest and the left shoulder, it would have been possible to believe that life would go on as it had in the past, with its great poverty, its small satisfactions, and the immense joy of Sabbath evenings. But little by little disturbing rumors had begun to spread. People said that the Jews were being exterminated, that Hitler had sworn to kill them all and that he was keeping his promise.

One night some Jewish partisans came to see the rabbi and asked him to flee the village with all the inhabitants. But the rabbi replied that their lives were in the hands of the Lord and that if it was decided that they were to die, they would die as well in the forest as in their homes. Then the partisans gathered some young people together and told them what was happening in Vilna and what had happened in other villages: one night S.S. and Ukrainians would surround the village and in the morning everyone would be taken to an out-of-the-way part of the forest, to the edge of a huge ditch. They also told that halfway to Warsaw, in a place called Treblinka, hundreds of thousands of Jews had arrived of whom nothing was left but their clothing.

"Give us weapons and we will defend ourselves," one of the young people declared to the man who seemed to be the leader of the partisans.

But the partisans did not have enough weapons for themselves. Then the young people began to go out at night with the partisans. In the beginning they had fought with sticks, then gradually each one acquired a grenade. They made an agreement with the partisans that they would defend themselves first in the village and that they would not leave it until they had set fire to it, taking with them all those who could follow them. Then they went to see the rabbi, and they told him:

"Rabbi, no one knows the Torah as well as you, but no one understands war worse than you; no one sings the praises of God better than you, but no one holds a gun as poorly as you. As it is no longer a question of praying but of fighting, after today we will be in charge."

Next, they explained their plan.

"Like the ghettos of the Rhine in the Middle Ages, when the Crusaders were coming," the one who had taken command of the group concluded.

The rabbi smiled. He was pleased by the manner in which they had addressed him, and answered nothing. After that he never again tried to prevent them from convincing the population of the village.

The wait lasted until the end of summer, and the young people went out at night sometimes to train for war. Then one evening the lookouts ran into the village and through the streets, shouting, "The trucks, the trucks!"

It was a fine evening in autumn, and the flaming colors of the setting sun were matched by those of the forest. No one slept that night. While the Jews prayed in the village, the Ukrainians and the S.S. sang drunkenly all around. The attack began before dawn. The partisans gave the order to open fire when the first column reached the center of the village. Some S.S. fell, and the others fled.

"We waited for the second assault with a kind of passionate joy. It was terrible, we did not even know how to use the weapons recovered from the first dead. When the village caught fire I grabbed my wife by the arm and began to run for the forest. Men were running in all directions, bullets were whistling, wooden cottages were crackling in the flames. From time to time a dull explosion shook the air. The smoke that rose everywhere choked us. I don't know how I reached the forest, but I remember suddenly seeing a bearded young man with shining eyes yell something at me and point the way with the barrel of his gun. After walking a few minutes in that direction, we met a few people from the village. Afterward a few more came and joined us. Then the partisans arrived. I heard them say that all the others were dead and that we had to leave. I looked around me and recognized none of the young people who had organized the resistance. The partisans made us form a column and placed themselves in front and in back of us. We walked until nightfall.

"We were dead with fatigue and I was beginning to go to sleep, when I heard screams immediately followed by shots. We left again. The gunfire went on for a long time behind us. During the night I learned that we were being taken to a camp of families which I had never heard about. It was a camp hidden in the mid-

dle of the forest in which Jewish families lived. Before dawn I
heard shots again in front of us, but it was so dark and I was so
tired that I don't know what happened. When the sun rose we
halted and we were ordered to eat. I looked at the group of partisans, who stood apart, and observed that there were much fewer
of them than the night before and that some carried two guns.
They were very thin and all wore beards. There was something
frightening in their faces, frightening and pathetic at the same
time. All at once I understood that it was to save us that they
were doing all this, that it was to rescue us from death that half of
their men had fallen.

"At one point their leader came over to talk to us. He told us
that we would reach the camp that night if all went well and that
there we could rest. We left again. We stopped several times and
we were ordered to lie down and not to talk. Night came. I fell
asleep on my feet. I staggered at each step, nothing mattered to
me any more but sleep. I was about to drop when we were told
that we were almost there. I recovered a little strength. Some time
later we slowed down and I sensed that we were arriving at our
destination. A few minutes afterward we stopped. The order was
given to crouch down and not to talk. I heard a whistle blast
come from the front of the column, then silence, then another
whistle blast, and I began to be afraid.

"I sensed that something was not right. I went over to my wife
and took her in my arms. Then I heard another whistle blast that
was different from the first two, and immediately the group of partisans that was serving as our rear guard advanced, passing the
column. We were last again and I was even more afraid. Suddenly I heard a shout and at the same time the forest exploded.
Gunfire burst out everywhere at once. We had been ambushed.
The camp must have been spotted and they were waiting for us.
This was why the sentinels had not responded to the whistle. Our
men defended themselves fiercely and now all the shots con-

verged around them. Suddenly, over the tumult, I heard a shout in Yiddish: 'Run for your lives!' Without knowing what I was doing, I stood up, and grabbing my wife by the arm, I began to run.

"I have the impression now that since that moment we have never stopped running, that we have run without eating or sleeping, pursued, threatened, hunted down by the peasants, the Germans, and the Polish partisans, as if the whole world were chasing us. Our real agony began with winter, when we no longer had even wild berries to eat. We knew that we were going to die and we found this long agony useless. One day a peasant told us, before closing his door in our faces, 'Go where you belong, to Treblinka.' I remembered the name and we decided to go there and die with all the Jews."

When Lalka returned he asked the two young people a few questions, then nodded to the Ukrainian guards. The young couple sat down quietly on the bench at the edge of the ditch, joined hands, and waited. The faces of the two Ukrainians were a mixture of incomprehension and incredulity as they pressed the barrels of their guns against the necks of the young woman and the young man. They seemed to be saying, "These Jews, they're not like other people."

When Kurland reported this story to the Committee that evening in the barracks, all were struck by the impression it left of an implacable destiny. For each man the revolt signified the possibility of freedom. Everyone would not succeed in reaching the forest, but each man knew that he had a chance. Now, all at once, they learned that life in the forest was more untenable than life in the camp, where, all things considered, you had some chance of surviving, at least as long as the S.S. needed the Jews and provided you were fit and worked hard. Of course it was necessary to testify, but as the tale of the young couple proved, the truth about Treblinka was known outside the camp. One day someone would talk and then it would be easy to start excavations.

It was at this period that the epidemic began to subside. There were still a few cases until the month of April, but they were increasingly rare. All this time Adolf had been almost completely occupied with the struggle against typhus. He was not aware of what was happening on the Committee, and he thought Galewski had said nothing more to him about the revolt because he was waiting for the Germans to relax their surveillance. One day he went to see him to tell him about a new recruit who might make an excellent military adviser. He was a former captain in the Czech army. His name was Djielo Bloch and he had just arrived.

"Do you believe the revolt is still possible?" Galewski asked him.

Adolf, who had lived day after day with the prisoners' struggle against the epidemic, was not familiar with the doubts that had assailed the members of the Committee since the death of Dr. Chorongitski. Less educated, simpler, more aggressive than Galewski, he did not ask himself questions. For him the revolt was a kind of natural need; it had appeared to him one day like a revelation and since then he had lived with it, as one day he would die for it. The failure of the first attempt had not affected him as it had the other members of the Committee. When the leaders, with their extraordinary capacity to dream, had been promised weapons, they had believed that they already possessed them, and mentally possessing them they had seen themselves using them. Adolf, however, was not a "ghetto dreamer," he was a man of action and, what is more, a man of war. This turn of mind, which denied him any larger conception, had protected him from the sudden disillusion which the other members of the Committee had felt.

When the epidemic had broken out he had seen it as the first obstacle to overcome before preparing for a new attempt. He knew from experience that what counts in a battle is the number of manned guns in the field and that you don't make war with convalescents, shut-ins and sick men. Sick men would be incapable of fighting and in the forests would become easy prey for waylayers of Jews. After the epidemic was checked, Adolf devoted himself once again to the revolt.

Adolf was on the platform when the convoy to which Djielo belonged arrived. By the bewildered but fearful look of the deportees Adolf realized that this convoy came from another country. One man had immediately attracted his attention: tall, very thin, wiry and smooth-shaven, with a long neck with prominent tendons, thin lips, and eyes that were green, intense, hard, and very deep.

Adolf walked over to the man and whispered, "Say that you are a carpenter." Adolf had observed that for some time during the selections the Germans had been particularly interested in manpower for the construction commando, whereas the shoemakers and tailors, who had once been very much sought after, no longer had much chance. This was the kind of detail to which he had attached considerable importance ever since Galewski had put him in charge of recruiting, for it helped him make the Germans select those whom he had chosen himself for his combat units.

Djielo looked at him, wanting to say something in reply, but remained silent. His gaze, after pausing for a fraction of a second, left Adolf's eyes before the latter was able to tell anything.

The aptitude tests had been abolished since the stabilization of the "personnel" at Treblinka. The S.S. confined themselves to selecting a few artisans and skilled laborers from each convoy. When the S.S. asked him his profession, Djielo said he was a carpenter.

Adolf saw him again in the afternoon. Djielo seemed still not to have realized where he was. One of his cheeks was cut, but his face still had the same impassivity.

"Have you been in the army yet?" Adolf asked him.

"I am a captain in the regular army." Djielo replied with a certain formality. "Captain Bloch of the Czech army," he continued, as if to introduce himself.

Adolf wondered how it was possible for these men to be so ignorant of what Treblinka was. The Polish Jews knew, but those who came from other countries all had this same absent air, these same mannerisms of civilized men.

"Kapo Friedman of Treblinka," he replied. Then, after a moment: "A *kapo* is a Jew who hits other Jews, and Treblinka is a camp where the Jews are exterminated."

Djielo paled a little.

Adolf was in the habit of revealing the truth about Treblinka to new arrivals. He did it in a dry way and immediately spoke of the revolt. He had noticed that by proceeding in this way the other man did not go through the bottom of the abyss as they themselves had done. Right away he gave him a hope to cling to, a reason not to let himself go. This was very important, for in this way the prisoner did not have to overcome an inferiority complex toward the Germans or a guilt complex toward himself. Even a man who arrived with his family knew that he had been chosen to participate in the revolt and if he agreed, as was always the case, he did so not in order to survive by sacrificing his family, but in order to fight. From the outset the German appeared as the enemy and not as the master. All at once the revolt seemed a necessity from which it would no longer be possible to turn back.

"Did you come here with your family?"

"No. I was alone."

"In that case it will be easier to explain. You have been told that Treblinka is a transit camp and that you were being taken to colonize the East. The truth is quite different. Do you see those concrete buildings down there? They are gas chambers. They drive the Jews inside, close the doors and start the motors. In half an hour everyone is dead, asphyxiated by carbon monoxide. Don't try to understand; it's impossible. Six hundred thousand Jews have already died like this. We are here to help. Don't try to understand this either. There are about a thousand of us. We will give you the exact figures if you're interested."

Djielo listened, fascinated. "How is it possible?" he repeated over and over, punctuating each of Adolf's statements.

"That's what people may ask some day if we don't get out of here."

"I don't see how we will get out if what you say is true."

Adolf paused a moment. Then suddenly changing his tone and looking hard at Djielo he said, "This is our business and this is why I have chosen you."

After a brief hesitation Djielo, thinking he understood, murmured, "An escape?"

"No."

"The Russians?"

"Not that either. According to our latest information the front is over six hundred miles from here, bogged down by snow, and anyway the Germans are still advancing."

"What then?"

Adolf paused for effect.

"A revolt."

"I see," murmured Djielo slowly, running a trained eye over the camp.

Adolf, following his gaze, answered Djielo's questions before the latter could formulate them, unconsciously assuming from the outset the attitude of a subordinate reporting to his superior.

"Yes, four rows of barbed wire plus an observation post every two hundred yards, equipped with a searchlight and a heavy machine gun, plus one guard to every five prisoners. The first real forest that will offer us any serious protection, against the Germans at least, is five miles away. Finally, the area is crawling with troops that will intervene at the slightest alarm."

"Is that all?" asked Djielo, with a slightly ironic note in his voice.

"And," continued Adolf imperturbably, "not one prisoner out of ten knows how to use a gun . . . But that doesn't matter," he concluded in a detached tone, "since we don't have guns anyway."

The report had pleased Djielo, for it proved to him that Adolf knew what he was talking about, that he knew the situation exactly, and that he was not building his plan on dreams.

"And what do we have in our favor?"

"What the Germans think of us. They have taken precautions as if they were guarding supermen—but in their eyes we are nothing but a mass of subhumans, incapable of the slightest gesture of courage."

"I see: the surprise element."

"Precisely, my captain—a handful of Jews against the conquerors of the world. We are adopting against them the tactic which they used against us and which worked so well for them. It was because it seemed improbable that we did not want to believe in the reality of the extermination until it was too late. They will have as much trouble imagining a revolt as we had conceiving of the extermination. We said, 'The Germans? That civilized people? Come now!' They will say, 'The Jews? Those subhumans? Really!' It's what they are saying already."

That night in the barracks they had had a long talk about what could be done. Afterward they formed the habit of meeting every evening, and out of these meetings had come the outline of a plan. Djielo had real military ability. Adolf provided him with all the information he might need, drew his attention to certain

255

points, and criticized his proposals in terms of what he knew to be the reality of Treblinka.

The revolt had found its military leader. Adolf decided to ask Galewski to appoint him *kapo* for his own protection.

"Do you believe the revolt is still possible?" Galewski had asked.

"And why shouldn't I believe it?" replied Adolf.

Galewski did not want to give the real reasons for his doubts. "What about weapons?" he asked.

"We have found a way to get some."

So utterly had Galewski abandoned the idea that Adolf had to insist in order to reveal his plan.

It was audacious but it had a chance. The S.S. had their boots and uniforms made by the *Hofjuden*. The bootmakers and tailors, who had their own workshops, were there only for this work. They were excellent craftsmen and had even succeeded in winning the confidence of the Germans, who treated them with a certain mildness, even bringing them cigarettes and alcohol on occasion when they were particularly pleased with the work of the Jews. Some S.S. even had shoes and clothing made for their wives and children. This led them to chat with the artisans, to talk about their families, the war, their country, the towns where they were born, and the little houses they dreamed of buying when "all this" was over. In the workshops of the tailors and bootmakers the Technicians of the extermination were transformed into petty officials. From time to time they even mellowed to the point of feeling sorry for the poor Jews, and one day one of them had even said, "What are you going to do? It's the war." The shops had become neutral territory, like locker rooms where the opponents would meet at the half and exchange their impressions of the game. Here even Lalka indulged in confidences. One day, for instance, he had explained that for him Hitler was like a God and that if he ordered him to kill his parents, he would do it. In short, at these moments the S.S. behaved like any man in the company of his tailor or his barber. By making them slip on jackets, boots and trousers, raise their arms, bend their knees, and turn in front of the full-length mirror, the artisans had acquired a kind of control over the S.S. and had even reached the point where they made the appointments themselves.

It was on this very point that Djielo's whole plan which Adolf was in the process of submitting to Galewski, was based.

"On D-day, the tailors and bootmakers will each make an appointment with a German every fifteen minutes, starting one hour before the time scheduled for the outbreak of the revolt. If the revolt is planned for three o'clock, starting at two o'clock a German will have an appointment every fifteen minutes in each of the two shops. Two Germans at two o'clock, plus two at two-fifteen, plus two at two-thirty, plus two at two-forty-five, in other words, ten Germans."

Galewski did not seem to understand.

"And what do you intend to do with these ten Germans?"

It was Adolf's turn not to understand.

"What will we do with them?" he inquired, confused. "What will we do with them? Why, kill them, of course!"

Galewski's face went through a number of transformations as he slowly realized what Adolf was proposing. It was so unlikely that he could not help making a joke.

"We ought to invite them all. Over the years we would innocently invite the whole German army, and we would win the war. Little David killing the great Goliath."

A certain brand of humor was a most astonishing aspect of life in Treblinka. An extreme form of the celebrated Jewish humor, a mixture of the tall tale and a gentle self-irony, it played the necessary role of release in this world of death. Today it is difficult to conceive of it, and the survivors sometimes have trouble remem-

257

bering that it existed. One of the female survivors told us about a joke she was in the habit of making. In the last months of the existence of Treblinka a number of young women were sent to Camp Number Two to work in a laundry where the prisoners' linen was washed. One of them had as much passion as lack of talent for singing, and all day long she insisted on humming songs of which she sometimes remembered the words but never the tune. This annoying habit had made her the butt of her companions' jokes. The survivor tells one of these jokes which she made herself.

"Rifka," she told her one day, "I thought I had gotten used to everything here, but there is one thing I can't stand."

"And what's that?"

"Your voice, Rifka, your voice!"

Earlier, at the end of the ghetto period, when with the best will in the world it had become impossible to preserve the slightest hope, some Jews had taken refuge in humor. The essential metaphysical question had become: "Do you believe in a life after the trains?" The standard consolation to friends whom you had to leave and whose sadness could be read on their faces had become, "Come on, cheer up, old man, we'll meet again some day in a better world—in a shop window, as soap." If the friend was in the know, he was supposed to reply, "Yes, but while from my fat they'll make toilet soap, you'll be a bar of cheap laundry soap."

To understand this humor is to understand the infinite love of life of the Jews. It is to understand both the abdication and the miracle.

That day Adolf had to wring out of Galewski the promise to have Djielo named *kapo*. When they met that night he was very depressed. He told Djielo that Galewski doubted whether the *Hofjuden* would agree to take so many risks.

"Perhaps he is right about the *Hofjuden*, but what he isn't saying is that he hesitates to take them himself," he added as an afterthought.

"And can't we do anything without them?" asked Djielo.

"Even with the *Hofjuden* it's risky, because we have no way of guessing the reaction of Camp Number Two, with whom we have no contact. By ourselves, it would be madness."

"We could force them by threatening to go into action anyway."

"No, what we have to do is convince them. Don't forget that it was Galewski who started the whole thing. It is he who is the real life of the revolt. He is the only one who has enough influence over the boys to make them all rise up at the same time. Right now he has lost his reason to fight, his blind confidence. We must understand him. He knows that he won't leave this place alive, that his life stopped when he got off the train. A man does not live so long with death, his own and that of others, without having these moments of weakness."

"So?"

"So, we must wait. I heard Kiwe say that we were still expecting many convoys. Well, as long as convoys keep arriving, they will need us and therefore they won't liquidate us."

"That won't last forever. Something has to happen before that."

"That's what I'm hoping. But where the new event that will get the revolt started again will come from, I don't know."

The men were exhausted, the revolt had lost its life, the Nazi machine seemed to have destroyed the attempt before it had even seen the light of day. Two men wanted to go on fighting, but all the others were on the point of giving up, renouncing the fight against death. Death had become too familiar to them. The real world, the other world had become dim in their minds. Had they ever been free? Had they ever been happy? Had they ever been men? All that was so far away, lost in the vague memory of another life.

But the dialectic of death involves that of life. This new event that Djielo was talking about would happen. This event was a man. A man who, on that night of the nineteenth of January, 1943, was riding toward Treblinka.

He was wounded, he was dying, his name was Choken.

XVIII

As soon as his car had passed the gate of the camp Choken took a stub of pencil out of his pocket and began to scrawl furiously on each piece of clothing, "This belongs to a Jew who died at Treblinka." He did not know where his fate would lead him and he wanted, from his first moment of freedom, to start fulfilling his mission of witness in every possible way. When his pencil was used up he took a knife and cut big clumsy holes in the shape of the Jewish star in the other garments. He worked this way all afternoon and part of the night, tirelessly, without pausing for a single moment, without thought of food or sleep. It was a kind of frenzy, like a need to speak, to throw off an intolerable burden. In spite of his apparent insensitivity Choken had been profoundly affected by what he had seen in Treblinka, and here alone in this car he exploded in a futile revenge on death and silence.

When he came to his senses and saw the car strewn with slashed clothing he realized that he must get away as soon as possible; the first inspection would be fatal. He tore off the grill that covered the little window and waited. Dawn was beginning to break when the train slowed down. After making sure that they were rolling through open country, he jumped onto the embankment. He lay for a long time after the last car had passed him. The grass smelled good, the night was soft. The receding sound of the train restored the darkness to silence. There was something glorious about the sky which was slowly brightening in the east. The taste of freedom was the taste of happiness. Everything was wiped out. The last fragments of the nightmare were vanishing with the red tail light of the train, which was growing dimmer and dimmer.

More than joy or happiness Choken felt then an extraordinary sense of liberation, of rebirth; the feeling a man must have on rediscovering a dear friend whom he believed he had lost forever. This friend whom Choken was rediscovering was himself, with his skin thrilling to the freshness of the morning, with his nose slowly rediscovering forgotten smells, with his eyes drinking in the infinity of the sky, with his tired body lying full weight on the loose and welcoming soil.

After lying motionless for a long time, he got to his feet and crawled toward a wood whose undergrowth looked particularly dense. Day was about to break and Choken, who had no Aryan papers, decided to hide. On the edge of the wood he found a little stream. He drank deeply, then he bathed. The water was very cold and Choken felt his arms and legs grow delightfully numb. With his naked body totally immersed in the stream, it seemed to him that the current, which was strong at this point, was washing from his skin, along with that odor of death which he had finally grown used to down there but was beginning to smell again, the last memories of hell. He dried himself with his shirt and then walked into the wood. He ate the crust of bread and the piece of sausage he had brought with him. Then, covering himself completely with a blanket of leaves, he went to sleep in the middle of a thicket.

Night had already fallen by the time Choken awoke. He got up at once. His mind was clear, his body rested. He decided to go to a village he had seen that morning a short way down the railroad track.

He reached the first house without difficulty. In the third, which he inspected cautiously through a window, he saw a solitary woman tending a baby. He knocked at the door and pushed it open firmly as soon as he heard her draw the bolt. The woman seemed frightened, but Choken had so much assurance that she did not dare say a word. He asked for something to eat and followed her into the other room. The child was moaning softly in the big basket that served as his cradle. Choken walked over to him.

"He is sick," said the woman in a voice that shook with stifled sobs.

Choken was about to bend over the cradle when he heard screams, shouts, and cries of protest coming from the other end of the village. He stiffened and listened to try to figure out what was happening. The noise redoubled and seemed to grow louder, as if the people who were making it were getting closer to the cottage. He wondered whether he had been seen and whether he was the one they were looking for. He turned quickly and ran his eyes around the room in search of an exit. But the woman had noticed his uneasiness and, as if to reassure him, she said in a neutral voice devoid of emotion, "Oh, they're taking the Jews to Treblinka."

It was an observation which did not concern her. She might have been saying, "Oh, there's the ten-seventeen; the clock's slow."

Choken was paralyzed. The spell was broken. Once again he found himself plunged into the heart of the drama. It took him a few minutes to pull himself together. When he thought he could control his voice he replied, "The Jews! Yes, of course."

The woman studied him. The voices were coming closer and closer. Now he could distinguish the shouting of the Germans and the weeping of the Jews, an undertone which made a kind of unbroken murmur. It was the weeping of a thousand voices, an orchestra of grief chanting all of human misery.

Blinded with sorrow, abandoning all caution, Choken murmured, "The bastards, the bastards."

The woman, who had not taken her eyes off him, took a step toward the door. But Choken ran forward and had his back to the panel before she could reach it. She looked at him with hatred and said between her teeth, "Jew! You're a Jew too. I suspected it the minute I saw you."

The child was still moaning in his cradle.

Choken took out a handful of gold pieces and flinging them on the floor in front of him, said with all the contempt he could put into his voice, "Give me something to eat."

At this moment the column of deportees was passing the door of the cottage and the woman's answer was lost in the tumult. But Choken saw her stoop down and begin to pick up the money. Then the sound receded and soon nothing could be heard but the moans of the baby.

"My baby," she murmured with hatred, as if the Jews were responsible for the fact that he was going to die.

She walked over to him and caressed his face, then went toward a big pantry in the back of the room. She took out a hunk of bread, a few potatoes, and a piece of lard which she set on the table.

"Take it and get out of here," she said, without looking at Choken.

Not far from Treblinka there was an ancient Jewish hamlet named Czegow. The miller, the blacksmith, the butcher and the mason were Jews. The Jews had built the houses with their own hands. They had even laid out the streets. The population had been Jewish from father to son, just as it had been poor for generations. Choken had been to Czegow once, he no longer remembered on what occasion, but he had preserved a fond memory of the town.

As soon as he saw its first cottages he immediately recognized the village on the edge of the forest and on the threshold of the great plain, as poor as its sandy soil and the swamplands into which it disappeared at the other end of the horizon.

Having bought Aryan papers with his gold, Choken now traveled by day. He had walked all day, and fatigue was beginning to weigh down his limbs, to make his feet drag on the dirt path. Day was dying, the red sun was distorting the plain and giving the forest a look of mystery.

The village seemed untouched and for the first time since the night when he had plunged into the nightmare again, Choken felt peace descend upon him. Miraculously preserved from the tempest, the little Jewish village was still peacefully following the gentle rhythm of faith and eternity.

The darkness deepened, swallowing up the hundreds of little houses, and as Choken advanced they seemed to melt into the forest. The path made a sharp turn and the whole village disappeared. The silence was unbroken. Choken felt a nameless anxiety stir in him, a vague fear. He stopped to listen. Then, without making any noise, he moved forward again along the underbrush that lined the path.

The ground became firmer under his feet, and he knew that he was entering the village. A few more steps, and the first house was in front of him. By gliding along the wall he reached the window, and suddenly his suspicion became certainty: the panes were broken, the furniture overturned, clothing littered the floor. It was like a painful revelation: he had arrived too late, Czegow no longer existed.

He rushed through the village, searching desperately for a sign of life. The main street was strewn with debris. The door of the little synagogue, which had been torn off its hinges, revealed a devastated sanctuary in which the ark, the cupboard where the scrolls of the Torah were kept, had been profaned. Everywhere the emptiness and silence spoke of death. Without realizing it, Choken had crossed the village and now he found himself at the entrance to the little cemetery. He took a few steps and felt the earth grow soft under his feet. He found that the cemetery had not been spared either. Slowly he sank to the ground and wept with rage, helplessness and hate.

That night he slept in one of the ravaged beds of the village. In the morning he had recovered his calm. He combed the village painstakingly to make sure no one was left alive. He chose some warm clothing against the winter which was impending, and without turning around, he left by the path by which he had come. He had made up his mind: he was going to kill and kill again until he died killing. Only death would cure him of his hatred, only death would satisfy his need for vengeance.

The day after his arrival in Wengrow the great raid began. He let himself be led away and put on the train without offering the slightest resistance. He wanted to try to rouse the Jews to the very end. The voyage amid these broken creatures, full of a horrible and resigned calm, was worse than death. He could not make up his mind to desert them this way. He could not give up, for he lived only for vengeance and felt nothing but hate.

The train was approaching Treblinka when he decided to jump. The bullets began to rain down when he tried to rise. But his rendezvous with death was not for that day.

He arrived in Novoradomsk in the morning. He had decided to stop at that town on his way to Warsaw, because one of his cousins lived there. He was given a warm welcome until he mentioned Treblinka. The town lived in a peaceful torpor. His cousin begged him not to mention Treblinka to anyone.

266

"But you believe me, don't you?" Choken asked him.

"Of course I believe you; but there's no point in frightening the others."

"It's better to let them die?"

"Not die; hope. Hope is all they have left."

"What about dying like men?"

"When you have to die, what difference does it make whether it is like a man, a Jew, or a sheep?"

The conversation had gone on this way for a few hours. Then Choken went out and began to harangue the crowd. After a quarter of an hour the Jewish police arrived and took him first to prison, then before the Jewish Council. The president of the Judenrat accused him of deliberately spreading panic in order to buy up gold and jewels at a low price. Choken smiled and said nothing. When he was taken back to prison, he escaped.

He reached Warsaw early in the month of January. There he was listened to, often with indifference and sometimes with hostility, but he was allowed to speak.

The saddest case was that of a man who, while listening to him talk about Treblinka, suddenly went berserk and tried to attack him, crying, "Swine, you dare to claim that my wife who is young and beautiful is dead! You are a liar and you have come here to torture us." The wife of this man had been taken to Treblinka a month earlier. He had refused to accept her death and even told people that she sometimes wrote to him.

Choken had trouble controlling him and left him with a certain sense of shame. From that day he suffered a great crisis of doubt which led him to the brink of despair. It was then that he decided that the only possible combat was the one Galewski was waging in Treblinka: the combat after death. He was thinking of getting arrested and taken to Treblinka to see Galewski again, when one night three young men accosted him in the street and pushed him under the arch of a carriage gateway. Two of them seemed to be students; they were thin and had the same burning eyes. The third was a giant whose unshaven face had a disturbing quality. They questioned him at length on Treblinka, and Choken suddenly realized not only that they were well informed about what was happening there but also that they knew every word he had said since his arrival in the town. He had just come into contact with the Jewish resistance organization of Warsaw which had controlled the ghetto for some time, and which three months later was to lead it in a battle as fierce as it was hopeless.

When the interrogation was over, one of the two students, who seemed to be the leader, asked Choken if he wanted to fight with them. Choken agreed and they led him away at once.

The raids had practically ceased in Warsaw, where there were only eighty thousand Jews left out of the four hundred thousand who had been concentrated there before July 1942. In the minds of the organizers of the resistance the final liquidation of the ghetto was certain, and the only problem was to find out when it would take place. The plan was solely defensive. The problem was to transform each house into a fortress and to make the Germans pay a high price for each Jew when the final raid began. The defenders did not have the slightest chance of getting out alive.

For the defenders of Warsaw, as for those of Bialystok, victory was no more possible than retreat. Worse still, their struggle might remain forever unknown and might not even serve the honor of the Jewish people. There exists a heartbreaking testimony of what the fighters in the ghettos felt on the eve of the final battle. It is Mordecai Tenenbaum's last letter, written to his sister in the land of Israel the night before the last raid. This letter, which left Bialystok a few hours before the outbreak of the insurrection, miraculously reached Palestine.

Will anyone ever know the story of our heroic struggle? . . . We shall all disappear without leaving a trace. Itzak is no more, nor Zywia, nor Fromka, nor any of our old comrades. . . . The men look at me with supplication and shame: "Not yet; next time maybe," they seem to say. How people long to live! . . . Now it is really over. Tomorrow the great raid will begin. If I really saw the necessity for it we could, at the price of my dignity, see each other again. But I don't want to. There's no need. And you won't cry, will you? That won't help anything. I know it now.

They did not conceal from Choken that they were going to die, that there was no question of any other alternative.

"Our only freedom is the freedom to choose between two ways of dying and even that may be for nothing," one of the leaders of the resistance told him. "We are like the defenders of Massada who, in that stronghold at the end of the world, sacrificed themselves right to the end, when the revolt against Rome had long since been drowned in blood, when the Temple was in ruins, when Judea had ceased to exist. Why fight when all was already lost? For the honor of Israel? But the dispersion had already begun, and they had no way of knowing that we would survive exile. For an example? But it was a battle without a witness, and history would never have known if Flavius Josephus had not later decided to write *The War of the Jews*. For faith? Perhaps; or rather from faith. They did not reason, they did not look for a meaning for their combat. They fought and died, that was all.

"How many other such struggles have there been that we don't know about, that we never will know about? It may be because throughout our history we Jews have agreed to fight without hope, but without despair either, with faith in God and in Israel, that our people have survived. Today we can argue that the Jewish people are dying and that therefore our fight is perfectly useless and our hatred futile. But who knows whether from these ashes our people will not rise again, stronger than before?"

Choken, who had been stationed in the foremost bunker, waited for the day of the battle with intense emotion. The ghetto was surrounded; no one left it any more. A silence of death hung over the streets which a few months before had been so full of life. At dawn and at twilight columns of workers passed, dreary condemned men, living ghosts. Whole buildings were empty of all but memories, precise and already cold memories which recalled lives interrupted in the middle of their daily toil. A laid table told that a family had been rounded up just as they were sitting down to eat, a gutted partition that a hiding place had been discovered, unmade beds that death had entered in the middle of a night's sleep.

The first attack began before daybreak. It was the ninteenth of January. The guards—Ukrainian, Lithuanian, Latvian, White Russian—marched at the head, then came the Polish police, and finally the special S.S. units. They advanced without fear, occupying the middle of the road. The Jewish commandant let them enter the lines of defense before opening fire. The gunfire burst from everywhere at once, and those mortally wounded and those frightened to death fell with a single movement. From all the houses an immense cheer rang out. The counterattack began in the early afternoon. Choken's bunker held out for three hours. Then, blinded by the roaring fire of the tanks and the field artillery, hastily brought up as reinforcements, it was hemmed in by flame throwers.

After fighting for every step of every story, the commandant of the bunker gave the order to retreat. The defenders had no alternative but to jump out the windows. Choken, who was wounded, jumped first, shouting, "Long live Israel!" He was out of ammunition and did not want to fall into the hands of the Germans alive. But when he saw the ground getting closer and closer, in a last reflex he doubled up his legs and brought his arms in front of his face. When he regained consciousness the first thing he saw was a ring of machine guns which were covering him and a few other men. Without moving he weighed his chances. He would have to leap across the few yards that separated him from the nearest guard, seize his weapon, fire, and make his escape at the same time. The chances of success were minimal; everything would depend on the rapidity of his leap.

It was when he tried to get to his feet that Choken realized that he had lost, that he would not leap, that he would never leap again, and that he was going to die. His right leg remained outstretched, inert, broken.

Then, from the depths of the distress that assailed him, one idea rose: to reach Treblinka and find Galewski, to tell him that the fight was possible and that the only victory would come from the bottom of the abyss.

With the help of another deportee Choken managed to get to the *Umschlagplatz,* where the convoy for Treblinka awaited them. All night he struggled against delirium and death. The convoy had been loaded very quickly and fortunately the car was not full. Choken was able to lie down. The pain in his leg became bearable and only the bullet he had received somewhere in his chest in the course of the morning's fighting was causing him real suffering. He felt that his death was very near and the voyage seemed interminable. The cold and the fever shook him with long chills, which became a continual trembling by morning. He passed out several times, but so great was his will to hold out until Treblinka that each time he recovered consciousness. His whole being was strained toward this single purpose to see Galewski again.

The convoy stopped several times before it entered the camp. Suddenly the doors were shoved violently open and the orders and shouts began to ring out. The able-bodied men got off first;

then the "blues" got on to collect the baggage and the wounded.

"Easy, friends, I'm wounded," said Choken to the two Jews who were bending over him. "It is absolutely necessary that I see Galewski."

They looked at him, astonished.

"I have been here before, I escaped. And now . . ."

There were many wounded in this convoy and the "hospital" was overflowing. The "blues" put Choken a little to one side, and asked Kurland to try to take him last so they would have time to find Galewski.

Choken had closed his eyes to spare his remaining energies. Galewski did not recognize him right away and seeing him unmoving, believed him dead. He was about to go away when Choken, feeling a presence above him, opened his eyes.

"Galewski," he murmured, "it's me, Choken."

"Choken?" replied Galewski, incredulous.

Without giving him time to respond, Choken went on, "There's nothing you can do for me. I'm going to die. But that doesn't matter, because I've found you."

And he told his story.

"This is why I wanted to see you. You must do something. Something that will make a mark, that will go down in history as an extraordinary victory. There are plenty of heroes, as many as there are cowards, but they all end up in Treblinka. What we need is a victory: the victory of the dead."

Choken's voice was growing weaker and weaker and Galewski was forced to bend over to hear what he was saying.

"There is no vengeance possible and hatred is sterile. It's not to die in a desperate battle that we need, it's not to kill Germans that matters. What we need is a victory and witnesses to tell about it, witnesses, Shlomo, witnesses of the victory of the Jews over the S.S. Goodbye, Shlomo, until we meet in the land of Israel."

Galewski did not have to bend down to know that Choken was

dead. As if to echo his friend's last words, his lips began to recite the *Kaddish*.

"*Yiskaddal veyiskaddash* . . ."

But more than a prayer it was a vow that Galewski was uttering, the vow to fight to victory as Choken had fought to the death.

Suddenly he started when he heard Lalka call him:

"What have we here, Galewski?"

"It's nothing, *Herr Untersturmführer*—a dead Jew"

XIX

THAT SAME EVENING Galewski called a meeting of the Committee. One fact was bothering him. The prisoners, who had learned what was happening in Warsaw, had become excited and had refused to carry two of their comrades who had been wounded by the explosion of a grenade to the "hospital."

Galewski began by introducing Djielo. There was an astonishing contrast between this man, sure of himself and in excellent physical condition, whom Adolf's welcome had saved from the vertiginous fall to the bottom of the abyss, and the others, emaciated, sick, with their skin covered with blotches, the aftereffects of half-cured diseases, and their shifty eyes, which looked at you only when you managed to catch them. They were so used to seeing each other that they had come to believe that they had always been like this, and that if not all men, at least all Jews were like them. Djielo with his battle dress, his boots, his tanned and healthy skin, and his clean-shaven face looked like a kind of archangel to them. When they saw him they realized that the revolt was assured.

Djielo spoke:

"I do not know whether my help will mean much to you, but I

do know one thing: I owe you my life. I also know that you did not save me for no reason. I hope I will be worthy of the confidence you have placed in me. Here is the plan that I propose. The only weak point is still the problem of weapons. The real solution would be to get them from the camp armory. We will talk about the possibilities of such an undertaking after I have presented my plan."

Short sentences, dry voice; this was a leader talking. Everyone felt it and was reassured by it.

"The operation will proceed in three phases: preparation, execution and withdrawal. I personally attach the greatest importance to the first phase, for if we have any chance of succeeding it will depend on what happens during this period. We must have the advantage of an effect of absolute surprise. Nothing about our plans must leak out. We must do everything we can to allay the suspicion of the Germans. Our meetings may seem suspect and attract the attention of an informer. The first point we must take up is what to do about informers. They must be either bribed or eliminated. I, personally, lean toward the second solution."

"Impossible," said Galewski. "That would reinforce the suspicions of the Germans. During the typhus epidemic doctors started to let them die, and Kiwe made the doctors responsible for their lives."

"We are taking a great risk by letting them stay alive."

The problem was debated for some time, and everyone came to the conclusion that it was just as impossible to kill them as it was dangerous to try to bribe them for the purposes of such an important project. In the end Kurland found the solution; Djielo had put him on the track when he had asked whether it was possible at least to intimidate them.

"There are two kinds of informers," Kurland explained, "the professionals and the amateurs." As camp historian, Kurland had studied all the intricacies of the system. "Informing at Treblinka

275

is very well organized, that is, by German standards. There are three professionals: Chatskel, Blau, and Kuba Yakubovich. The first is an idiot, the second a monster, and the third a sad case. The way he became a sheep reveals much about the power of a man like Kiwe.

"Before he got sick Kuba was an extraordinary man. A former student of medicine, he spent his nights tending, helping, comforting the others. By day he worked and was beaten, by night he took care of people. It was Dr. Ribak who told me his story, which should serve as a text for those who think they have the right to judge other people. One day Kuba got sick too, and he was taken to the infirmary. He found himself confined to his bunk, unable to move, at the mercy of the good will of his killers. The inevitable happened. One morning Kiwe bent over him with a smile and asked him kindly, *'Bist du nicht gesund?'* That's when Kuba broke down; he burst into tears. But do you know what Kiwe did? He patted his hand and said affectionately, 'There, there, don't cry. We'll take care of you, you'll get well, and you'll soon be out of here.' Then he left. Poor Kuba did not know what had happened to him. The next day Kiwe came back with a bag of oranges, the day after that with some sausage. One week later Kuba was cured and he began his career of licensed informer.

"These three nobody can touch; anyway, they are so well known that everyone mistrusts them. Whenever they approach a group, conversation ceases; when they speak to someone, he turns away; better still, their arrival is heralded like that of the Germans or the Ukrainians. So it isn't they who collect the information, but a bunch of little amateurs whose spying services they buy by the piece and who therefore imagine that they enjoy Kiwe's protection. But Kiwe doesn't know them, so they are the ones we must get rid of."

"But isn't there a chance that their immediate superiors will notice something?"

"Not if it's done discreetly enough. They may think it's a new epidemic of suicides."

The Committee discussed the idea and approved the proposal to hang a certain number of informers to look like suicides, but it reserved exclusive right to pronounce sentence after thorough investigation. Adolf was given the job of choosing hangmen from the men in his combat units.

Continuing his report, Djielo proposed as a second measure that they not reveal anything about the plan to anyone, not even those who would play a part in the action. Everyone agreed except Galewski.

"The incident this afternoon proves that the men are beginning to react. For the first time in the existence of Treblinka, prisoners deliberately disobeyed. The fact has both positive and negative implications for us. It raises the hope that everyone will follow, but if it is repeated the Germans will reinforce their precautions. Left to themselves, the men may do anything at all. But if we tell them to be patient, that something is being done, we will considerably reduce the risk of a desperate action. Whatever we do, let us not forget that this revolt will not be the work of a handful of men, but of the majority. All the men will leave here with the same message, but the chances of survival in the forest are so slim that it will be by the grace of God if a single one remains alive when it's all over."

Djielo did not understand this collective dimension of the movement. He was a Jew, but he was a soldier. But Galewski's argument presenting the mass of the prisoners as an uncontrolled explosive force made him hesitate.

"To let everyone in on it is to allow no margin for the slightest failure, like that of Dr. Chorongitski. If we set a date we won't be able to postpone it, for then this explosive force you're talking about will blow up in our faces."

"Perhaps," answered Galewski, not altogether convinced.

In the end it was Galewski's point of view that won out.

Undeniably Djielo was the military leader of the revolt. But this revolt could not be the work of one man or a group of men. The Committee was organizing it, channeling it, recruiting it, but the real actors were the anonymous mass of the prisoners. The revolt, like the extermination, was a collective phenomenon. A whole people was rising up because it had the sense of a mission to fulfill. Each individual knew that he had little chance of surviving, but he was also sure that at least one "chosen one" would live to tell the story and that therefore the mission would be fulfilled.

The case of Joseph Rapoport illustrates this state of mind admirably. Rapoport, short, rugged, powerfully built, with an amazingly innocent expression on his seamed face, was twenty years old when he arrived in Treblinka. One day as he was working on the sorting square, a German came and asked for ten volunteers for a little job that would take an hour. He presented himself and was taken to Camp Number Two. He never left again. Every day the great trap doors of the gas chambers opened before his eyes, disclosing a mass of murdered bodies so densely packed that death had welded them together. The camp was surrounded by a sand embankment which concealed everything around it from view. His universe was reduced to the bodies below and the sky above. Bodies and sky, sky and bodies, and being beaten and running and cold and hunger and death.

One winter day a raven, attracted by the smell of the bodies, lighted in the middle of the yard. All the watchtowers opened fire at the same time, making the bodies jump under the impact of the bullets. The bird, surprised, tried to fly away. The fire redoubled, until a bullet hit it. The incident acquired a symbolic value for the prisoners, who said to each other, "If even a bird can't leave the camp, how can we do it?"

A strange intuition had always told Rapoport that he would

278

leave Treblinka alive, but at the sight of the bird his hope failed him. That night he had a dream: he was in the yard surrounded by bodies when suddenly a loud noise rent the air, rooting everyone, Jews and Germans, to the spot, motionless, stiff as statues. The noise grew even louder, and an enormous airplane appeared and stopped in the middle of the sky. A door opened in its side, and from it dropped a rope ladder the end of which came to earth at Rapoport's feet. Then, before the transfixed multitude, he began to climb. The airplane left. He was saved.

The day of the bird was the only moment when he ever doubted that he would leave Treblinka. He did not know how he would get out, or rather, the methods which he imagined or dreamed belonged more to the wonderful than to the workable. Sometimes he flew away, sometimes he dug a tunnel, sometimes a band of partisans attacked the camp and freed him—him, Rapoport, and him alone. He was the witness. In the future he saw himself as a multimillionaire, going from country to country, everywhere surrounded by throngs of listeners who would come to hear him talk. He talked on and on without end. He was the witness.

Today he lives in Israel, and when he tells the story his face becomes transfigured with pain. Mystic of hell, prophet of the abyss, he returns to this place which he knew he would leave some day, but from which he will never escape.

The problems of general strategy having been settled, Djelo proceeded to the immediate preparation of the revolt. He quickly outlined the method he had conceived for procuring weapons.

"Even if we manage to lure the S.S. to the tailor shops and kill them, we will not have many guns. Worse still, we will not have a single grenade. Now grenades would enable us to spread panic among the Germans and Ukrainians from the outset. However, there is a way to replace the psychological effect of grenades. It will require great coordination, but it is feasible. Adolf tells me that every week a special commando washes down all the barracks in the camp with a liquid disinfectant. This disinfectant is stored in the garage along with a number of barrels of kerosene. Rudek, the Jewish foreman of the garage, is one of the most reliable unit leaders. We did not want to ask for his consent before speaking to you, but Adolf assures me that he will agree. So either we would have to let the men in charge of the disinfection in on the revolt or"—Djielo turned to Galewski—"have our own men put in charge of this work."

Galewski nodded his head to indicate that it was workable.

"On D-day these men will fill their pails with kerosene instead of disinfectant and wash down all the barracks."

It was a brilliant presentation, and everyone could picture the camp being consumed by fire.

"The disinfecting takes place every Monday morning, so D-day will have to be a Monday.

"We have few firearms at our disposal, so we will have to make a number of various sidearms like rods, shovels, and so forth; this will be the job of the iron and tin workers. In this connection Adolf has suggested the idea of making vitriol pistols out of rubber bulbs. There is plenty of vitriol in the camp, it will be easy. Well handled, it's an effective weapon. Those who possess them will have to stand beside a German or a Ukrainian a few moments before the launching of the attack and immediately spray him with vitriol and disarm him.

"Let us now proceed to H-hour proper.

"*H-hour minus 60:* The tailors and bootmakers kill their Germans and take their pistols, which they hide carefully.

"*H-hour minus 5:* The incendiary commando take up positions near the barracks at a ratio of two men to a barracks.

"Each of the vitriol throwers picks out a German or a Ukrainian. These men will have to be excellent shots, for their job will be to start neutralizing the watchtowers.

"A commando made up of particularly reliable men goes to the doors of the tailor and bootmaker shops and prepares to receive the weapons. Adolf will take personal charge of this commando.

"Finally, every man who is provided with a sidearm or club unobtrusively picks out a German or a Ukrainian.

"*H-hour:* It would be unwise to choose a shot as signal to attack, because shots are heard every day in the camp. If we decide to take four o'clock as H-hour, the signal would be the whistle of the train that brings the prisoners back from the work camp. This detail will be worked out later.

"The first minutes will be the most crucial, for at that time we will be under fire from the watchtowers without being able to fire back. So, as the fire breaks out and the guards are attacked, Adolf's commando, armed with the weapons recovered from the Germans, will rush to the armory and take it by storm. Each man will grab a gun and take care of one tower. Meanwhile the combat units will converge toward the armory to get weapons and will immediately take up their battle stations.

"The mass retreat will have to proceed to the south, in the direction of the forests. Two units, which will later act as scouts, will therefore head for the southern part of the camp while the other units will move to the west, the south and the east to protect the others.

"At this point the camp will be surrounded and reduced to cinders and to silence."

The evocative power of Djielo's voice was extraordinary. The other members of the Committee looked at him, fascinated. This man seemed to them a messenger from heaven, a kind of angel armed with a flaming sword, come to lead them to victory. They no longer doubted this victory. It was there, before their eyes, red as the burning of the camp, invincible as this archangel in battle dress.

"It is then that the third, and perhaps the most difficult, part will begin: the withdrawal. At that moment we will be the masters of the camp, but the Germans will be starting to react. We can anticipate their counterattack in two phases. An immediate attack from the nearby garrisons will occur within the half hour. A second attack will mobilize much larger units and will probably take the form of a real combing of the region. If all goes well, we have nothing to fear from the first counterattack. Very likely the enemy reinforcements, not understanding very clearly what is going on, will converge on the camp in scattered formation. But since there are no garrisons between the forest and the camp, the withdrawal will encounter no resistance from the front. Two combat units will be enough to guide the movement. The weight of the German attack will fall on the rear.

"We will join battle in the camp itself to enable the mass of the prisoners to reach the forest. Then we will ourselves attempt a withdrawal movement. I will tell you frankly that this retreat in the open field is against all the instructions in the military manuals, and that the chances of success are extremely slim. We will undoubtedly beat off the first attack but what will happen afterward God alone knows.

"However, we may assume that the mass of the prisoners, guided by the two combat units, will meanwhile have reached the forest. Night will begin to fall, and it is doubtful that the heavy enemy reinforcements who will then arrive on the scene will immediately launch a combing operation. As a rule you never comb at night, especially a forest. Besides, the Germans will not yet have recovered from their surprise, and they will have no accurate idea of the extent of our forces. We may therefore assume that, stunned by our resistance, they will prefer to use the night to prepare a vast search net and not start the combing operation until morning.

"Given the importance which the enemy will attach to recap-
turing all the prisoners, and allowing for the stupor he will feel,
he will do everything in his power and will undoubtedly bring in
tanks and armored cars. This probability means we will be in no
position to fight the next day. So, once it reaches the forest, the
troop will have to break up into many little groups, each of which
will try to reach the heart of the forest separately. Some will be
recaptured, but others will get away."

Djielo paused for a moment. Then he concluded in a curt and
emotionless voice, "As for ourselves—well, I don't think our purpose is to save our own lives."

After a long silence the discussion slowly resumed. The problem of weapons was debated again, and Djielo admitted that his
solution was only a last resort. The Committee concluded unani-
mously that they would have to study the possibility of stealing
weapons from the armory.

Then Kurland raised the problem of Camp Number Two:

"The fact is that we don't know what is going on down there.
Those men are in on the last phase of the cycle of death, and their
testimony will be essential to history."

It was decided to try to establish contact with the prisoners of
Camp Number Two.

The hour of the curfew was approaching. Night had already
fallen. Silence reclaimed the room. In the doorway the silhouette
of the sentry appeared and disappeared at regular intervals.
Djielo, who had remained standing throughout the meeting, sat
down on one of the wooden bunks, yielding to the enchantment
of hope. Every one of them wanted to hold on to this moment.
They did not dare to move. They all felt that now the revolt
would take place, that this day had marked a decisive step, and
that it would no longer be possible to turn back.

WHEN HE HEARD about the act of insubordination of the prisoners who had carried their comrades to the infirmary instead of taking them to the "hospital," Lalka immediately gave the order to look after the wounded. Thus he sanctioned the disobedience of the Jews.

And yet the crime committed by the prisoners merited immediate punishment, and this punishment could only have been general liquidation. . . .

It is necessary to understand Kurt Franz.

January 1943 was the dead season for convoys at Treblinka. After the extraordinary abundance of summer, autumn, and early winter, there was a lull in the arrival of the deportees. But this slowing down did not mean that the camp was about to close its gates; on the contrary, Lalka had just been informed that fresh convoys were to arrive from the farthest reaches of Europe. Furthermore, the typhus epidemic, in spite of the extraordinary resistance of the Jews, had just cut the working forces in half and considerably lowered the output. Consequently, the clothing and belongings of the deportees were piled up on the sorting square, some already sorted, others waiting to be. For this work Lalka required considerable manpower, but since the rhythm of the convoys had slowed down, he was not sure that he would be able to fill out his gangs in either the quantity or the quality he needed. The fact is that his prisoners had become highly specialized. This was the first reason why he could not allow himself to liquidate all of the prisoners after this grave act of insubordination. The second reason was that Treblinka, that perfectly running machine, was capable of receiving a vast number of deportees on two hours' notice. So that the machine would be able to 'treat'' them properly, all the wheels must remain in place, the machine must keep on running—the furnaces must remain lit, to borrow an expression from industry.

In addition to technical reasons, Lalka had other motives for temporarily sparing the camp. Kurt Franz was not a common jailer or an ordinary head of a prison camp, some former cavalry officer pining for his squadron. Franz had not arrived at Treblinka to take over a camp that was already running. When he arrived the site was nothing but a dismal wasteland dotted with birch groves. He witnessed the laying of the first barbed wire, calculated the dimensions of the first common grave. He spent his first nights in this place in a field tent. He remembered how in the beginning all was chaos and old night, and it took a lot of imagination to foresee what this new world would become. The first convoys, the cries, the panic, the disorder: it was all engraved in Franz's memory. Then came his first efforts to organize this abyss —the appointment of *kapos*, the specialization of the workers, the division into three social classes—and the world emerged from limbo, life began. And suddenly the "flood" that threatened the whole structure: that idiot Max Bielas who got himself assassinated. Would the camp be destroyed? Would his work be condemned? Already sentimentally attached to it, he managed to save it after a terrible night of passionate debate. It was Noah's

Ark. Life began again, but on new foundations. By unremitting effort Franz succeeded in turning the camp into an extraordinary machine whose every wheel, perfectly oiled, turned smoothly, processing convoy after convoy, without a cry, without a hitch, with fantastic rapidity.

This work had become his life. He was attached to it, like a captain to his ship, like a baron of industry to the empire created by his hands. So it is that sometimes our works bind us to them to the point where we become their slaves. Lalka felt this passion of the creator for his creation to the highest degree. He knew, of course, that some day he would have to destroy it with his own hands, without leaving a single trace, but that day was still distant. In the meantime its inevitable disappearance only increased his love for it.

So once again, Treblinka was saved, just as God, in spite of his terrible wrath, each time spared the world, his handiwork. It is the dialectic of creation.

The act of insubordination of the prisoners nevertheless revealed a flaw which was in urgent need of correction. Lalka's policy, as we have seen, was based on a double process: administer enough oxygen to keep the little flame of hope alive and at the same time take a certain number of measures designed to convince the prisoners of their subhumanity, if possible, by compromising them.

The creation of the office of "shit master" was one of these measures. The character gotten up in this way was so ridiculous with his big alarm clock, his whip, his beard, and his cantor's costume that even the Jews could not help laughing at him. They laughed at this puppet who, with his whip dangling from his shoulder, begged them with tears in his voice to come out of the latrines when the three minutes were up. He would never have dared either to hit them or to report them, but since he knew he would be held personally responsible for infractions, he had no alternative but to plead. And no one could resist the humor of the situation presented by this old man the dignity of whose costume and the solemnity of whose function only accentuated his absurdity.

"I beg of you," he would say, "do it for me. I beg of you, come out!"

But the others, squatting, looked at him, tall and majestic, and they could not help laughing. Then he would become angry and threaten to whip them, his voice breaking with emotion, lifting his enormous whip and vainly trying to crack it.

The prisoners could not help laughing, but it was themselves they were laughing at, it was their religion they were mocking, for the "shit master" was one of them and his costume was part of their religion.

When Lalka would ask at roll call, "Rabbi, how goes the shit?" and when the false rabbi dressed as a cantor would answer, "Very well, sir!" it meant that at Treblinka a rabbi was good for nothing but to take care of the shit. By laughing in spite of themselves, the prisoners were compromising themselves. After surviving their families, after helping to murder their brothers, they were mocking themselves and their religion.

This principle was now to be extended into other areas.

Just as the Lord, when the world was finished, created a seventh day and made it holy, Kurt Franz, the Prince of Hell, decided to make Sunday a holiday and to sanctify it in his own way. The rest was intended to replenish the oxygen supply and the sanctification to convince the Jews yet again of their subhumanity. The morning would be devoted to rest and the afternoon to great diabolical fairs. Their organization gave Lalka a chance to prove his capacities.

He began by choosing the performers. He did it with that meticulous care which we have already encountered so often, in him as in his colleagues.

"First and foremost, music!" Lalka began with the orchestra.

He ordered the "blue" and "red" *kapos* and foremen to alert him to the presence of any musician in future convoys.

Providence was with him. A few days later he was advised that the celebrated Warsaw violinist and composer, Arthur Gold, had arrived in Treblinka. Lalka had never heard of Arthur Gold, but he was assured that he was one of the most distinguished Jewish musicians of Warsaw. With no time to lose, Lalka retrieved his man on the road to the gas chamber, naked and half frozen. The too-perfect system had almost swallowed him up. At once Lalka had him brought warm clothing and a cup of tea. Then when the other was somewhat recovered, he explained to him what he wanted: an orchestra worthy of Treblinka. Torn between astonishment and relief, Arthur Gold did not know what to reply.

"You will have everything you need in the way of men and instruments. You will have only to ask me for what you want, and you will have it at once. In return, I want an orchestra. If the orchestra is good, you will become the most important Jew in the camp, but if it is bad, you will return to your place in line."

And the very next day Lalka went to Warsaw to buy Gold's records, to make sure he really was a good musician.

Without losing a moment, Gold went to work. Snatched from death *in extremis,* he spent exactly one night realizing what Treblinka was and reconciling himself to it. When the first convoy arrived the next morning he was on the platform ready to start recruiting his musicians.

His first days at Treblinka were spent between the platform and the sorting square: the platform in the morning for the musicians, and the sorting square in the afternoon for the instruments. Soon he had everything but a drum. That was no obstacle; Kurt

Franz went to Warsaw himself to procure one. He was a man of his word.

Rehearsals began at once. The prisoners selected for the orchestra could be excused from work simply at Gold's request. Lalka often came and sat in the barracks where they took place. He would slip quietly into a corner and listen, savoring the pleasure of having an orchestra of his own. When he was pleased with the work he would go over to Gold and congratulate him in terms that were more than laudatory. On certain days he even offered his opinion and since it was not always without foundation, discussions began. Lalka criticized and Gold explained, all this in an almost friendly tone, in an atmosphere of mutual understanding. Lalka had subjugated Gold. Gold impressed Lalka, who in his presence became again just another music lover respectful of the talent of a master. In every German, beside the relentless worker, there lurks the music lover, and Lalka was no exception to the rule. With that extraordinary faculty for forgetting that certain Germans have, as soon as he crossed the threshold of the barracks the relentless worker, the meticulous Technician became a sensitive music lover, full of attention and delicacy. Nothing else mattered to him but this music, nothing else existed but this barracks resonant with harmonious chords. Once an unsuccessful musician, he suddenly possessed his own orchestra, like a Renaissance prince.

Lalka had a deep love for music. Gold was an excellent musician. The orchestra rapidly became a fine one. But although the music was good, the musicians made a shabby appearance in their faded and threadbare suits. This did not matter much at rehearsals, but it was incompatible with the impressive quality Lalka wanted the spectacles to have. He ordered the tailors to make uniforms for the musicians. He designed the uniform himself: a white dinner jacket trimmed in blue, with musical notes on the lapels, and white trousers with a band of blue silk at the seam.

Gold was entitled to wear a white frock coat and a pair of polished shoes. Then they retrieved some laquered music stands with
signs bearing the inscription *"Gold Kapelle."*

The working out of all these details had required a certain period of time during which Lalka had begun to attend to the rest of
the program. From successive convoys he had rescued a dancer,
Boris Weinberg; a *chazan* (cantor of a synagogue), Salver, who
had a very fine voice and who also sang opera; a song writer,
Yajik; two actresses whose names have been lost; and a play-
wright, Schenker, who had written a great deal for the Young
People's Theater of Warsaw. All were requested to prepare, each
in his field, a number that could be included in the great pageant
of Treblinka. Lalka offered them the same bargain that he had
proposed to Arthur Gold: either they would give satisfaction and
they would have nothing to complain of, or they would demonstrate their incompetence or bad will and they would take the
road to the "factory." Everyone started to work under the direct
supervision of Lalka. Schenker wrote an edifying playlet about
some good prisoners who force a shirker to work. In a long per-
suasive tirade they explain that work has a sacred virtue which
is independent of its conditions or purpose. Yajik wrote a number of humorous sketches on camp life in which the scapegoats were the privileged Jews of Treblinka, the *Hofjuden* and
kapos. Lalka provided the themes himself. The actresses rehearsed the tirades, the dancer did warming-up exercises, and
the singer practiced scales. Treblinka was suddenly transformed
into a boarding school the day before the big annual celebration.

The show was almost ready when the boxers arrived. They belonged to two traditional sports clubs whose rivalry had been the
delight of the Jewish population of prewar Warsaw: the Maccabees and the Athletic Union. At the beginning of the ghetto period they had all gone to work in the same factory and they had
just been rounded up together. One of the *kapos,* knowing

Lalka's fondness for boxing, had informed him of their presence in a convoy. Lalka had rushed to the rescue and offered them the traditional cup of tea of welcome, followed by the just as traditional bargain: comfort or the "factory."

The boxers had been forced to work in the commandos, but their position as Lalka's protégés protected them from beating and bullying. Lalka shrank from no sacrifice and he even had boxing gloves made for them. Organized according to club, the boxers began to train. Since they worked during the day, they waited until evening to put on their gloves and pitch into each other according to the rules of the noble art. It was an unexpected distraction for the prisoners, and every evening after roll call the yard of the ghetto filled with shouting groups surrounding the boxers who trained for the great spectacle in pairs. One of the survivors relates that at that time Treblinka became "mad for boxing. . . . On free evenings in the yard you could see groups gathered around two idiots with black eyes and swollen noses, sparring without mercy."

Lalka, looking on, thought delightedly that only men who had lost all self-respect could behave like this. It was the result of the treatment they had been subjected to since the beginning of the ghetto period. It was the proof of the excellence of the system. Kurt Franz told himself that the danger of an explosion had been averted.

Lalka decided to go further. The carpenters received the order to construct a collapsible ring which would serve as a stage for the spectaculars. It was in this festive atmosphere that one day at roll call Lalka announced that he had kept the promise he had made the day he took command of Treblinka.

"Next Sunday," he said, "you will not work. The day of the Lord will be devoted to rest and enjoyment. It will be this way every Sunday. You will work for six days and on the seventh day you will relax." Then he motioned to the orchestra, which was making its first public appearance for the occasion. Gold raised his baton and the orchestra struck up the first movement of *Cavalleria Rusticana.*

Lalka had insisted on personally planning the Sunday celebration down to its smallest details, and nothing was left to chance. It was a winter Sunday, gray and cold. The sky, murky with snow, softened the din made by the carpenters who were assembling the ring. When they arrived, gloomy and silent, carrying the lumber, the prisoners thought it was a gallows they were coming to erect. The hammer strokes rang out dull and muted throughout the morning, and the ring appeared, reassuring and unexpected. Incredulous, the prisoners had begun to approach. They were soon shooed away so that two sides of the ring could be furnished, one with armchairs and the other with benches. At lunch the prisoners had been entitled to half an egg in addition to the daily ration.

At two o'clock, whistle blasts give the order to fall in. The benches are reserved for the *Hofjuden* and the *kapos,* the common prisoners must sit on the ground. Everyone guesses that the armchairs are reserved for the Germans. The prisoners sit down around the still-empty ring. At first there is silence; then the conversations spring up and become animated. Suddenly a voice cries: "Begin!" This does it: Treblinka has become a theater, the ring a stage, the prisoners spectators.

A few more minutes of impatient waiting, and the orchestra appears in full regalia. The musicians sit in the ring opposite the still-empty armchairs. Suddenly there is a long whistle blast. Gold freezes. The crowd hushes instantly. Galewski shouts, "Attention!" Everyone stands. The silence is absolute. The Ukrainian sentries at the gate of the Ghetto present arms. The Germans appear, at their head, chatting gaily, Lalka and the administrative director of the camp. As they go through the gate the orchestra

launches into a symphonic arrangement of the Treblinka anthem
which Gold has just composed. Lalka smiles, very relaxed. He
nods briefly to Galewski, who salutes him; then, followed by all
the Germans, he sits in an armchair. At Galewski's order the
prisoners sit down again, the "aristocracy" on the benches, the
masses on the ground. The anthem is finished and the orchestra
waits. Some small children, sons of the *Hofjuden,* appear carrying programs. They distribute them to the Germans. Lalka seems
as immersed in the study of the program as if it were a menu in a
restaurant. Pleased, he looks up and nods at Arthur Gold Salver, the cantor, comes forward and bows deeply. The spectacle is
about to begin.

As a curtain raiser Salver sings the great air from *Lohengrin.*
Treblinka-Bayreuth roars with the suffering of poor Lohengrin.
The voice is very fine, very big, alternately majestic and menac-
ing, but poor Salver's hands are cold and when he lifts them to
express his passion, he takes the opportunity to rub them together
vigorously, and Lohengrin becomes a slave. Lalka gives the cue
for the applause. Very elegant, he taps the palm of his left hand
with the ends of the fingers of his right hand. Conditioned, the
prisoners do not spare their applause. Since, for once, nothing is
being asked of them but to applaud, they are eager to prove their
good will. Then, too, it warms them up a little.

Part two: a change of scenery. Treblinka-Bayreuth is transformed into Treblinka-Pigalle. The deep forests become a night
club. Yajik jumps into the ring. 'Good afternoon, ladies and gen-
tlemen, at this time the great Music Hall of Treblinka is happy to
bring you some scenes from everyday life. They were written to
amuse you, and yours truly hopes you will see no malice in
them." Lalka was Yajik's muse, and the aristocracy is not spared.
Kapos and *Hofjuden* are the scapegoats; one is ridiculed for his
mania for imitating Lalka, another for his too-well-polished
boots, a third for his Prussian haircut, yet another for his affected

elegance. It is done with considerable wit, and each shaft hits home. Their class consciousness coming into play, the men now applaud without waiting for Lalka's signal. Moniek, who is said to be very impressed with Kurt Franz, is represented as a worm enamored of a star. Moniek is not very popular, and only the first term of the comparison is retained. Even the informers are entitled to a couplet: "Once upon a time there were three little sheep, with a hey nonny nonny. . . ." Kiwe's face darkens, but Lalka's is wreathed in smiles. The holiday promises to be a great success. Yajik leaves the ring during the applause. Instinctively he returns and bows. The applause redoubles.

The dramatic presentation has less success. The play seems to be a parody of Soviet neo-realism. But Lalka is waiting. With two sharp and imperious handclaps he calls everyone to order. The prisoners hasten to obey him, especially since the boxers appear, jumping up and down to warm themselves. The Maccabees against the Athletic Union in three rounds. In the audience the bets are on. The Maccabees are the favorites at five kilos of oranges to one. They win the first two rounds easily, but lose the third even more easily. It is fast, even too fast. The curtain is about to fall and the dream to end. Treblinka is about to become Treblinka again. The prisoners, sensing that the program is ending, experience a feeling of frustration. They would like to dream a little longer, to forget for a few more moments what they are and where they are, not to remember just yet that they are only condemned men, outlaws from life, that in a little while it will be cold in the barracks, that the nagging hunger will keep off sleep for a long time, that tomorrow morning before dawn the whistle of the locomotive driving the first convoy of Jews to be gassed will make them jump.

But Lalka has saved a surprise, the main attraction of the show. He calls Moniek over and says something to him. Moniek listens, astonished, turns around and climbs into the ring. The

294

show will continue with amateur fights; volunteers are requested to come forward. Kurt Franz himself will award the prizes to the victors. The men hesitate, feel their muscles. One man gets up, then another, then a third, and two more. They come forward, a little embarrassed. They have to put on the shorts of the boxers, who have dressed in the interval. The first pair climbs into the ring to the cheers of the crowd, which realizes that it is going to be amused. The two bruisers raise their fists in salutation. Obviously they are more used to street fighting than they are to boxing. Lalka stands up. "You aren't women and you aren't here to be nice to each other." And he concludes, "May the best man win!" The fight is on. Caught up in the game, the two protagonists do not spare their efforts. Suddenly it is no longer a game; one of the adversaries had landed an illegal punch, the other closes in, his fists forward, urged on by the crowd, which noisily demonstrates its sympathy. The adversary, hurt, falls down, landing a vicious kick on the way, the other howls with pain and rage and attacks again.

That night in the barracks the prisoners looked at each other dazed and ashamed. At the hour of the *Kaddish* many could not hold back their tears when they thought of their families who slept nearby. They felt that they had reached the depth of degradation. Not content to let themselves be humiliated, they had also humiliated themselves by providing a spectacle for their killers. The implacable logic of the system had led them close to the ultimate corruption, that of the soul. That day they seemed to have lost their last particle of humanity.

This final fall, this ultimate degradation is perhaps the most characteristic and the most tragic as well, for its underlying reason lies precisely in the extraordinary life force of the Jews. In spite of all the humiliations, in spite of all the conditioning processes, in spite of the inevitability of death, in spite of the agony of their people, of which they were the witnesses and the accomplices, the prisoners had not renounced life. Inexorably they had climbed back from the bottom of the abyss as soon as the pressure of death had begun to relax. As a piece of cork held under the water bounces to the surface as soon as it is released, as a spring expands as soon as you relax the pressure, as the water in a dam breaks through the embankment at the first fissure, so the prisoners hurled themselves into life at the first sign of spring. Their death had been only a hibernation.

For the Jews the real enemy was not Hitler or Kurt Franz, it was death, and even more than death, despair. Hitler, Kurt Franz, and the Technicians, those Prometheuses of death, were only the instruments of a system which was infinitely greater than they. Effective instruments, to be sure, as the results have proved, but instruments all the same. Wars may be made with men, but they are declared in the name of principles, and the victor is not the one who has lost the least men, but the one whose principle is saved. The real stake of the war that the Nazis made on the Jews was life itself. When people talk about the war of 1939–45, they confuse two wars that have absolutely nothing in common: a world war, the one Germany made on the world, and a universal war, the war of the Nazis against the Jews, the war of the principle of death against the principle of life. In their war the Jews were alone, but it could not be otherwise. One of the leaders of the great Warsaw uprising expresses this solitude in a pathetic message: "The world is silent. The world knows, it is not possible that it does not know, but the world is silent. God's representative in the Vatican is silent; London and Washington are silent; the Jews in America are silent. This silence is astonishing and horrible."

But to live is to recreate conditions for life. Life does not exist in a vacuum. Paradoxically, the first victory of the Jews of Treblinka had been the phenomenon of the friend who pulled the box away. Later there had been the hope, real or imaginary, first of escape, then of the revolt. Finally, when life had recovered its rights, had come the distractions: the nightly boxing in the yard of the Ghetto and the great spectacle that had just ended. It was because the love of life had not deserted them, it was because they had never doubted it at any moment, that the prisoners entered so profoundly into the game of Lalka, who seemed to have trapped them just as easily as the Technicians of Vilna had trapped their Jews.

That night the barracks were full of funereal murmurs. Nothing mattered to the prisoners but their shame. Mortified, they looked at each other as if to say, "Are we not worse than they, we who have made a spectacle of ourselves? Have we become so corrupt that they can make us laugh at ourselves on the graves of our brothers?"

What was left of the great moments of enthusiasm when the barracks seemed about to explode? What was left of that fierce will to live, to bear witness, to revolt? Where were the leaders? Where were the Just Men who had appeared? What were they doing now? There had been a Committee, what had become of it? Had it foundered too? Had it been defeated even before the battle? The prisoners did not know the names of their leaders, but they knew that they existed, that they were among them, invisible. And their voices rose, full of reproach and incomprehension: "Why have you forsaken us?"

Lying side by side, motionless, Djielo and Adolf listened to the complaints of their brothers. They were silent. They would have liked to get up and announce the great news: the time of the revolt had come at last. But the Committee had decided to reveal nothing until the last moment.

XXI

IT ALL BEGAN the day the masons were given the job of constructing a concrete building between the two barracks of the Germans. When Moniek reported the news to the Committee, Galewski realized that something important was about to happen. All the buildings in the camp, with the exception of the gas chambers, were made of wood. What made the Germans suddenly want to build in stone when cement was so difficult to find? Even more astonishing was the fact that the available space between the two barracks was only a few yards wide. The construction could therefore be of only limited proportions. These points had bothered Moniek and this was why he had mentioned it to the Committee.

Everyone agreed that this construction was strange; like Moniek, they assumed that it was undoubtedly designed to become a strong room. He was commissioned to find out about this new project. He had no trouble obtaining the plan for the job and brought it the next day. They all leaned eagerly over the blueprint to try to discover its secret. Three points became evident: the room would not communicate with the German barracks, the window would be very narrow, and the walls would be twenty inches thick. The conclusion was obvious: this was neither a habitation nor an office. What then?

"An armory!"

They said nothing for a moment. It was too good. A coincidence.

"A gift from God," murmured Kurland. "The manna in the desert. God has heard us. He is on our side."

Galewski kept a cool head. "Let's not celebrate too soon," he said. "We aren't sure that it really is an armory. And building an armory still isn't the same as having weapons. We still have to go and get them—get into the armory, take out the weapons and bring them here—without betraying anything for a single moment. Then we will have to hide the weapons for a certain length of time before the revolt, which means that during this time we will be at the mercy of any German who enters the armory."

Djielo agreed, and he immediately proposed that they take only grenades. In his opinion every gun was probably earmarked for a German. At any moment the owner was liable to come for it without warning. The grenades, on the other hand, were anonymous and they would be enough to set off panic. But the thickness of the walls ruled out the possibility of storming the armory.

"So we must have the key," continued Galewski, turning to Moniek. "I depend on your locksmiths. The door will certainly pass through their shop."

The building was not yet started, no one knew what the Germans would put in it, but everything was already planned. The carpenters and locksmiths were notified; everyone had the feeling that he had become the cat, after having been the mouse for such a long time.

At the end of a week no door had yet been ordered at the carpenters' shop, and the members of the Committee were beginning to wonder what was going on.

The building was up by the middle of the following week, but still nothing had been done about the door. The door frame had not even been finished; it was still a gaping aperture, much wider than the plan specified. One of the masons had told Moniek, "It looks as if they intend to put in iron bars." The Committee was at its wit's end trying to guess what invention the Germans were going to find. Moniek spent his time going back and forth between the different workshops of the carpenters, the locksmiths, and the metalworkers. The musical and dramatic rehearsals had begun, and a strange atmosphere reigned over the camp. The Committee met again to study the situation. It was a plenary meeting; Adolf and Djielo attended it. Galewski was the most pessimistic.

"I believe," he began, "that we are approaching the end. It may not be upon us yet, but we can already see it. The number of convoys is decreasing. They are all coming from Warsaw again. Now, Treblinka was created to exterminate the Jews of Warsaw, and according to our calculations half a million Warsaw Jews have already arrived. I don't know how many of them there were in all, but there can't be very many left. There is considerable danger that we won't survive the last of them by very long. I have the impression that this orchestra, these spectacles that are being prepared are designed to allay our suspicion. The end of Treblinka is near and we cannot wait indefinitely."

He had spoken in an unsteady voice full of emotion. His breathing was irregular. He was sick, very sick.

"Exhaustion," according to Dr. Ribak, who had added in a professional reflex, "You should take better care of yourself. Actually, what you need is to take a very long rest, not to worry about anything, to get plenty of sleep and also to have a more balanced diet."

"What would you say to a cure at Baden-Baden?" Galewski had asked without smiling.

"Of course, that would be just the thing," the doctor had replied, entering into the game.

As he listened to him, Djielo realized that Galewski was sick.

"You ought to rest a little," he said.

"At Baden-Baden?" They all smiled.

Djielo continued the discussion. "I think you are right," he said, turning to Galewski. "On the other hand, we have no reason to panic. We have a way of knowing when the camp will be liquidated. As long as all the clothes and belongings have not been sent away, the Germans will need us and won't liquidate us. So we need only watch the stock piles. Given the rhythm of work and the size of the piles, we can estimate our reprieve at over a month and a half. A month and a half is plenty of time."

"You're right," murmured Galewski, "but you know, sometimes I don't have the strength. And then, I want so much to see this revolt."

Djielo respected Galewski a great deal. Adolf had told him about Galewski's role in the birth of the movement, and he knew this tired and sick man was the one who of all of them had done most for the revolt. But he understood that the moment had come to assume full responsibility.

"This revolt is your work and we are only carrying it on for you. But sometimes, as you say yourself, you feel that your strength is failing and this alters your judgment of the situation. Unlike you, I believe that we are becoming the real masters of the game, that we have the situation in hand. The Germans are trying to put us to sleep, but it is we who are going to put them to sleep. I agree with your analysis of the reasons for this sudden rush of artistic activity. I think they are doing this to make us believe that Treblinka will last forever."

Kurland, who did not see what Djielo was driving at, said, "In that case the situation is really very serious. They mistrust us—as well they should," he could not help adding.

301

"But that is where we will counterattack. We must catch them off balance."

Adolf had got the point. "The Germans must believe that we believe that life will go on. Trap them in their own game, beat them on their own territory."

The others looked admiringly at the two men of war.

"Everyone gets his turn," said Kurland. "That was how they brought us this far: we knew nothing about their intentions."

"Precisely," said Djielo. "Their barometer will be our reaction. Well, we are going to laugh at their farce, and while they are sleeping peacefully, we will light the fuse."

After a moment of enthusiasm the members of the Committee were returning to their great preoccupation when Moniek asked, "What about weapons? We don't have any yet."

But Djielo remained optimistic. "We're too impatient," he replied. "We must not forget that the Germans' are not at our disposal."

So great was the audacity of the others that they were ready to believe that they were. Ever since they had imagined them, the weapons had already been theirs.

"The trap is set. Whatever they think up, we'll have the key. Let's wait and see what happens."

Djielo could not understand what the other members of the Committee were feeling in their hearts. He had never seen the Germans as superior beings; quite the contrary, in fact, since at the time of his first contact with them it was he who had deceived them. He had not gone through the stage of the "forked stick" and he did not retain that vague feeling deep down, that fear which his comrades could not shake off. For them this revolt had a further dimension: the destruction of a myth, the recovery of their humanity. It was this dimension that gave them their irresistible strength, but which conversely made them doubt themselves at times. Their struggle had a psychological aspect which Djielo knew nothing about.

The key arrived a few days later. "On a silver platter," Moniek commented with keen satisfaction as he turned it over to the Committee.

The Germans had brought the locksmiths an old door all faced with iron which they had gone to one of the neighboring villages to get. Quite thick and hewn from a wood harder than iron, it was further reinforced horizontally by long steel fittings which half covered its surface. It had taken six men to carry it.

The locksmiths had understood the problem at once. The soft wax was ready. Silberstein had been kneading it in his pocket for over a week. The lock was a little rusty and did not work well. He had to take it apart and put it back together again right under the noses of the S.S. According to plan, Silberstein had begun to work and he was waiting for the German to look away for a moment to take the imprint. But the S.S. man, who was suspicious, remained planted in front of Silberstein, his eyes riveted on the lock. He had been told not to take his eyes off it for a single moment, and he was obeying to the letter, his face hard, his eyes set. The other Jews tried to distract him, but he seemed not to hear what they were saying. Silberstein dragged out the work, trying to find a way to get rid of the busybody. He made him change his position twice, claiming that he was standing in his light; the other moved obediently, but without losing sight of the lock. They tried to deafen him; pretending to be busy, all the workers began to bang on something in unison. The noise became infernal but the S.S. man did not budge.

Then Silberstein had an idea. On the workbench right in front of the guard lay a heavy hammer which was used for riveting. By moving around a great deal he managed to gradually push it to the edge of the table directly over the feet of the S.S. man, who was beginning to grow impatient. Silberstein then pretended to try to unscrew a bolt that had gotten jammed. Red-faced, he seemed to be making great efforts. The bolt suddenly gave but Silberstein, carried along by the impetus, "accidentally" knocked the hammer off the workbench. A roar was heard and the S.S. man began to hop on one foot. While the workers rushed over to him, Silberstein hastily took the lump of wax out of his pocket, clapped it onto the latch, and immediately whisked it out of sight. The operation had taken thirty seconds, during which the bellowing S.S. man had distributed a few blows at random to the obsequious Jews who had come to his aid. When he returned to his post in front of the lock Silberstein looked up humbly in apology and plunged into his work again. Five minutes later, clasping the real key in his hand, the S.S. man left, escorting the door. Before crossing the threshold he turned to deliver a parting shot at the lazy and good-for-nothing Jews who only pretended to work.

When Moniek came into the locksmith's a few hours later for his daily inspection, a beautiful brand-new key was ceremoniously presented to him.

"This is it," he concluded. "It's our move now."

Galewski held the key in his hands with a dazed stare. The dream had become reality. The armory was not even finished and already the Committee possessed its key.

Even Djielo was very excited. "It's our move now," he repeated, as if talking to himself.

A few barracks away, Arthur Gold's orchestra was rehearsing. In the yard the boxers were training, and the shouts of the prisoners came to them in bursts. Night was falling slowly.

"It's our move now," Galewski echoed.

When the armory was inaugurated a few days later, Marcus, a young man of sixteen who acted as the Germans' valet, was sent to inspect. The masons had begun the construction of a large building that was to serve as a water tower and he took advantage of the activity to slip into the armory. The Germans were so sure of themselves that it was not even guarded. It was the cave of Ali

Baba: automatic rifles, machine guns, and guns, gleaming with oil, reared their barrels on weapons racks. Marcus spotted the grenades in one corner. There were three cases, pretty cases made of white wood with fifteen grenades in each. After checking to make sure the window opened, he left as unobstrusively as he had come.

That evening Marcus made his report to the Committee, which now met every day to work out the final details. He told what he had seen with a kind of ecstasy. It was decided that thirty grenades would be enough for the first attack and that it was not necessary therefore to take all three cases. When he had finished, Marcus gave a military salute as he had seen the Germans do, and left full of pride.

Moniek had been given the job of deciding how to get the cases out of the armory and into the potato cellar, where it had been decided to store them. He made his report.

Under the influence of Djielo, its new leader, the Committee had acquired the atmosphere of a general staff. Moniek began in a crisp voice slightly imitative of Djielo's: "The window opens onto the back of the barracks, a place that is usually deserted, so there is little risk of being surprised. However, we will have to station a sentry at each corner of the building. It would be impossible to take out the grenades one at a time and have the prisoners carry them around in their pockets. That would take much too much time and would create a traffic which the Germans might notice. They obviously do not suspect anything, but they are distrustful by nature. The business with the key showed us that. After looking around a little, I have found what we need: the masons' horse-drawn cart, a regular delivery wagon. They use it to pick up different materials all over the camp, and the Germans don't pay any attention to it any more. It is also used for rubbish. So there's no problem, we'll be able to take it to the potato cellar easily."

Salzberg had started when he heard the cart mentioned, and his face had paled slightly.

"The only problem," continued Moniek, turning to the old man, "is that the driver of the cart is your boy, Heniek."

Salzberg had realized this at once and had pictured the face of his son, who had just turned thirteen. Short, skinny and a little sickly, he looked eight. His face was sensitive and his skin had an unhealthy pallor which further heightened the brilliant black of his eyes.

Moniek had stopped speaking, and everyone was looking at old Salzberg.

"My son will do his duty as well as the rest of us. We can count on him."

"Can we also be sure of his discretion?" asked Djielo.

"Yes."

"Even if he is caught?"

"I'll give him a vial of poison. Fear nothing, he is a good Jew."

Moniek finished his report: "In addition to the two sentries, we'll need a third man to transfer the two cases which Marcus will hand out the window to Heniek's cart. Heniek won't be strong enough to carry them. The operation will have to take place in less than a minute. The only ticklish part will be Marcus' exit, but if he can get in without being seen, he can get out, too."

There remained only two points to settle: the definite date of the revolt and the most opportune time to inform the prisoners.

There was no longer any reason to wait, and the sooner it took place the better. D-day was set for the following Monday.

"Since we will have grenades," added Djielo, "the signal will be the explosion of a grenade."

It was then that Galewski was seized by a strange premonition. He was never able to explain the source of his sudden certainty

306

that the revolt was going to fail, that their martyrdom was not yet over, that they had not yet reached the last of their stations of the cross.

"It was the same feeling I had the day Berliner killed Max Bielas," he told Kurland later. "Everything was worked out down to the last detail, and yet I knew that it was not over yet. When I thought about the revolt I did not see what could prevent it from taking place, but in spite of this I felt that we had not finished. Was it because I sensed intuitively that we had not yet seen all of this hell on earth, or was it the presence of these hundreds of thousands of bodies that bothered me? I knew with absolute certainty that the hour of the revolt had not yet struck."

A premonition of this kind cannot be explained. When you consider it after the fact it assumes a miraculous quality. It is also possible that it was simply a coincidence. Perhaps it was only the overwhelming fatigue that weighed him down that made Galewski so profoundly dubious. At any rate, his tone was so convincing that everyone agreed not to alert the prisoners.

"We must not tell them," he repeated. "I know we must not. If all goes well they will still have time to get ready, but we must not tell them anything, their despair would be too great."

Adolf was the first to agree with his opinion. He remembered their first meeting, in front of the door to the train which Choken had just boarded, and the terrible night that they had spent together talking and making plans in spite of the certainty of death. All had seemed lost; during that tragic night Galewski's assurance had acquired a prophetic dimension. Since then, in spite of the moments of doubt that had assailed Galewski, or perhaps because of them, Adolf had a confidence in him which was more mystical than rational, more intuitive than reasonable. He admired Djielo very much, the way you admire a good leader. What he felt for Galewski was different. Djielo was certainly a better organizer, a better leader, but Galewski sometimes seemed possessed of an inspiration that was other-worldly. Djielo was an assimilated Jew, and this was terribly apparent. It was Nazism that had made him become aware of his Judaism. To be sure, after that he had assumed it courageously. Although his Aryan appearance would have permitted it, he had not tried to hide. But his Judaism was merely negative, it was more an attitude than a living reality. He was Jewish because his code of values forbade him to deny his identity, but it would take only the death of the last anti-Semite for him to cease being Jewish. A fine attitude full of nobility, but so un-Jewish! His Judaism was not a faith, it was a tragic challenge delivered to the world. Djielo was more like a Polish aristocrat than a Jew of the ghetto. He regarded the revolt as a mission in the military sense. He did not live it, he organized it. Galewski was his opposite. He did not know how to use a gun and had no idea what the word *strategy* meant, but he lived the revolt. As he had given it birth, it was what kept him alive.

It was these considerations that caused Adolf to side with Galewski. The others soon followed him, except Djielo, who took a long time to come around. In the end he yielded to superior numbers. Only the men in the combat units would be alerted. The unit in the camouflage commando which, from the forest where it worked, might not hear the sound of the grenade, would attack its guards at exactly four o'clock and would return to camp immediately to station itself at the western entrance. The grenades would be entrusted to a special commando. The unit whose job it was to seize the armory and then to attack the watchtower would slip among the masons after the noon break.

The incident was forgotten, Djielo had resumed his role as leader.

"Three units will attack Camp Number Two simultaneously. We have found no way to make contact with the prisoners down there. The attack may be difficult but we have no choice.

"By the time the units arrive, the guards of Camp Number

Two will have recovered from their surprise. It will be sheer butchery."

"What are the chances?" asked Galewski.

"Slim."

And a terrible problem arose. Should they run the risk of jeopardizing the attempt for the sake of the two hundred prisoners in Camp Number Two? It was Kurland who provided the answer.

"Two hundred men more or less are of no importance. Naturally, their testimony would be very useful, but if we must run the risk of losing over half of our forces without the certainty of rescuing our comrades from their hell, I don't think it's worth the trouble. Our mission is too serious for us to pay attention to sentimental considerations. We must show the world that even in the bottom of hell man does not abdicate. We must tell of our martyrdom. Therefore it is essential that the revolt take place, that it succeed, and that there remain at least one witness to relate both the martyrdom and the supreme revolt. No matter what it costs us, our duty is to abandon our comrades."

Salzberg still hesitated.

"But have we really done everything we can to make contact with Camp Number Two?"

"The only way would be to go there. That is the worst misfortune that could happen to us. Many of those who are sent there would rather get the bullet in the back of the neck."

No one in Camp Number One had any experience of Camp Number Two, no one knew what went on there, but it was never mentioned without dread.

The Committee came around to Kurland's opinion but everyone felt a kind of remorse over what he could not help regarding as a betrayal. They completed the final preparations and adjourned gloomily.

"They act as if they are sad to be leaving," said Djielo to Adolf that night as they were lying on their bunks.

"They want a great victory that will inspire the world and they are afraid that it will be a rout. They need something to balance the extermination. I don't know whether you have noticed it, but as time goes by they get more demanding."

"How about you?"

"I, too, perhaps."

"But we have done everything in our power."

"Not really."

"What else could we have done?"

"Get ourselves transferred to Camp Number Two."

Djielo said nothing for a long time. Then he said slowly, "I don't think I'll ever understand you."

"Neither will the Germans."

Djielo raised himself onto one elbow and looked at his friend.

"What pride, Adolf! What pride!"

"Guilt, Djielo! Nothing but guilt!"

The week dragged on slowly. Preoccupied with their various jobs, the members of the Committee forgot this last meeting. They had always imagined that it would be the finest, and it had ended almost in sorrow. Surrounded by shouting and music, they lived in an unreal world. Chance decreed that there were no convoys during these last days and they had to make an effort to remember what Treblinka was and what went on there.

Then Sunday arrived and amid the fanfare of the holiday, Treblinka went completely insane. The last day of Treblinka: the apocalypse of hell, the end of the nightmare. The world of madness and death was going down amid a lunatic display of fireworks. Its death was true to its life: unreal, distorted, monstrous.

XXII

Monday morning it seemed as if the sun did not want to rise. The sky was leaden, heavy with snow, as dismal as the morning after a party.

Adolf met with his unit leaders before the start of work. The long file of prisoners was waiting in front of the kitchen window to receive the mugs of warm colored water that they were served instead of coffee. Still and dreary, they formed a long ribbon across the yard. Adolf's men surrounded him attentively, their faces hard and impenetrable. They listened and from time to time nodded their heads imperceptibly; even then, their features remained absolutely immobile. Five statues of wood or bronze come from the depths of history, risen from the heart of the abyss, eternal; five anonymous men, five Jews burning with shame, passion and faith; five Jews who were going to die, who wanted to die for an ideal that was three thousand years old; five martyrs in the cause of their people, five brothers in blood and in death, five Just Men—five Jews.

Adolf spoke in a deep, hoarse voice. "This is our last meeting before the revolt and no doubt the last we will ever have. You all know your missions, but I will repeat them for you one more time.

"At three-thirty, half an hour before the attack, each unit will send one man to the potato cellar, where he will be handed three grenades. He will say, 'Today the earth trembles and quakes,' and the answer will be, 'It is the Day of Judgment.' This man will unpin a grenade in his left pocket and blow himself up if anything goes wrong on the way back. If that happens the others will immediately go to the armory which they will hem in with grenades, while all the men in the units, wherever they are, will also go to the armory in scattered formation. The units will reform there. Let me emphasize this point: in case of a premature outbreak, every man must try to reach the armory, alone if necessary, and any way he can. So make sure that each man possesses a sidearm.

"After the first grenade has exploded it will no longer be possible to stop the insurrection. In theory, everything should proceed normally as planned. The Germans are drugged; yesterday's performance showed us that.

"I will repeat the entire plan of action. The men have rejoined their units. At ten minutes to four, you will gather them quietly around you. The signal will be given at four o'clock by the explosion of a grenade. You will immediately throw yours, hitting a guard if possible; then you will rush toward the armory. There will already be someone on the spot when you arrive. Two men in each unit will enter the armory. They will receive the guns and automatic rifles for the whole group.

"Each unit will then proceed to its combat position, killing any Germans or Ukrainians it finds on its way. When you have reached the barbed wire the camp will have to be scoured. I will already have started to take care of the watchtowers, you will help me finish the job. We will cut them down in no time. While the gunner is held in check by our weapons, two men will go and burn the tower. Remember the bottle of gasoline. Next Meir and Moshe's units, which are to clear the path to the forest, will pull up the barbed-wire fences. If that isn't possible the men will throw some of their clothes over them. Then they will shout "To the forest!" This will be the signal for the retreat. The mission of the other units, including Haim's, which will have returned to the camp by then, will be to drive the prisoners to the south. We must have no illusions; by this time we will no longer control the situation, if indeed we are still alive. There, that's all. Are there any questions?"

There was one, but nobody asked it. They understood that Camp Number Two was to be sacrificed. Adolf looked at them one after the other. Then he went on in a voice which was fraught with the emotion that gripped them all:

"We shall now take an oath on the honor of the Jewish people to fight to the death for the glory of Israel."

After the oath was taken Adolf began to recite the *"Sh'ma Yisroel."* "Hear, O Israel, the Lord is our God, the Lord is One . . ." The five leaders joined in, slowly, in muted and restrained voices, stressing the syllables as if to give more meaning to every word: *"Sh'ma Yisroel, Adonoi Elohenu, Adonoi Echod."*

It was more than a prayer; it was a fierce and passionate act of faith. They were asking nothing, they were affirming their love— exclusive, uncompromising, and painful—for God and for their people.

Old Salzberg woke his son long before the Ukrainians arrived to make their usual uproar. He made him say his prayers as he did every morning. Then he looked at him for a long time before giving him his last lesson in Judaism.

"Soon we will be separated. In a few hours, I will no longer be at your side to guide you. Suddenly, I am afraid for you. What will become of you? You will live, my little Heniek, I know it, I am sure of it, but will you be able to remain a real Jew? After all these miseries, will you not long to be like other people? Listen to me, Heniek: Do not forget that you are Jewish. If you were to forget that, it would be worse than death. Tell the world what you have seen, tell how we died and how we rose again. And never forget that it was not as men that they tried to destroy us, but as a people, that it was not Jews that they tried to banish from the earth, but the Jewish people."

When his father had finished, Heniek bowed his head to receive his benediction. It was his only answer, it was more binding than any oath.

As soon as Kurland arrived at the "hospital," he dug up all of his notes, which formed the record of Treblinka. It was a jumble of figures, anecdotes, and personal reflections, including everything from a breakdown of the camp working force to philosophical and prophetic essays in which he had tried to find a mystical meaning in what was happening. Certain notes from his special advisers were not even copied over. Those of the banker Alexander, for example, whose pages were so crammed with columns of figures in his small handwriting that they looked black. For history, Kurland had already transformed the deaths into statistics. Every day began like this: "December 9, 4 convoys, 24,000 dead"; "January 2, 1 convoy, 2,000 dead." Sometimes there were summaries by month and country. The shipment of Jewish goods back to Germany was recorded in the same way: "25 carloads of hair, 248 of clothing, 100 of shoes, 22 of fabric, 40 of medicine and medical instruments, 10 of down, 200 of assorted rags, 260 of blankets, and 400 of assorted objects—pens, combs, dishes, handbags, wallets, canes, umbrellas," et cetera. Alexander liked precise records and he had even gone so far as to estimate the total number of diamonds shipped in carats: 14,000.

Kurland wondered whether these pages would ever reach posterity and whether the world would ever even know that this spot had seen hundreds of thousands of Jews die and a handful survive to their greater shame and their supreme glory. Then he took out some other papers, his complete works. They were plays, all of which were set in the "hospital." He sometimes read passages from them to the *Hofjuden* at night in the barracks Such were these Jews who, "with the blade of the sword at their throats," did not give up hope; such were these men who died but did not abdicate from life. While they were being killed they wrote plays— for their own sake, for no reason, to stay alive. Because life, no matter what it is like, must be lived, and because to live is not merely to survive; it is to laugh, to think, to write.

As he had every morning, Djielo managed to shave and found time to do a few gymnastic exercises.

Water was scarce and the Ghetto's single well was hard to get to, because it had to meet the needs of a thousand prisoners. They did not all wash, of course, but the water was also used for drinking. So Djielo used part of his coffee. For him it was a question of discipline. He felt it was more important to shave than to drink coffee. It was a kind of defiance of the living conditions in the camp, his own way of affirming his humanity.

The exercises he forced himself to do proceeded from the same spirit. "A man who lets himself go is a man who is going to die," he would tell men who were astonished to see him use up his energy this way, and he would add, "It is never strength that is the first to fail, but the will to live."

Next, he rapidly reviewed all the details of the operation to assure himself that nothing that was in his power had been left to chance. Then he tried to imagine how the revolt would go off. He had too much military experience not to know that what really happened would bear little resemblance to what had been anticipated, that after a certain point the flow of operations would slip out of his control, and that then, for lack of a communications service, he would no longer be able to correct the course of events. At this point the revolt would be carried along by its own momentum and nobody, neither the Germans and Ukrainians nor the Jews, would be in control of the situation. Its success would depend on the force of the human flood formed by the mass of the prisoners. This was the great unknown.

Djielo forced himself to stop thinking. The die was cast. His role was almost over; it would come to an end sometime that afternoon when, entrenched in the camp with the other members of the Committee, he would fight to the death to hold back the German reinforcements as long as possible.

Galewski thought he would not be able to get up when he woke to hear the Ukrainians arrive. His work was done, he had no further reason for living. He wished he could wait for death, lying motionless on his wooden bunk, resting at last; lying motionless with no further need to think or fear or fight or hope. He had long since passed the limits of human resistance, and he should have died long ago. Only this task that had been thrust upon him had kept him alive, as if it were giving him back that life that he had breathed into it. Now it was over. Berliner was dead, Choken was dead, Chorongitski was dead, and he was going to die too. God had been more generous to him than to Moses, who died before he could enter the Promised Land, and had not been permitted to witness the fulfillment of his mission. Moses was dead, but Israel had come out of Egypt. Galewski was going to die, but the prisoners would escape from hell, the Jewish people would continue to live, an impregnable fortress of faith and of the spirit, for once again they had triumphed over death.

Gathering his remaining forces, Galewski rose to face his final ordeal, to answer the final summons. As he turned the camp over to him, Lalka immediately noticed his weakness. He walked over with his cold smile of death and looked at him for a moment.

"So, Galewski, not feeling well? *Bist du nicht gesund,* as our friend Küttner would say?"

Galewski stood petrified before this unfathomable expression. For him Lalka was more than a man, he was a kind of angel of misfortune all-powerful in evil, a spirit of death. He decided that Lalka knew everything and that he had been waiting for the last day in order to destroy the Jews more surely and to kill their last spark of life, their last human defiance. The camp stopped breathing. After a long moment which seemed an eternity to those who knew the secret of the revolt, Galewski managed to say, "I feel very well, thank you, *Herr Untersturmführer.*"

His voice was firm, and Galewski did not understand where he had found the strength to utter these words.

Lalka kept looking at him as if he had not heard his answer. Then he turned and left without a word.

Shaken, Galewski watched him walk away. He was sure that Lalka knew. He tried to reason with himself all morning long, to tell himself that he was too nervous and that he was imagining things, but he could not shake off a throbbing apprehension which made him jump at the sight of every German.

At exactly eleven o'clock Heniek stopped his cart opposite the window of the armory.

He glanced swiftly at the two corners of the building where the sentries were conscientiously raking the gravel paths. They seemed to be doing their work with particular care and bent over from time to time to pick up invisible bits of paper.

Just then the prisoner who was to load the cases of grenades into the cart passed the corner of the building. When the man had come within five yards of him, he whistled the opening bars of the "Hatikvah." The spot was deserted and silent, and the notes stood out with extraordinary clarity in the cold air, hesitant at first, then more assured.

Marcus' head appeared behind the windowpane just as the prisoner arrived under the window. Heniek looked at the two sentries again: they were raking calmly, the path was clear. He nodded and the window opened. Marcus' head disappeared and was immediately replaced by a case. The prisoner gave a little jump, grabbed the case, and crouched back down with the case hidden between his doubled-up knees and his bent torso. His eyes flickered to either side, then he made a dash for it. The case disappeared under a pile of rubbish in the bottom of the cart. The window had closed again. The prisoner took up his position underneath. Heniek looked at the two sentries again, gave another nod, and the maneuver was repeated, just as swift, just as precise, just as silent. The window closed, the prisoner retraced his steps, and Heniek had raised his whip to start his horse when the sentry who was posted at the corner of the building in front of him crouched down and remained squatting. It was the signal that a German was approaching.

Heniek froze, his whip raised. The back of the crouching sentry hypnotized him. Suddenly he saw him move, his eyes clouded. When he recovered, the sentry was peacefully raking again. It seemed to him that he had spent an eternity with his arm raised, but when he turned his head to look at the other sentry, he saw the prisoner who had loaded the cases pass the corner of the building. The film that had been stopped for an instant started again; he lowered his arm, the lash of the whip unfurled, curled, and cracked. Heniek felt a jolt: the horse had started to move.

Work had just resumed after the short midday break when Lalka sent for Galewski. It did not matter any more; the grenades were theirs, nothing could stop the revolt now. The decision had been made to launch the attack no matter what happened. Salzberg, who was to give the signal, was kept informed of changes in the situation by a number of liaison officers who followed Lalka's and Kiwe's every move.

Lalka had that good-natured manner which he affected at times when he wanted to seem pleasant.

"You are tired," he said to Galewski. "I appreciate the sense of duty which keeps you from admitting it. However, as much in the interest of your health as of the proper functioning of the camp, you must resign from your post."

Nothing mattered to Galewski now, and he offered a feeble defense.

"Naturally, you will retain the advantages that your position gave you: you will remain in the *Hofjuden* barracks and you will not be required to do any work. We know how to show our gratitude to those who serve us faithfully."

Galewski wondered whether he was dreaming. He bowed, said "Thank you" and assured Lalka that he would be at the disposition of his masters for anything that they were pleased to ask.

As he dismissed him Lalka added, "Your successor will be Kapo Rakowski. He will assume your duties tomorrow."

According to the new arrangements that had been made that morning after the successful theft of the grenades, the men in the combat units stayed close to their leaders.

Adolf and Djielo, who were both working in the shipping commando, avoided each other's eyes. There was too much between them and they wanted to avoid the risk of its showing inadvertently and arousing the suspicions of one of the Germans.

All the *Hofjuden* were in on the secret of the revolt. The tension that reigned in the barracks reached a climax that was almost painful. No one dared speak, for fear his voice would come out a scream. Some remained motionless, lost in thoughts of their own; others prayed, and you could see their lips move almost imperceptibly. You could hear a pin drop as the tension mounted, silent and dramatic.

All at once the door of the shoemakers' workshop opened violently and banged against the wall. All the shoemakers jumped and looked up, trembling with fear and impatience, their nerves horribly taut.

"Does anyone know anything about weapons?" asked the prisoner who stood in the doorway.

"Yes, I do! What's the matter?" Simek Goldberg almost shouted, jumping to his feet.

"Quick, Galewski needs you!" cried the other in a voice that trembled with emotion.

Goldberg rushed out. They did not dare run for fear they would be noticed.

"The grenades," the man explained. "There's something they don't understand."

Goldberg felt reassured. These idiots knew nothing about weapons.

"What about the Germans?" he asked.

"Sleeping!" replied the other, who could not catch his breath.

"Everything's all right," said Goldberg to reassure him.

Then he noticed the tall hesitant form of Galewski and the prisoners who were standing guard around the cellar.

"It looks as if something is missing on the grenades," Galewski told him after greeting him.

His voice was so weak that Goldberg could hardly hear him. A case was open at Galewski's feet. Goldberg dashed over to it. He started to lean over but immediately stopped in the middle of his movement. Just as Galewski opened his mouth to ask him what was the matter he straightened up unsteadily.

"The other case, where is the other case?"

Galewski pointed to a spot a few yards away, where it lay half buried under the potatoes.

Goldberg ran to it, leaned over, opened it feverishly, looked inside, and dropped his arms. His body seemed to sag.

"Well?" asked Galewski.

"We've had it," replied Goldberg in a flat voice that trembled a little.

On his knees he contemplated the case, his eyes vacant, sunk in a profound distress.

"What do you mean? What's the matter?" said Galewski, coming over.

Without moving, as if hypnotized by the case, Goldberg replied in a voice that was almost indifferent, "The fuses, there aren't any fuses."

XXIII

ONE NIGHT THE weather became milder, and the next day the snow began to melt. Spring had arrived. Then there was the sun, pale and decorative at first, then more and more cheerful. From far away in the countryside the prisoners again heard the shouts of the peasants returning to their fields after the long winter. And there were the birds, their songs and their flight, and the hearts of the men began to beat again in spite of themselves.

The abortive revolt was only a painful memory that was growing dim when suddenly, a train . . .

Early one afternoon there arrived a convoy that had originated in Germany. Passenger cars, baggage cars, order and discipline: the German Jews, the great disabled veterans and holders of the Iron Cross, First Class, were entitled to favors. They died like the poor, but they traveled like middle-class citizens. This shameful train of death had crossed Germany in all innocence, as thousands of other trains crossed it every day. Everything would have gone off without incident if a red light had not stopped the convoy for a few seconds in a station of the Reich. A young woman, the wife of a high-ranking officer of the Wehrmacht, was waiting on the platform with her two young sons. She thought it was her train. She got on. The mistake was understandable, for the train was not guarded.

So, the young woman got on. She suspected nothing. The train left. No doubt she realized by their yellow stars that her traveling companions were Jewish, and probably she realized that she was on the wrong train. However, she did nothing. Her companions told her what they had been told before their departure, that they were going to colonize the eastern provinces.

There were no survivors of this convoy, and we do not know what happened during the trip, what the young woman said and did.

The train crossed Germany, then Poland; after transferring from one line to another, it arrived at the branch line of the quarry, and from there it pulled slowly into Treblinka, whose station had just been rebaptized with a name which meant nothing. "Obermaïdan," the young woman must have read under the clock, which still pointed to three o'clock. She saw the arrows, the signs, the ticket window, the false doors, and the flower beds, and she probably did not notice that the gleaming rails of the tracks which, since she had left Germany, had formed two long uninterrupted lines, suddenly ended in the rank weeds that spring had produced. Probably she did not understand that the trip was over or where her wrong train had led her, for she said nothing at first. She did not scream or try to escape when she landed on the platform.

It must have been when she entered the barracks that served as dressing room and beauty salon that she suddenly realized that "Obermaïdan" was not an ordinary station. The survivors remember that she was very beautiful. She cried that she was not Jewish and that she was an officer's wife. Her papers proved it. Then she showed that her sons were not circumcised.

Lalka seemed embarrassed. He conferred for a while with

Kiwe, then left. The young woman had accidentally discovered the terrible secret and all the prisoners stopped to see what would happen. Kiwe made her undress in the middle of the yard, and then ordered her to undress her children. They cried and she tried to console them through her own sobs: "It's nothing, my darlings, it will soon be over, don't cry, we are going to a wonderful country where your papa will soon join us." But the children still cried. Kiwe laughed. The prisoners saw them disappear into the stream of the condemned.

Galewski, who had witnessed the scene, reported it to the Committee that evening.

"It reminds me of what Chorongitski used to say. There will be no witnesses. All traces will be obliterated and not one of those who saw the massacre will remain alive. We now know where we stand. Our revolt is acquiring a universal meaning. It is not only for our people that we must succeed, but for the whole world, which does not know and which may never know. We must set a new date today."

Djielo looked at Adolf and replied, "Begin again? Yes! But this time Camp Number Two must be included. That way the failure of the first attempt will serve some purpose."

Everyone looked at him.

"How?" asked Galewski.

"There's a way," replied Djielo. "I have talked it over with Adolf. We have been thinking about it for a long time."

"What is it?"

"To go there."

All the men on the Committee, which now had nine members, looked at him in disbelief.

"It's madness," began Galewski. Then, after a silence during which he seemed to be thinking it over, "But how would we go there?"

"That is our business we'll tell you about it when the plan is ready."

"There's no way," said Kurland.

Djielo looked at him for a moment in silence and then said slowly, "Yes, there is! By getting ourselves transferred."

It was Adolf who had initiated this idea the evening of the first failure when he had met Djielo in the barracks.

As soon as Goldberg had informed him that the grenades were unusable, Galewski had mastered his fatigue and instantly become the leader again. There was only one way to avoid disaster: to take the cases back to the armory and to alert all the unit leaders, especially Kleinmann, who was somewhere in the nearby wood with his camouflage commando and was preparing to attack his guards.

Galewski no longer felt his fatigue; he felt as if he had never been sick. He was one of those men who are bothered rather than reassured by favorable signs, but who forget all their fears when danger threatens to become disaster. A pessimist when things were going well, he became an optimist when they could not get any worse.

Djielo and Adolf were working at the other end of the camp, and although they were *kapos,* they were not allowed to leave their place of work during the day. This privilege was reserved, and very sparingly at that, for the *Hofjuden.* So Galewski had not only to decide upon but to try to carry out the maneuver single-handed.

The first thing to be done was to send a messenger to inform Djielo, Adolf, the unit leaders, and the commando in charge of burning the barracks. Galewski sent immediately for Henochsberg, a prisoner who worked in the potato cellar. He instructed him to go and tell Djielo that the operation was canceled and that he, Djielo, was to get word to the unit leaders before they sent their men for the grenades. Any suspicious traffic might attract the attention of the Germans and prevent the return of the grenades to their starting point. After that, Henochsberg was to warn the incendiaries. He did not ask any questions, he had understood.

"Then," finished Galewski, "you will come back and go on with your work as if this were any other day."

As soon as Henochsberg had left, Galewski went to find Salzberg and Moniek in the Ghetto. They had already been told. They were white-faced and silent.

Galewski understood that they knew as soon as he saw them. The psychological factor would be paramount. He came straight to the point.

"I have sent word to Djielo, Adolf, the unit leaders, and the incendiaries. There remains the problem of the grenades, and Kleinmann. We can return the cases to the armory, it won't be any harder than taking them."

Turning to Salzberg, he added, "We must put everyone back at his post again: Marcus, your son, the sentries. Exactly as it was a little while ago. The Germans suspect nothing, I am sure of it now. . . ."

Then, to show that it was only a postponement, that nothing was lost, that the fight would go on, "In a few days we'll send a weapons specialist to see what happened."

Salzberg looked at him without a word, amazed to suddenly see the old Galewski again. Seeing him still hesitate, Galewski added, "If we succeed, it will be an extraordinary proof of our superiority. It will be a sign that far from being defeated, we are stronger than ever."

"You're right," said Salzberg, and he left.

Then Galewski turned to Moniek, who still had not said a word.

"About Kleinmann, I have an idea. Its success depends on

you. It's very difficult, I'll be frank with you. It will take nerve
and daring. And it's risky."

"Count on me," was Moniek's only reply. He had recovered.

"Here it is. You are the only one who has a chance of getting
out of the camp. Lalka seems to respect you more than the other
kapos, and the Ukrainians know it. You will run to the guardhouse and tell the head officer that Lalka has given you a message
for the S.S. man who is with the camouflage commando. He has
no telephone and won't be able to check. He will have to make the
decision himself. It's so improbable and these primitives are so
naïve that you have a chance of succeeding. Everything will depend on your confidence."

Moniek was less convinced of the possibilities of success than
Galewski was.

"Let's hope they're as stupid as you say."

"Even more so. It's their only excuse for doing this work."

"So, I arrive and I tell him, 'I must take a message to the S.S.
man from Lalka'?"

"No. First, you run up to show him it's urgent; that way he
won't think it over too long. Then you won't ask him to let you
leave, because in all probability he will refuse. You begin by asking him where the camouflage commando has gone today. That's
not a secret, he will answer you. Then you tell him that Lalka
orders him to give you an armed escort. He will ask you why, and
you will answer carelessly that you have an important message to
take to the S.S. man who is guarding the commando. He'll be all
mixed up; he won't know what to do, caught between the fear of
letting you out without a written order and the fear of holding up
the transmission of an important message. It will be up to you to
turn the balance in your favor. To do this you must press him,
confuse him. Go even faster if you feel him weakening, but go
into reverse if he resists. Make him understand that it's all the
same to you, but that Lalka may not be pleased. This will im-

327

prove your chances: when he sees that you don't insist on leaving, he will be less suspicious and will be forced to think about his responsibilities. And if he doesn't fall into the trap, that will provide you with a way out! If you see he is not giving in, say you will report him to Lalka."

"And then what? When I don't come back, do you think he won't check?"

"There's a chance, they are so terrified of Lalka."

"And suppose he checks anyway, or suppose he lets me out and reports afterwards?"

"It will be up to you to decide whether you are capable of holding out under torture. Otherwise . . ."

Moniek looked up. His eyes shone. His face wore a strange expression, a faraway smile that moved and impressed Galewski.

"What do you think the chances of success are?"

"One out of four that you will succeed in warning Kleinmann, and one out of ten that they will never suspect anything."

"That's good enough for me," replied Moniek.

He was about to turn and go when Galewski detained him.

"Run through it again," he said.

Moniek hesitated. He almost said that he knew it by heart, but then changed his mind:

"I run up . . ."

Marcus, who had kept the key to the armory, was standing by and waiting for the explosion of the grenade to rush to the door and open it. It was he who was in charge of distributing the weapons. He was seventeen, and since his arrival in Treblinka he was without father or mother, uncles or aunts, or family of any kind. He was alone, he was the last of his line. But he had seen so many misfortunes at Treblinka that it had taken the edge off his own. His drama had become the drama of the Jewish people as a whole. Since it was a drama too passionate to be lived every day, he had buried it deep in his heart with the ancient dramas that made up the whole history of this people. These tragedies had hardened his heart and made his body supple. Inside this child's body, behind this pathetic face, a kind of wild animal now throbbed.

Marcus jumped when Salzberg clapped him on the shoulder.

"The grenades are no good, we have to take them back to the armory."

The child's eyes brimmed with distress. For a moment, Salzberg squeezed his arm in a gesture that expressed both authority and love.

"I know how you feel. We'll succeed the next time. Nothing will stop us, I promise you."

All the sentries were at their posts. Heniek was waiting by the potato cellar. The cases had already been loaded into his cart.

Moniek thought to himself that all he had to do was kill his guard and he would be free. He glanced at him stealthily. The other was walking beside him, indifferent, unsuspecting. The idea that he was almost free meant nothing to Moniek. It was not escape that he longed for, but revolt.

As he came within sight of the camouflage commando he quickened his step to outdistance the Ukrainian. The latter, knowing he could not run away, let him go. Moniek planned his course so he would pass Kleinmann. When he reached him he murmured, "Operation canceled, do nothing." Kleinmann nodded his head imperceptibly to indicate that he had heard. Moniek passed on, pretending not to see him, and quickened his step again so the Ukrainian would not hear what he wanted to say to the S.S. guard, who watched him approaching without showing any surprise.

"Wiernik asks that you also bring back some timber. I was sent to tell you to save time."

329

His guard arrived. He turned and told him that he had delivered his message and must return at once. The Ukrainian agreed and they left.

"Success," said Moniek to himself. "If we do that well with the grenades I don't care if they do catch me, I'm willing to die."

The carpenters had greased the lock well. It opened noiselessly. Marcus moved away a few inches. A group of workers approached carrying buckets, shovels, and boards. Marcus turned his back and hugged the wall right next to the door. "Now," whispered an invisible voice. He opened the door and closed it behind him in a flash.

At each corner of the building a worker raked listlessly. A few yards behind the little cart a man was walking slowly. Suddenly the cart stopped, and after a short silence Marcus heard a soft whistle: the "Hatikvah." He leaped forward and opened the window.

Moniek was the first to reach the Ghetto. He entered the barracks, where Galewski was waiting for him. Without a word he dropped onto a bunk. His hands were trembling. Respecting his emotion, Galewski did not ask him any questions. After a long moment Moniek raised his head. He made an effort to control his voice.

"It's all right," he murmured. "They know."

Galewski leaned over and took his hand, which he pressed very hard as if to stop its trembling.

It was a moment of great emotion. Suddenly Moniek broke it. "What about the grenades?"

"I'm waiting. They're supposed to come and tell me as soon as it's done."

Silence fell again.

Galewski saw Marcus arrive at a slow walk. Marcus came in, put his hand in his pocket, and took it out slowly.

"Here you are!" he said, holding out the key. "Next time I hope it'll be a one-way trip."

Rumors had leaked out, and a strange atmosphere reigned in the barracks. Voices were more hushed than usual. The men were discussing something more serious. It was a kind of momentous hush. The group of religious had just finished the prayers. The room vibrated silently.

"They were extraordinary," murmured Djielo.

Adolf did not answer at once.

"It was Galewski who amazed me most. Decidedly I understand him less and less. The situation was hopeless."

"Nothing is ever hopeless," Adolf answered then, continuing to stare into space.

Djielo changed the subject. "Why didn't you want to postpone the thing to a specific date?"

"Because I have an idea. It's something I have felt strongly about for a long time. I wanted us to talk about it before anything was decided. Actually, I think I've already mentioned it to you: —you remember." He paused.

Djielo thought it over and hesitated before asking in a whisper, "Camp Number Two?"

"Yes, Camp Number Two. We have to go there. It's not a revolt to save a few lives that we must stage, but something big that they'll still be talking about a thousand years from now."

Djielo lacked that typically Jewish quality of always looking for the hardest way, always wanting to do better, never being satisfied with the possible, and undertaking against all odds what is logically impossible. He lacked that quality, but he lacked neither courage nor resolution. The idea of getting transferred to Camp Number Two would never have occurred to him. The chances of success were too slim, and Djielo, as a good soldier, took only calculated risks. An enterprise with less than a fifty-fifty chance of success did not strike him as viable. To him such an idea smacked more of poetry than of the art of war. And indeed, to believe such an enterprise workable was just as mad as to refuse to believe in the reality of the extermination in the ghettos, as the majority of the Jews had done. For a Jew, however, logic, reasoning and calculation are no deterrents to hope. In the ghettos everything proved that they were being exterminated, and yet they continued to believe madly. In Treblinka everything proved that they had no chance of success, and yet they had dared to try. It was the same impulse, they were the same men; only the situation had changed.

Adolf is a hero beyond compare. So is Choken, so is Galewski, so are all the members of the Committee, all the unit leaders, so is Marcus, and all those who took part in the revolt. They are heroes beyond compare whom circumstances snatched from anonymity, but there is no essential difference between them and the mass of the prisoners. Like the rest they allowed themselves to be led to slaughter, like the rest they became the accomplices of extermination. Their virtues and their defects are Jewish virtues and Jewish defects. Adolf's mad idea had germinated in a Jewish brain.

Djielo would never have thought of it. It seemed mad to him but he could not help replying, "How do you propose to get there? I doubt that the Germans will accept our applications without an argument."

"When a prisoner makes a mistake there are three kinds of punishment: a beating, Camp Number Two, and the 'hospital.' For the *kapos* the alternatives are slightly different: demotion, transfer, execution. All we have to do is make a mistake serious enough to deserve more than demotion but not serious enough to deserve death."

"Brilliant," Djielo replied.

"Of course, we'll have to weigh our move carefully.'

"Of course." Then, after a moment's reflection, "I believe it's possible, or at least not impossible. They will never suspect that we would go there voluntarily."

The day had been taxing; they fell asleep quickly.

The next day Treblinka woke as usual. The day was like any other. It was at evening roll call that Kapo Radowski officially took command of the camp.

Over six and a half feet tall and almost a yard wide, with a huge mop of black curly hair and coarse features—that was Rakowski. On the border line between man and monster, he possessed Herculean strength and an insatiable appetite. During the great era of speculation the prisoners had called him the King of Speculation, and the Germans, to whom his prowess had been reported, *Oberspekulant*. Kiwe did not like him, but Lalka, who was fascinated by his strength and truculence, protected him. He had been a farmer, and his Jewishness was limited to his birth and a mechanical respect for the Sabbath. He could drink a fifth of vodka straight out of the bottle without showing the least sign of intoxication.

His appointment was one of the greatest days of his life. He promised to do anything they wanted. He was interested in only one thing: living well.

Later, when Lalka decided to keep a few women and girls in Treblinka to take care of domestic chores and provide distraction for deserving prisoners, he was the first served: *"Quia nominor Leo."* The Germans organized a "religious" wedding for him, and he was given a small private room for his love nest. He also engaged in resistance, but outside the Committee, which mistrusted him a little. He formed a group with which he planned to escape. But as his recruits seemed too weak, he got the idea of

333

making them engage in sports to put them in good physical condition. Lalka, to whom he submitted the idea, agreed, seeing it as a way to divert the prisoners' attention from their impending extermination.

Helpless and discouraged, the Committee left him alone. It was on the point of considering drastic measures when fate came to its aid.

Rakowski had two mortal enemies at Treblinka: Kiwe, whom he laughed at, confident of Lalka's support, and Chatskel, the informer, whom he scorned openly, and to whom Kiwe had secretly promised the post of Jewish commandant of the camp. These were two enemies to be reckoned with. But Rakowski was incapable of fearing anyone or anything, with the possible exception of hunger. When he was in a good mood he amused himself by sparring with Chatskel, and when he was hungry he shut himself in his room with his wife, whom he had chosen in his image, and gorged for hours on end, to the huge delight of Lalka. He generally had five meals a day, all washed down with wine and vodka. Totally unaware of danger, he bought openly from four Ukrainians at once without even taking the trouble to hide. It was his own way of responding to disaster.

The great life lasted three months, then the trap slammed shut. The Germans, whose superiors must have decided that the work was taxing, were entitled to one week's leave every three weeks, which meant that they spent one third of their time outside the camp. Kiwe waited patiently for a time when he would be in camp while Lalka was on leave. It took three months.

The day after Lalka's departure, Kiwe walked into Rakowski's room in the middle of the morning as he was having his second breakfast. The table was loaded with food and drink.

"*Also, Rakowski!* You're speculating as much as ever!" he said.

Rakowski replied with a smile that they were gifts. His mistress, who was lying half naked on the bunk where he was sitting, looked at Kiwe in terror. Kiwe made her dress and took them both away. The fact of receiving gifts was not sufficient, but Kiwe had planned carefully. As soon as they had left, Chatskel came in and hid a bag of gold under Rakowski's bunk. Kiwe then sent two S.S. men to search the premises. They found the bag easily.

When it was shown to him, Rakowski understood that he had been framed. He did not try to defend himself. He had lived like a prince, he wanted to die nobly.

"Bravo!" he told Kiwe. "Go to it!"

But Kiwe could not help feeling a kind of fear in the face of this giant. He sent for four guards and two head guards to take Rakowski to the "hospital." He even had the prisoner's hands tied behind his back. Then the procession left. The impassive colossus towered over the six men who bracketed him. A spindly dwarf, Kiwe followed a few steps behind. The episode had been brief, but when they saw the cortege go by all the prisoners understood. Rakowski had never had any scruples about beating them, and the prisoners had little fondness for him, but not one could help feeling a sense of pride at the sight of their brother marching to his death with so much assurance and contempt. For the first time in Treblinka, perhaps, the killers looked like what they were: it took seven of them to kill a single man, unarmed and bound.

The group passed the former Roll Call Square where the deportees from the convoys undressed and then started the long trek across the immense sorting square to the "hospital." Everyone—German, Ukrainian and Jew—stopped his work and watched with fascination as the funeral procession slowly passed. Kiwe was nervous; Rakowski seemed so extraordinary that he was afraid that at the last moment he would break his bonds and run away or kill him or do God knows what. It was an absurd fear, but he felt you had to be ready for anything from this colossal Jew.

335

When they reached the middle of the sorting square Kiwe slowly drew his revolver, paused, aimed carefully, and fired. Rakowski shuddered. The six guards, who had been warned ahead of time, leaped aside to get away from Rakowski and all fired at once. Rakowski gave a kind of bellow, snapped his bonds with a sudden effort, and charged forward. But in the middle of the gesture, he rolled onto the ground. He moved again for a moment and then subsided, his face smeared with blood and dust. Panic-stricken, the guards fired again for a few seconds before they stopped, dazed.

Rakowski was dragged to the ditch of the "hospital" like a vanquished bull.

Lalka would not hear of an informer as the Jewish commandant. As soon as he got back he reappointed Galewski.

Rakowski's reign had represented an important stage in the life of this world of death. A belligerent puppet, he had amused both Lalka and the Committee, although toward the end he had almost jeopardized the latter's plans.

Thanks to Galewski's strange premonition, the Committee had succeeded in saving the situation *in extremis*. If the prisoners had been in on the plan their explosive force would have been difficult to turn off. But in order to be able to begin again afterward it was necessary to keep the Germans convinced that the Jews believed that the camp would not be liquidated. The first measure by the Committee to this end was to allow a few rumors of what was afoot to leak out. It was Adolf who was charged with this mission. The night of the first spectacle, which was to have been the eve of the big day, the prisoners had felt a profound shame. So there was a danger that, filled with remorse, they might boycott the festivities. It was necessary, therefore, to present participation in the celebrations as an act of resistance. In the upside-down world that was Treblinka, amusement had become a duty.

Meanwhile, Lalka methodically pursued his policy of sedation. To divert the attention of the prisoners while awaiting the manna of the promised deportees, he initiated a program of major construction designed both to put the final touches on his masterpiece and to lull the suspicions of the Jews. It was an old Technician's principle to make the Jews believe that work equaled life. It was one of their first arguments at the time of the ghetto, and its logic had long deceived the Jews. The Technicians said, "Work and your life will be spared." The Jews thought, "They need our labor, so they will let us live." This was a mistake, of course, and the Technicians gained on two grounds: in the first place the Jews worked for them, and in the second place this work, which they saw as security, disarmed them morally and psychologically. Since work was to insure their salvation, they did not bother to look for another path.

Faithful to this old ruse, therefore, Lalka began to build. Treblinka was suddenly transformed into a giant construction project. A main street was laid out from west to east under the direction of an S.S. officer, Kurt Seidel, who gave it his name. It began at the great western gate and ran all the way to the station. The gate was reconstructed in wood in the style of a medieval city gate. Two towers connected by a fortified footbridge flanked the heavy double gate. The southern tower was converted into a guardhouse and was also decorated in the medieval style. Treblinka was becoming a fortress of Teutonic knights.

Along the main street Lalka tore down the old barracks, which were reconstructed in the style of those Middle Ages which the Technicians seemed to miss so much. Under the direction of Sudowich, an agricultural expert, who was one of Adolf's unit leaders and who along with several others was to become a member of the Committee, gardens were designed. An athletic field was prepared. The Ukrainian barracks were named "Max Bielas Quarter." Additional barracks resembling medieval houses were con-

337

structed on the left side of the street. The workshop of the *Goldjuden* was installed in the first. The second was for the Germans' dentists, the third for the barbers. Then there was the Germans' laundry, where young Jewish women worked. The last barracks was used as a food store. Behind it lay the Ghetto.

Halfway up the main street there branched off to the left another, smaller street which first climbed north and then veered off to the east and ended in Camp Number Two. It acquired the name "Aussiedler Strasse" (Street of the Deportees). Later, in early spring, an offshoot of this road was built to the west; it led to a zoo that was being laid out. It was a park with lawns and flower beds and little paths covered with fine white gravel. On the lawns Avraham Silber, who had a certain artistic sense, designed decorative motifs and German emblems with little multicolored stones. In a shady corner of the park an ornamental lake was dug and in the center was placed a stone frog, sculpted by prisoners, from whose open mouth a fountain was made to spout. All around the lake rustic benches were installed for the relaxation of the lords of the manor. In the center of the park was a hexagonal building covered with little birch logs. On each side of the building were the cages: there was a cage for the birds, a cage for the squirrels, et cetera.

Manpower was plentiful, and the enthusiasm of the architects tireless. To the right of Aussiedler Strasse were built a cattle shed, a stable, and a pigsty. Behind the zoo the camp kitchen garden extended to the barbed wire. Treblinka had become a complete, self-sufficient world. The right side of the main street was reserved exclusively for the Germans. Beside the guardhouse was a paved area where a light armored car was kept. Beyond, to the south, lay the German gardens complete with tables, chairs, and even umbrellas. On the other side of the paved area rose the German buildings flanked by a high tower in which water was stored and on which a huge flag bearing the swastika was planted. A

338

wing was added to the original buildings, and the whole interior was redesigned very luxuriously with guest rooms, bar and bathrooms. The labor was provided by the prisoners, and the raw materials, from the bottles on the bar to the mattresses on the beds, by the convoys.

From one of the last convoys of January Lalka selected a wood carver who had considerable talent. He had him do a series of multicolored panels carved in bas-relief. Under the arrow reading *"Zum Bahnhof"* at the end of the main street, a panel was hung representing a group of Jews with beards and glasses carrying luggage to the station. Opposite Aussiedler Strasse, which led to the stable, the cattle shed, the pigsty, the zoo, and Camp Number Two, the panel represented all the farm animals being watched by a young shepherd. The entrance to this street was decorated with a porch. A globe showing the four cardinal points was placed over the lintel. Surmounting the Street of the Deportees this way, it symbolized world Judaism, which would be deported in its entirety. The symbolism was continued over the porch which marked the Ukrainian quarters. Here a huge sun of painted wood shone forth, indicating that the sun had risen over the Ukraine with the arrival of the Germans. In front of the gate to the quarter there was also a panel depicting a group of Germans and Ukrainians marching fraternally to war. Under the panel an arrow read *"Zur Kaserne."*

The panels which embellished the shops hung from chains like signs. They represented a scissors for the barber, a tooth for the dentist, and a spear of wheat for the bakery.

In front of the Ghetto the arrow reading *"Zum Ghetto"* was accompanied by a huge panel depicting some Jews of cartoonlike appearance walking with their heads bowed and carrying heavy sledge hammers of the kind used to crush rock.

Treblinka, which had just been rebaptized *"Juden Staat"* (Jewish State), had become a peaceful little town with its "factory," its station, its streets, its shops and its signs—a town that was situated somewhere outside time and space. Time had stood still there one day and since then the wooden face of the clock always pointed to three. The town was called Obermaïdan, but no map mentions this name. The working methods were the most modern, two hundred laborers worked in the "factory" under the direction of alchemists of death. The first town of the Thousand Year Reich was born. It had everything: a history, music, cruelty, science, horror, lies and madness.

The construction was almost finished when one day the heavy gates opened to admit a procession of seven cars. In the first, stiff as a ramrod, sat a little man who looked like a fanatical schoolteacher and who wore a pair of steel-rimmed spectacles on his ferretlike face. The German Jews recognized him at once from having seen his picture on so many posters and in so many newspapers. It was S.S. Reichsführer Heinrich Himmler himself, patron of the Technicians. His court accompanied him, respectfully staying a few feet behind. He inquired at length into the functioning of the "factory" and seemed pleased with what he heard. He wanted to see everything. He would demand explanations, nod his head, and walk away. Occasionally a faint smile would distort his face. He left before dark, followed by his long cortege.

A few days later an acrid black smoke began to rise from Camp Number Two.

The Committee met at once. They had to know. Since Lalka had initiated his policy of extensive construction, Yankel Wiernik, the carpenter from "down there," came to Camp Number One every day. He was the first man to return from hell. He was very closely watched, and at first they did not want to take the risk of talking to him. But when the thick black smoke began to pollute the atmosphere, they approached him.

340

In a whisper, Wiernik revealed, "They are digging up all the bodies and burning them "

When the Committee met that night Galewski said, "Djielo and Adolf are right. We must get into Camp Number Two at all costs. We must find out how fast they are burning the bodies. When we know that, we will be able to determine almost precisely what day the camp will be liquidated. They have just turned over the hourglass."

And so the countdown began. . . .

XXIV

MUSIC, DEATH, SPRING, and the great funeral pyres upon which the dead and numberless witnesses of the massacre were consumed. The impression of unreality grew stronger from day to day. The madness of this world exceeded all bounds. Soon the earth would open and swallow Treblinka up. The camp would sink like a ship, leaving behind fields as innocent as the calm, flat, luminous surface of the sea after a storm. Lost dramas, eternal serenity.

Djielo and Adolf carefully finished the preparations for their transfer to Camp Number Two. They had already agreed on the method and they were only waiting for the opportunity. Being quiet and efficient, they were well thought of by the Germans; this gave them an additional chance of avoiding the "hospital." Their plan was simple. While working on a shipment of the clothing and personal possessions of the deportees, they would deliberately make a mistake in counting the bundles.

Their principal chance lay in the fact that there was a surplus of *kapos* in Camp Number One since the typhus epidemic, which had eliminated half of the prisoners and spared the *kapos,* whose living conditions were easier. Indeed, it was because of this su-

perabundance that Djielo and Adolf belonged to the same commando. For this reason the chances of pardon were very unlikely.
Since the chances of the "hospital" were also slim, the solution
was to make an obvious mistake. The Germans attached great
importance to bookkeeping and Adolf knew they would be furious over the mistake that he was preparing with Djielo.

While they waited for the propitious moment they worked out
an intercamp communication with the Committee. After several
days of investigation, Galewski found a method. It was not the
easiest. The "road to heaven," that long path down which the
deportees were led to the gas chambers, began in Camp Number
One and continued into the territory of Camp Number Two. This
path, which was covered with white sand, was raked and cleaned
every day. But to make the two camps even more airtight, the
Germans had entrusted the cleaning of the part that was located
in Camp Number One to a gang from this camp and the other
part to a second gang from the other camp. In this way no prisoner from Camp Number One entered Camp Number Two, and
vice versa. The gangs arrived, each accompanied by two guards
who had been instructed to keep them at least ten yards apart.

"You can't say that they don't take precautions," commented
Galewski. "But strong as they are, there is a way to outwit them.
Of course it requires the complicity of both gangs. That of the
gang from our camp is certain." He turned to Adolf and Djielo.
"Your job will be to obtain that of the other gang. The dialogue
will take place indirectly. Let me explain. The man who has a
message to deliver will address it to a member of his own gang,
shouting loud enough to be heard by the other gang. Naturally
the message will be contained in a seemingly innocent statement,
for we are not absolutely sure that the Ukrainians do not understand a few words of Yiddish. The answer will be delivered in the
same way. With a little practice it will be possible to have real
conversations this way."

The two speleologists of hell listened impassively. Galewski

343

asked them whether they had understood. They nodded their heads in silence.

The problem of the date of D-day was brought up next. The Committee did not know the situation in Camp Number Two and as they would have to wait until it was prepared for the attack, they decided that Djielo would send word when he had completed the mobilization. They would decide then.

"Down there we will be in a better position to follow the development of the situation," Djielo added, "for every day we will see the sand run out. From now on it is no longer the number of convoys that determines our life expectancy but the number of bodies. Himmler has just given us a new reprieve. It will be the last."

To facilitate their task the Committee decided to ask Wiernik the carpenter, who seemed to be a personality in Camp Number Two, to find some way to have them appointed *kapos* or foremen.

The Committee had already replaced Djielo and Adolf. Two new members had been elected, the engineer Sudowich, and Rudek, who was head of the garage. The two newcomers had great admiration for Adolf and they watched him leave on this hazardous mission with some apprehension.

Djielo continued, "I think we had better say our goodbyes now. The opportunity we are waiting for may arise from one moment to the next. No one can say what will happen when we get caught in the works. For the Jewish people and for God, we will succeed."

There was a moment of hesitation. Then Galewski rose and took the two men in his arms.

"I'll miss you," Rudek told Adolf.

"See you soon," replied Adolf. Then, after a moment, "Next time don't forget to give us some pretty fireworks with your garage!"

344

Rudek smiled and hugged him.

Djielo nodded to Adolf, and in the awkward silence that had fallen, they left. The others saw their silhouettes appear framed in the doorway and then dissolve into the mass of the prisoners, who were enjoying a few last breaths of fresh air before being shut up for the night in the immense barracks-dormitory.

The air was sweet and the sky was luminous in the west. Life must be beginning again in the other world.

The opportunity came a few days later. There had been no convoys for a while and the commandant of the camp had to send for a special train to come and collect the belongings. To know in advance how many cars would be required, he had Djielo and Adolf find out how many bundles were available. They deliberately gave a figure that was much higher than the truth. The train arrived and was loaded, and it was noted that five cars would have to go back empty.

The next morning Djielo and Adolf, their faces swollen, their bodies raw, were led half conscious through the "road to heaven" to Camp Number Two. Only by a miracle had they escaped death. The Germans had reacted much more violently than they had anticipated. The five hopelessly empty cars rankled in their minds.

The sky darkened as Djielo and Adolf got closer to Camp Number Two. The smell, which from Camp Number One was only a vague scent, bitter and slightly sickening, became stifling. Unconsciously they breathed less and less deeply. Slowly they began to hear the sound of a motor in two alternating tones: a slow regular hum which periodically became a more violent sound, gasping and deafening. As they came still nearer they discovered behind these mechanical noises a loud roar like the sound of a forest fire. The heavy door of solid wood opened as in a dream. They took one step, then another, and stopped suddenly, ready to faint.

345

Nothing that they had seen up to then could be compared with the hell which they suddenly discovered before their eyes. To the left yawned an immense ditch and moving around it were three excavators, mechanical giants which jerkily plunged their long jointed arms to the bottom of the pestilential pit and lifted them more slowly, loaded with dismembered bodies. The bodies seemed to lean forward as if to escape or to dangle their heads like drowned men. Each long steel arm ended in a monstrous set of jaws which closed gradually as they rose, inexorably eliminating anything that was too long, severing heads, torsos, and limbs, which fell heavily into the ditch. After that the mechanical arm would describe a wide circle, pause, shudder, and brutally open its jaws, hurling to the ground its cargo of damned.

A few dozen yards away, immense bonfires roared. As the flames reached them, the faces of the dead suddenly came back to life. They twisted and grimaced as if contorted by unbearable pain. The liquid fat and lymph that suddenly exuded covered their faces with a kind of sweat that further reinforced the impression of life and intense suffering. Under the effect of the heat the belly of a pregnant woman burst like an overripe fruit, expelling the fetus, which went up in flames.

Between the ditches and the fire a race of slaves scurried.

Djielo and Adolf let themselves be led wordlessly to the barracks, which rose at the other end of the big yard. The head *kapo*, Singer, greeted them with these words:

"Welcome to hell. Here the work is hard, but the food is adequate. You will receive new clothing every two weeks and your linen will be washed every week."

Seeming not to have noticed their stupor he added, "So we won't waste time, you will start work at once."

Djielo and Adolf followed him. They had not uttered a word.

What the early days of Camp Number Two were like, no one remembers. The prisoners had become animals, wild animals. All day, while they were busy carrying the bodies, they were beaten; not just occasionally, but without interruption. In the evening they fought among themselves for food, and at night for a place to sleep. The slightest word was a pretext for bloody brawls, which always resulted in several deaths. You had to choose between food and sleep. Anyone who took time to eat had to give up the idea of sleeping for lack of room, and anyone who wanted to sleep had to run to the barracks as soon as work was done. When there was enough room for everyone in the barracks, the fight for survival limited itself to food.

Two men played a leading role in the moral rehabilitation of the prisoners. First, Pinhas Alter, the fanatical Hasid and friend of Berliner, and later Dr. Zimmermann, *kapo* of the "dentists." Pinhas Alter, whose physical stamina matched his moral strength, spent his nights taking down the bodies of hanged men and separating brawlers. Alone, inspired by an extraordinary faith and a fierce love for God and for life, he slept only a few hours in the morning when the prisoners, prostrate with fatigue, had fallen every which way on the floor. Before falling asleep too, he would pray at length, praising the Lord for the interest He showed in His people, thanking Him for the ordeals with which He tormented them, assuring Him that His wrath was even dearer to him than His kindness. Pinhas Alter died of exhaustion at the beginning of the typhus epidemic.

Dr. Zimmerman, who carried on his work, resembled him in nothing except determination. The son of a family of poor artisans, he had worked his way through medical school to become one of the most celebrated doctors in Warsaw. In the presence of doctors, even Jewish ones, the Technicians felt a kind of uneasy respect. Dr. Zimmerman took advantage of this respect to obtain more tolerable living conditions for the prisoners. Meanwhile, for long hours in the evening he urged them not to despair and to pull themselves together. He forced them to bathe when they had finished work and to clean their shoes, which were covered with shreds of skin, blood and rotted flesh, before re-entering the barracks. At his suggestion the Germans appointed a barracks guard whose job it was to see that these regulations were followed.

After several months of effort Dr. Zimmerman managed to recreate almost normal living conditions in Camp Number Two. As in Camp Number One, there were the era of escapes and the era of speculation. By a strange osmosis the two camps tended to resemble each other. In Camp Number Two, however, the living conditions and morale were such that a dream world was created among the prisoners. When they were not working, the prisoners met in groups in the barracks and talked about their former lives. All claimed that they had been millionaires and that they had lived in marvelous apartments. Every day they would add new details about a cure at Baden-Baden, their hunting preserves, or their property on the Baltic. It was an inexhaustible mirage. They loved other people's lies as much as their own, and by a kind of tacit agreement it was forbidden to question a single detail. One day Moshe, a former cab driver, almost got knocked down for shouting during one of these sessions, "All millionaires, but where the hell are the poor people of Warsaw?"

There was another evidence of this need for the dream, this need for hope in this apocalyptic world. Every time the prisoners gathered to drink contraband vodka, before bringing the mouth of the bottle to their lips they would each repeat the wish that all Jews have made at the end of the Passover ceremony since the destruction of the Temple: "Next year in Jerusalem." This wish, which is at the same time an oath of loyalty and an act of faith, was their way of affirming their absurd and desperate hope, their will to live, their denial of death.

An orchestra was formed, a "shit master" was appointed, roll call became a ceremony, and life was organized. There was a touch of originality with respect to Camp Number One: a sentry

was posted at the gate of the barbed-wire fence which marked off
a little space around the barracks where the prisoners could relax
until lights out. The job was filled by a young man whom everyone knew as Motele. He was dressed like a Cossack, wore the cap
of a Russian soldier, and had been given a wooden gun as a
badge of his function. His job was twofold: to prevent the prisoners from entering the barracks during the day and to present
arms to every German who passed. A kind of Jewish hooligan, he
played the part of a simpleton with the Germans. What he lost in
dignity he made up for in security. One of the S.S. officers, Karol
Petzinger, had a kind of affection for him, and never passed without addressing a few words to him. The survivors remember an
anecdote in connection with this strange friendship. Petzinger arrived one day in a very good humor. Motele grasped his gun
firmly and presented arms.

"Well, Motele, and how are you today?" Petzinger wanted to
know.

"Very well, thank you, sir. I would be even better if the war
were over."

"Soon, soon, Motele, a little patience."

Motele who was still presenting arms, asked innocently, "Still
advancing in Russia?"

"Of course we're advancing, but Russia's a big country, you
know; it takes time to get to the end of it."

"Of course," replied Motele with an air of absolute credulity.
"But just how far along are you?"

"What do you mean?"

"Well, Kiev, for example, have you taken it?"

"Of course."

"And Lwow?"

"A long time ago."

The dialogue took place in German. Motele mentioned a few
more names of cities at random, and each time the S.S. officer

replied with a satisfied air. Then suddenly Motele threw out, "And when will you get the Clap?"

Petzinger thought this was the name of another city. He did not want to seem either ignorant or doubtful of victory. With unshakable assurance he replied "Soon, soon."

Motele did not waver. The prisoners who had formed a circle around him began to retreat, but Petzinger walked off smiling, very pleased with himself.

Life was following its deadly course when Himmler arrived. He came to sign Treblinka's death sentence. The Germans wanted to wipe away all traces before closing shop. A few days later the earth opened.

But it is one thing to kill and another to burn, as Lalka would learn from humiliating experience. The soil of Treblinka contained seven hundred thousand bodies, or an approximate weight of thirty-five thousand tons and a volume of ninety thousand cubic yards. Thirty-five thousand tons is the weight of a battleship. Ninety thousand cubic yards represents a square tower nearly three thousand feet high and ten yards across. The task was gigantic, superhuman; the problem apparently insoluble. With an output of one thousand bodies per day, which seems at first glance a good rate, you would have to allow seven hundred days, or almost two years, without stopping a single day; provided, moreover, there was not a single convoy more to process. The future was dim, not to say hopeless, and anyone but a Technician would have given up from the start. Lalka, however, set courageously to work. The orders of the supreme leader of the Technicians were not questioned, even if they seemed impossible to execute.

He began by having one ditch opened. The bodies appeared, arranged in an orderly fashion, head to foot, and emitting a pestilential odor on which Kiwe, stopping his nose, commented, unconsciously parodying a remark made by a king of France: "They smell even worse dead than alive." It was not in the best taste, but it relaxed the atmosphere.

Lalka then had several dozen quarts of gasoline poured on the bodies and gave the order to light the fire. A huge flame burst forth with a roar and a thick curl of black smoke began to rise. Rolling back on itself it fell, engulfing the spectators. The fire rumbled for a long time in the artificial haze of its smoke, then began to die down more and more rapidly. The smoke whitened and thinned, revealing the frozen forms of the spectators. Suddenly the fire went out, releasing a last sluggish curl of smoke. The S.S. approached anxiously. The bodies were still there, barely singed by the blaze. One, two, three more experiments were made, with just as poor results.

At the German mess that evening consternation prevailed.

But if it is not necessary to have high hope in order to undertake, neither is it necessary to succeed in order to persevere. Lalka's fertile brain had conceived another method. Arriving at the yard at dawn, he had the excavators dig a very wide and shallow ditch to the middle of which the prisoners carried one hundred bodies, forming a pile as tall as it was wide. After the gasoline was poured and the prayer said, the pile was ignited in its turn. Flames, smoke, haze, anticipation, hope: the fire subsided, the smoke lifted, the bodies were still there. They were a little more burnt than they had been the day before, but the failure was apparent, as Lalka admitted to himself.

In the days that followed the experiment was repeated by varying the shape of the piles, the quantity of gasoline, and the position of the fire, but the results were just as disappointing. At the end of a week some hundred bodies could be regarded as completely burned and even then it had taken several hundred quarts of gasoline to arrive at this result. By rapid calculation Lalka estimated the number of years necessary to finish the job at one hundred and forty. Even for the Thousand Year Reich, it was a long time.

Then an S.S. officer remembered having heard through a colleague in one of the small local camps that you had to alternate layers of bodies with layers of tree trunks. The idea seemed good. Several cords of wood were ordered and a new start was made. At first gasoline was used sparingly and the trunks did not have time to ignite. Then the wood was soaked with all the inflammable liquid available. A tense moment: the match was applied, the flame burst out, the smoke rose, fell back and dispersed. All rushed forward and—oh miracle!—the fire continued to roar. A profound silence fell as if to enhance the sweet sound of victory. When nothing was left but a little heap of ashes, a great ovation arose. Congratulations, felicitations, cries of long life to the beloved *Führer* and immortality to the eternal Reich.

Tired, the celebration over, the ashes cool, the Germans added up the figures. The cost price turned out to be exorbitant: besides gasoline, they needed as many tree trunks as bodies. The matter was not feasible, for even if they could contemplate cutting down the forests of Poland, gasoline was becoming increasingly scarce. A German army had surrendered in Stalingrad, and the rich oil fields of the Caucasus had vanished like a mirage.

The next few days were devoted to a number of experiments in which the quantities of gasoline and wood and the diameter of the wood were varied. The problem was twofold: first, to reduce the quantity of wood to a minimum, and second, to try to replace gasoline by kindling and small fires. Men and corpses were sorely tried, but in spite of the undeniable strides that were made, it became evident that the enterprise had failed, that Treblinka was unable to solve the problem. Profound despair; after a night of agony Lalka decided to report his defeat to his superiors and to ask for their help.

Blond and slight, with a gentle face and a retiring manner, he arrived one fine morning with his little suitcase at the gates of the kingdom of death. His name was Herbert Floss, and he was a specialist in the cremation of bodies. Self-educated, he had perfected his art in the little local camps to which the vagaries of fortune had brought him one after the other. He had never visited Treblinka before, but he knew the camp by reputation. At that time Birkenau, the extermination camp at Auschwitz, had not yet established its supremacy, and Treblinka was still the great center of spiritual attraction for the Technicians. Floss was conscious of what this appointment represented for him: it was a promotion, even an ordination; he had heard that there were several hundred thousand bodies.

He reported at once to the administrative director of the camp, who, after wishing him good luck, sent him to Lalka. As he showed him to his room, Lalka began to explain the situation. The cremator listened attentively, then asked to be taken to the spot without delay.

Once there, he asked for information about the placement of the ditches and their approximate capacity. He seemed to attach particular importance to the age of the bodies. At each detail that was given him he replied, "*Tadello:*" (splendid), with a pleased little smile. He submitted his plan that evening.

That night a group of prisoners from Camp Number One left the camp under heavy escort to unbolt the tracks of a nearby railroad. The next morning the masons received the order to build, not far from the ditches, four cement pillars two and a half feet high to form a rectangle twenty yards long and one yard wide. Floss supervised the work. He shouted a great deal, but he was very awkward and seemed incapable of striking a prisoner. Running in all directions, shouting, explaining, gesticulating, he fell down several times. The prisoners did not dare laugh, but they gave him two nicknames: "The Artist" and "Lefty," because

355

of his clumsiness. When the cement of the columns was dry, Floss had the rails laid on them with much shouting and fuss.

The first bonfire was prepared the next day. Herbert Floss then revealed his secret: all the bodies did not burn at the same rate; there were good bodies and bad bodies, fire-resistant bodies and inflammable bodies. The art consisted in using the good ones to burn the bad ones. According to his investigations—and judging from the results, they were very thorough—the old bodies burned better than the new ones, the fat ones better than the thin ones, the women better than the men, and the children not as well as the women but better than the men. It was evident that the ideal body was the old body of a fat woman. Floss had these put aside. Then he had the men and children sorted too. When a thousand bodies had been dug up and sorted in this way, he proceeded to the loading, with the good fuel underneath and the bad above. He refused gasoline and sent for wood. His demonstration was going to be perfect. The wood was arranged under the grill of the pyre in little piles which resembled camp fires. The moment of truth had come. He was solemnly handed a box of matches. He bent down, lit the first fire, then the others, and as the wood began to catch fire he walked back with his odd gait to the group of officials who were waiting a little way away.

The mounting flames began to lick at the bodies, gently at first, then with a steady force like the flame of a blow torch. Everyone held his breath, the Germans anxious and impatient, the prisoners dismayed and terrified. Only Floss seemed relaxed; very sure of himself, he was muttering abstractedly, *"Tadellos, tadellos . . ."* The bodies burst into flames. Suddenly the flames shot up, releasing a cloud of smoke, a deep roar arose, the faces of the dead twisted with pain and the flesh crackled. The spectacle had an infernal quality and even the S.S. men remained petrified for a few moments, contemplating the marvel. Floss beamed. This fire was the finest day of his life.

When they had recovered from their stupor, the Germans gave expression to their joy and gratitude. Herbert Floss became a hero. An event like this had to be celebrated in a worthy manner. The Germans sent for tables, which were set up opposite the funeral pyre and covered with dozens of bottles of liquor, wine and beer. The dying day reflected the high flames of the funeral pyre, the sky glowed at the end of the plain where the sun was disappearing with a show of fire.

At a nod from Lalka, the corks popped. An extraordinary party began. The first toast was made to the *Führer*. The operators of the excavators had returned to their machines. When the S.S. men raised their glasses noisily, the excavators seemed to come to life and suddenly flung their long jointed arms toward the sky in a throbbing and jolting Nazi salute It was like a signal; ten times the men raised their arms, each time shouting "*Heil Hitler.*" The manlike machines returned the salute of the machinelike men, and the air rang with shouts of glory to the *Führer*. The party lasted until the funeral pyre was entirely consumed. After the toasts came the songs, savage and cruel, songs of hatred, songs of fury, songs of glory to Germany the eternal. Treblinka, abandoned to the madness of men of another age, seemed to have become the sanctuary of terrible pagan rites. The Technicians had been transformed into barbaric and bloodthirsty demigods arisen from some mythology.

The next day the S.S. men became once again the conscientious, busy, meticulous Technicians they were. The experiment had been conclusive. Now they had to translate it from the experimental to the industrial realm. Herbert Floss attacked the problem.

An organized man, he divided the task into combustion proper and fuel; this second point was in turn divided into two parts: extraction, and carrying and loading. Combustion was limited

only by the number of fires, which could be increased at will. The
rate of production would therefore depend on the possibilities of
extraction, carrying and loading.

The solution of all these questions would take him a certain
period of time.

As a first innovation, the excavators would extract the bodies
and set them in a pile outside the ditch, where the prisoners
would find and transport them to the fires at a ratio of two prisoners per body. This was the first stage. Then Floss noticed that it
was difficult for the three excavators to put their loads in the same
place and that the prisoners were crowded for room. He divided
the prisoners into three teams, each of which served one machine: progress. But a bottleneck occurred at the fire. The number of fires was increased to three: progress. New problem:
below a certain level the bodies extracted were dismembered and
the prisoners transported them in pieces, a leg under one arm and
a torso under the other. As a result they transported many less.
Herbert re-enlisted the litters that had been used to carry the
bodies from the gas chambers to the ditches: progress. But it happened that limbs fell off along the way during the transfer, which
was done at a run. The litters were modified, the canvas was replaced by crates: progress. Then it was remarked that the rails
were sagging under the effect of the heat. New supporting pillars
were constructed within the enclosure: progress.

The output was now two thousand bodies per day. One evening at roll call Floss made a speech.

"Today we burned two thousand bodies. This is good, but we
must not stop here. We will set ourselves an objective and devote
all our efforts to reaching it. Tomorrow we will do three thousand, the day after tomorrow four thousand, then five thousand,
then six thousand, and so on until ten thousand. Every day we
will force ourselves to increase the output by one thousand units.
I count on you to help me."

356

A good-natured little man incapable of hurting a flea, sounding like the head of a factory to his workers, Herbert Floss then had each prisoner given an extra ration of bread.

The improvements continued. The mania for specialization was not peculiar to Lalka. Since the prisoners were losing time loading and unloading their litters, the crews were again divided into three: a crew of loaders, another of carriers, and a third of burners, which acquired the name of fire commando: progress. But the ten-thousand figure had still not been reached. The pyres were loaded during the day and lit in the evening. They now covered a distance of over fifty yards. It was possible to extend them even further, but the fueling had reached a plateau. It was at this level that the bottleneck was occurring. Floss discovered a further improvement. When the carriers reached the piles of bodies they stopped and rested while their litters were being loaded. This represented an enormous loss of time. To offset this disadvantage the excavators were ordered to lay their bodies not in a compact pile but in the form of an arc. The loaders were arranged along this arc and the carriers were instructed to walk along the line of the loaders. Herbert Floss had rediscovered the principle of the assembly line. The loaders were no longer responsible for one crate, but instead they threw a piece of a body into each crate that filed by.

It was at this point that the prisoners reacted. Three prisoners were responsible for counting the bodies. Their comrades, feeling that they were about to die of exhaustion, asked them to make The Artist happy and give him his ten thousand bodies. The next day Floss was informed that the goal of ten thousand bodies had been reached. He insisted on thanking the prisoners for their zeal in the work.

One day an excavator ran out of gasoline. The driver rushed out to get a can and the prisoners seized the opportunity to catch their breath. Just then Floss arrived. The prisoners, knowing that

357

he did not hit them, were not too afraid of him, and explained that the excavator had broken down and that they were waiting for it to be fixed.

"How long will it take?" asked Floss.

"Three or four minutes," they answered at random.

"Four minutes? You have just enough time to make one haul with the next excavator."

"For one haul," they replied, "we will lose more time going back and forth than we will waiting."

To which Floss replied, "One haul for the principle, to prove to yourselves that you aren't good for nothing. We'll call it the Haul of Honor."

Herbert Floss was mad.

XXV

THE FIRST MESSAGE from Adolf and Djielo arrived over a month after their departure. It was laconic. "Arrived safely in hell, starting the job," the *kapo* of the sweeping commando transmitted.

Carried along by its own momentum, Camp Number One continued to sink into insanity. Like a mad machine, or a runaway horse charging toward a precipice, the camp was rushing toward its end with a kind of infernal gaiety. The only certainty was the approaching end of Treblinka. Everyone knew it—the Germans, the Committee, and the prisoners—but everyone also pretended not to know it: the Germans, in order to reassure the prisoners, the Committee and the prisoners who were in on the secret of the revolt, in order to reassure the Germans, and finally the other prisoners, who knew nothing, in order to reassure themselves. There were still a few convoys, but everything happened in a dreamlike atmosphere.

One day a band of Gypsies arrived at the gate of the camp with caravans and baggage. They were happy to have finished their long trip; the Germans were happy too. In one hour it was all over. Another day, some Balkan Jews arrived. It was Sunday and the holiday was going full blast in the yard of the Ghetto. All at once the whistle of the locomotive rent the air. Lalka had the orchestra walk out on the platform, and the debarkation took place to music. When it was all over, Kiwe told a gang of prisoners who were returning to the Ghetto, clapping one of them on the shoulder, "Don't worry, there'll be plenty more like that one."

While the commotion continued implacably, while the ditches were being emptied and the bodies were going up in smoke, optimism had become compulsory at Treblinka, and everyone kept up his spirits in the hope of deceiving himself or others.

With its language, its new buildings and its Sunday celebrations, Treblinka now needed only one thing to play the farce: women. The first convoy corrected this situation. It was from Grodno and was bringing the last Jews in town. Contrary to custom, the women undressed in the yard. When they were naked, Lalka made them line up and inspected them. He wanted them young, fresh and pretty. Twenty girls and young women who found grace in his eyes were set apart. They were ordered to dress and were conducted to the Ghetto. Half of them stayed there and the other half were taken to Camp Number Two. The ten who stayed in Camp Number One were lodged in a room constructed especially for them, an extension of the barracks of the *Hofjuden*. During the day they worked in the German laundry, but in the evening they were allowed to stay with the prisoners in the yard of the Ghetto.

Their arrival transformed the camp. Fights broke out around these frightened and helpless women, who did not yet understand what had happened to them. Everything that Treblinka boasted in the way of *kapos* and privileged persons began to dress with meticulous care, to bathe and to show off.

When Lalka felt that the prisoners had risen to the bait, he decreed that deserving *kapos* and *Hofjuden* had the right to marry. There would be both a civil and a religious service. The young couples would be entitled to private rooms. Candidates were to apply to him.

This took place under the reign of Rakowski. He was the first to be served. The civil marriage was brief. When the young couple had reported to Lalka he said to the woman, pointing to the man, *"Das ist dein Mann"* (This is your husband). The service was simple. It reflected the fact that Lalka was the absolute master of love as well as of life and death. Next there was the religious ceremony. Kapo Meir, who was the leader of the group of religious, acted as rabbi. Tradition was respected in all its details. The Germans even went and got a nuptial canopy from one of the little Jewish hamlets near Treblinka. The ceremony took place in the evening after work. The S.S. officers attended and for the occasion Kiwe even donned an officer's white jacket, which he had just had made. After the benediction Lalka made a little speech in which he wished the young couple long life and much happiness. Gold's orchestra, in full uniform, played the wedding march.

After Rakowski, several other *kapos* married in the same way. It was the game. Chatskel, who had social ambitions, married Perele, the *kapo* of the women.

She had arrived with another convoy and she owed her appointment to the hostility which her nastiness had immediately aroused. She was a rather large woman who was not without her charms. Chatskel had singled her out himself upon her arrival. As there were many more candidates for marriage than marriageable women, Lalka had had the idea of forcing all approved candidates to come and help themselves when a convoy arrived.

Chatskel's marriage was the occasion for one of those humiliating jokes for which Lalka had a talent. The ceremony was to take place at the end of the day. During roll call Lalka made Chatskel step out of the ranks. He told him that he regarded him as a good servant and that in recognition of his loyalty, he and all the prisoners were presenting him with a gift. Rakowski stood a few yards away, imperturbable, holding in his two outstretched hands a pretty, rather sizable package tied with white ribbon. Chatskel blushed with pleasure and stammered his thanks. Lalka, who was looking at him kindly, added that he was not an ingrate, that he knew how to recognize loyalty, and that never had such a gift been so well deserved. Then he motioned to Rakowski to bring the package to Chatskel. Stammering more and more, the latter tried to return to his place with his package, but Lalka insisted that he open it.

Meanwhile the word had gone around and everyone was waiting impatiently. Chatskel untied the ribbon and opened the paper. Another piece of paper appeared which Chatskel also opened, then a third, a fourth, and a fifth, which revealed a little paper box. Chatskel realized by the smell what it contained and stopped, red with shame. It was too late: an enormous wave of laughter broke behind him.

They laugh, they will die, thought Lalka.

The most lavish wedding was that of Dr. Ribak, who married a woman doctor named Irena.

The case of Dr. Ribak sheds light on the atmosphere that reigned at Treblinka at that time. It shows what had become of this world of death and delusion, abandoned to the double intoxication of the Germans and of the Committee.

Dr. Ribak had arrived in Treblinka with his wife and two daughters. He had survived them because life is a duty. Working during the day, tending the sick at night, he had undertaken to assuage the pain and suffering of his brothers. The survivors remember the night he operated on a prisoner for a terrible abcess while the sick man's comrades gathered around him and sang so the guards would not hear his screams. With makeshift equipment, without medicine, he spent his nights waging his desperate battle against death. In one night he would save ten prisoners through his courage and tenacity, but the next day twenty would be led to the "hospital." And yet he never stopped. Another time he spent a whole night giving a blood transfusion to a prisoner who was dying of exhaustion. The next day the prisoner succumbed during the "race of the dead." That very evening Dr. Ribak began once again to tend, operate console and cheer. He knew that the battle he was waging against death was a hopeless one, but he did not want to think about it Driven by an irrational imperative, every night he tried to pick up the threads of the tapestry of life which the Germans had ripped out during the day. He replaced Dr. Chorongitski after the latter's death. He saw this new position only as a way to obtain medicine for the prisoners. He would bring it back after work under his white tunic and give it to Kuba Yakubovich, the orderly, who would distribute it at night in the barracks. This was during the typhus epidemic.

When the women arrived the doctor began to dress with more elegance. The prisoners noticed him at night in the yard of the Ghetto in conversation with Dr. Irena, a young widow of about thirty, who had arrived in Treblinka with her two young children. Some time later Dr. Ribak officially announced his candidacy.

Lalka did a great deal for these two people who had decided to play the game of life. After the religious ceremony a reception was held in the tailor shop. The Germans provided the buffet, and Lalka opened the ball with the bride. The party lasted well into the night, flinging its shouts, its bursts of laughter and its waltz strains into a sky that glowed from the bonfires of Camp Number Two.

Galewski, who attended the party, was frightened for a moment by the game he was playing. He had personally encouraged the festivities from the beginning. Instead of opposing the German efforts in this realm, the Committee had acted as an amplifier and expanded the range of the celebrations. Galewski thought of the other prisoners, shut in without air, so crowded on their huge wooden bunks that when one man turned over all the others had to turn over at the same time, and he wondered how they were welcoming such demonstrations. He thought, too, of the corpses that were being burned in the other camp. He remembered the early days of Treblinka: the suicides, Choken, Berliner, Chorongitski. There was something unimaginable, incomprehensible in what was happening right now. And he himself—what was he doing here, drinking and listening to this music? What frightened him the most was that he could drink without throwing up, that he could listen and forget his brothers. Of course, it was strategy; but strategy did not explain everything. When he returned to his barracks he discussed the problem with Salzberg and Kurland.

"I know," he began, "the Germans are trying to deceive us and we are trying to deceive the Germans. But this does not explain why Ribak loves this woman, why she loves him, and why I enjoyed going and having a drink down there."

"I enjoyed it myself," replied Kurland. "And yet I live the tragedy of the Jewish people every day, even more directly than you."

"Have we really become slaves? Have we really ceased to be men?"

"We are neither slaves nor men, we are inhabitants of Treblinka."

Then Salzberg spoke up. He had retained an extraordinary moral consciousness, and although he did not criticize this type of celebration, he avoided taking part in it.

"And in what respect are the inhabitants of Treblinka not men? Who can say that if he were placed in this situation he would not behave in the same way?"

"Men who do not love life," replied Kurland.

"But is it a curse to love life, then?" Galewski asked in a low voice.

The question hung in the air. The echoes of the party reached them through the door, which contrary to custom had been left open. The night was soft: a spring night full of music, sorrow, and hope.

Kurland broke the silence which had fallen among them. "We should submit the case of Ribak to our rabbis. Is it a sin to marry under such circumstances? Or is it an act of faith in life?"

"But a man can live without going that far," said Galewski.

"No, you do not live in the air. To live is to eat, to hope, to love; to live is to act. You love life the way you love a woman, with your heart and with your body too."

After a silence during which he seemed to be reflecting Kurland added pensively, "Yes, life is like a woman: perhaps you should not love it too much if you are afraid to suffer. . . ."

Then after another silence, he added, "But I feel sorry for men who have never loved."

If Ribak's love affair received official confirmation, there were others that were born and developed in misfortune. Treblinka had become a very complex society, and beside the sacred tie of marriage the great myths of Love were also represented.

Yajik, the satirical song writer, a young man of twenty-one, lived the story of *Romeo and Juliet* with a girl of seventeen. He knew how to laugh and to make people laugh. He had lost his whole family when he arrived at Treblinka, but a kind of miracle had preserved in him the heart of an adolescent. She was seventeen, with two long black braids and a face like a flower. She was an orphan too, helpless, distracted with grief. The first time he saw her, Yajik forgot Treblinka. She was so lovely, so sweet, so pure, so frail she was like a miracle, like a dream in this world of madness, death and hate. He brought her an orange, and she smiled at him. From that day he ceased thinking of anything but her. In the daytime he talked about her and at night he dreamed about her. During the few moments of freedom between the end

365

of the working day and lights out, they would sit in a corner of the Ghetto yard, and he would take her hand in order to forget, to make her forget. Without speaking, looking at each other shyly, smiling occasionally, they silently lived their pathetic love, savoring every moment, which might be the last. He was twenty-one, she was seventeen.

June lengthened the evenings interminably and mingled the light of the days with the glow of the nights, which were long luminous with the setting sun. When lights out sounded they parted, each day more reluctantly. One night Yajik tried to go to her in her barracks. Hidden in a corner of the yard, he waited for the doors of the prisoners' barracks to be closed, but the last watch caught him. His position as comic saved his life, but next evening at roll call he was sentenced to twenty-five lashes. He counted them, weeping with pain, humiliation and love.

At Treblinka, Romeo and Juliet did not have the right to die in each other's arms.

His name was Shlomo. Everyone knew her as Malka. He was *kapo* of the red commando, she worked in the German laundry. He had been a butcher's boy, she had just finished school. He was handsome, with a savage beauty, dark and very strong; she was blond and slender, and her eyes were porcelain blue.

When they met for the first time he was wearing boots and riding breeches, and was carrying a long whip in his right hand; she was naked and preparing to die. She could have tried to escape in the ghetto she had come from; a German officer, charmed by her beauty, had even advised her to do so. She had been unable to leave her family and had chosen to die with her own. Standing in line, naked, she was now waiting for death to come and deliver her from this final humiliation. In a last gesture of pride and defiance toward her killers and toward death, she did

366

not try to hide her nakedness. Arrogant and scornful, she let them admire her and wished to die.

Shlomo the *kapo* had come to amuse himself. He was one of those whom Treblinka had corrupted. When he saw her, beautiful and contemptuous, abandoned and inaccessible, he felt a sudden surge of emotion. The civil marriage took place on the spot. *"Das ist dein Mann,"* Lalka told Malka. She managed to hold back her tears until evening, but when she entered the barracks the sobs that had choked her all day burst out. The religious ceremony took place a few days later.

Meanwhile Shlomo, the brute with the savage beauty, had been transformed. The sadistic *kapo* had become a bashful schoolboy. Every night Malka wept with despair and longed for death. Bending over her, respectful, almost humble, sharing her despair, he would talk to her for hours until, overcome by fatigue, she fell asleep. Then, not moving, he would let her sleep, watching every movement of her beautiful face.

These few hours, which were illuminated by the fire of the funeral pyres, became moments of unspeakable happiness for Shlomo. He also talked to her at these times, long meaningless phrases, or words, or sometimes just her name, which he would repeat interminably: "Malka, my little Malka, my queen, my love! Malka, I love you. Is it my fault that we met in this hell? I love you, Malka, I love you. Soon we will be dead and you will not have smiled at me. Forgive me for saving your life, since we must die." Sometimes he also began to rave. "I will save you, Malka, we will leave this place and then we will really get married. We will forget, we will go to the land of Israel, our land, Malka, and we will have children; they will be blond, like you, and strong and happy. I will protect you, Malka, I will defend you, no one will harm you. Oh, Malka, my little Malka, how I love you."

Little by little, Malka had formed the habit of pretending to be asleep and had begun to listen to the mad dreams of her "husband." And imperceptibly, overcome by the power of his words, she felt something stir in her, a slight shudder of life which had the sweetness of love and the bitterness of death. One night as she was pretending to sleep, moved by the long passionate litany of her desperate tormenter, she suddenly threw herself into his arms, weeping with grief and hope. The day before, she had heard about the Committee. That morning she slept peacefully for the first time.

In the days that followed she tried to get more information about what was going on. After being made to swear not to say anything to Shlomo, she was told what was being prepared. She was also asked to pretend to be happy at Treblinka, to pretend to forget what it was. After that she began to drink in order to forget, to deceive herself, to give herself courage. Then overcome by Shlomo's love, she began to love him too. In her own way she had gone through the same process as all the other prisoners and now she wanted to live, she wanted to believe that life still existed, that one day the nightmare would be over, that there was a land full of sun somewhere in the south by a sea that was always blue, and that this land was the land of the Jews. She wanted to live, to be happy, to have children. She was in love. She too began to wait impatiently for evening, to wait for the moment when she would again see Shlomo, who, seeing her come back to life, felt more desperately in love than ever.

One night she no longer had the courage to keep the secret of the revolt to herself and she told him what she had learned. That night Treblinka completely disappeared for them. Insanely, they began to make plans. They would flee together and would hide in the forests until the end of the war; then they would leave for the land of Israel. They would get married. They would live in a *kibbutz*. It would always be summer. The sky would be blue and so would the sea. They would have children who would be as beautiful as the summer, and as happy as the sun, and one day they would tell them so that they would remember.

They had forgotten Treblinka, but Treblinka had not forgotten them. The catastrophe struck a few days later. Ferele, who was jealous of Malka, informed against her to Kiwe one day when Malka was drunk. At Treblinka, drunkenness was punished by death. Mad with despair, Malka insulted Kiwe when she was led before him. The scene took place during the day, and Shlomo was not there. A prisoner who had seen Kiwe take Malka away informed him at once. Shlomo rushed to Kiwe and begged him to spare his wife. Seeing a way to recruit a new spy, Kiwe agreed not to kill Malka.

"She will go to Camp Number Two," he declared.

Shlomo knew what this meant and begged Kiwe again, but the latter had his plan.

"She'll come back if I am pleased with you."

At once Shlomo thought of the revolt. The three of them—Malka, Kiwe and himself—were standing beyond the sorting square, beside the "hospital." Malka was looking intensely at Shlomo. She felt that he was hesitating, that he was ready to reveal the secret of the revolt. He seemed not to see her, with his head bowed, lost in his pain and uncertainty.

Suddenly he looked up and she realized that he had just chosen betrayal. He was about to speak when she broke in. "Goodbye, Shlomo. I'll see you soon, when all this is over!"

Shlomo did not immediately realize what Malka meant, but he read such entreaty in her eyes that he stopped. They looked into each other's eyes for a moment. Then Malka added, "Don't say anything, my darling, you'll spoil everything."

Shlomo understood.

"See you soon, Malka. Soon we'll be together forever!"

Smiling at him, she turned and left.

When he saw her disappear Shlomo realized that he could not live without her, that even freedom had no meaning without Malka. What did he care about the revolt, what did he care about vengeance, what did he care about freedom? All he wanted was to see Malka, to live with her, no matter where, no matter how. Blinded by love, he no longer cared about anything but Malka, and he was determined to do anything to see her again. He spent the next few days in terrible confusion. Ten times he was ready to go and give information about the revolt, but ten times he saw Malka's face with that intense, imperious and pleading look. He could not disobey that look. He knew that if he did she would never forgive him.

The idea came to him one evening as he was sitting in a corner of the Ghetto yard, watching the smoke rise from behind the high sand embankment. Every evening he spent a long time like this, contemplating this smoke, which had become a kind of symbol. This evening he realized that without Malka he would die. So he decided to go to her. Lalka was on leave; as soon as he returned Shlomo would ask him as a favor to transfer him to Camp Number Two. No doubt he would die there too, but at least he would see her first.

Lalka laughed loudly when he made his request. He found the idea amusing and agreed after warning him that "down there" he would no longer be *kapo* and that he would spend his days carrying corpses. But Shlomo did not care; he was ready to do anything to see Malka again.

He left the next day.

Carried along by its own impulse, the "great life" continued to expand. Cautiously at first, then more and more openly, a kind of cabaret had opened in the Ghetto. The idea had appeared after Dr. Ribak's wedding. At first Gold had formed the habit of com-

ing to the tailor shop to play music every evening before lights
out, and privileged persons who had certain liberties had stayed
with him. One day someone brought his wife, then all the wives
came. There was music, men and women; people began to dance.
Summer was coming and the dancing made them thirsty, so they
brought drinks.

When Lalka heard about what was going on, far from forbidding it, he provided the drinks himself and encouraged the S.S.
men to go there. The first contact lacked warmth, but the S.S. men
knew how to make people forget who they were, and soon
their presence was ignored. In addition to the dancing there were
night-club acts. The ice was broken between the Jews and the S.S.
This did not prevent the S.S. from killing the Jews during the day,
but the prospect of having to part company soon mellowed them a
little. They had been together for such a long time, they had so
many memories in common; and then this camp was a kind of
joint production. The early days had been hard, God knew, but
they had lived through them together, they had suffered together,
each in his own way, of course, and now they were going to part.
The Jews would go back to their own people and the S.S. would
be transferred to another camp, with prisoners whom they would
not know. Ah, how difficult life is!

Other S.S. preferred to go and listen to the Jews in the big
barracks sing their funny sad songs for long hours in the evenings. The S.S. men would sit under the windows, leaning against
the walls of the barracks; lost in nostalgic dreams, they would
listen, deeply moved, to the songs of death and hope that wafted
into the glowing night. There was one song that they particularly
liked. It was a funeral song which Kapo Meir sang like an interminable sob. All the sadness of the earth flowed through these
strange notes, which ascended, shrill as a harrowing cry and descended again, slow and solemn as a majestic burial. Long into
the night the barracks resounded with the songs of the Jews, and

the nostalgic S.S. officers listened with emotion. The best-known song told the story of a Jewish mother who was so sweet and good that she made her love shine upon every member of her poor family. Still another said that even when he is poor and utterly destitute the Jew is nevertheless rich, for he has his God. Sometimes the voice of the singer was mingled with the sobs of the prisoners, and the S.S. officers were moved almost to compassion, but the next day the whips remained firm in their hands. These rushes of sentiment never outlasted the night. A man can have a fine voice, but this does not keep him from making a fine corpse.

The high point of these festivities was unquestionably Arthur Gold's birthday. An immense buffet was laid in the tailor shop, which the S.S. officers decorated themselves. Handwritten invitations were sent to every member of the camp aristocracy. It was to be the great social event of the season, and everyone was eager to wear his finest clothes. The clothing stock had been plundered for the occasion and several smoking jackets even appeared, a sediment left by a convoy which must already have returned to dust after having been first carrion and then ash.

Galewski, who had resumed his duties following Rakowski's reign, was present. Very pale, his face emaciated by his long illness, he tried to smile. The women had done each other's hair and had put on the finest dresses in the store, simple for the girls, long and decolleté for the women. Kiwe had brought out his white jacket again. Lalka was in good form and talked at length about what would become of Treblinka after the war. To hear him talk, it would be wonderful.

"Paradise, that's what!" said Gold, who suspected nothing.

There was a slight chill, which Galewski and Lalka hastened to dispel. This was the only delicate moment in the course of that memorable evening.

"On earth," Galewski had added.

Lalka laughed, and the good mood was restored at once. Ar-

thur Gold outdid himself in the toasts that preceded the festivities. He insisted on thanking the Germans for the way they
treated the Jews.

"Some," he said. "complain a little, but they are forgetting that
every people must think first of itself. What the Germans are
doing is in the interest of Germany. Who can say that another
people, our own even, placed in similar circumstances, would
not have done the same? . . ."

Meanwhile, even the Ukrainians got into the act. Since they
were not allowed to enter the Ghetto at night, they formed the
habit of coming and watching the parties through the gate. At
first they came alone, then they brought the young Ukrainian
girls who worked in the camp with them. One evening a Ukrainian brought an accordion, and the others began to dance. The
scene attracted some Jews who, with the onset of summer, were
more and more uncomfortable in their "cabaret." The nights
were soft and starry, and if it were not for the perpetual fire
which suffused the sky with its long suppliant flames, you would
have thought you were on the square of some Ukrainian village
on Midsummer Eve. Everything was there: the campfire, the
dancing, the multicolored skirts, and the freshness of the night.
Friendships sprang up. Just because men were going to kill each
other tomorrow was no reason to sulk. On the contrary, they
must take advantage of these nocturnal truces. The Jews, not
wanting to be outdone, brought their orchestra. They provided
the music, and the Ukrainians the dancing. In the two thousand
years that Jews and Ukrainians had been living together this was
the first time they found themselves gathered together around a
campfire. To think that they had had to wait for this to discover
that they were all human beings, after all, and that Jewish musicians were perfectly capable of playing for Ukrainian dancers!
Unfortunately they were soon going to part, so they had to seize
the opportunity. Meanwhile they exchanged bottles through the

373

gate, offered each other cigarettes, and talked about the villages that had had to be abandoned.

It was July; Treblinka was one year old. Born out of chaos, Treblinka was sinking into madness. Eight hundred thousand men, women, children and old people, sane and mad, beautiful and ugly, short and tall, had been exterminated. Their bodies were almost all burned. The curtain was falling on the next-to-the-last act of the drama. As in ancient tales, the adversaries were fraternizing before the showdown.

The ghettos had also known these explosions of merrymaking, this thirst for pleasure, this desperate need to forget before the end. While in the streets of Warsaw men who no longer had the strength to move were slowly dying of hunger, the cabarets of the city were bursting with music and frenzied laughter.

In Camp Number Two also the "great life" had been organized. While Djielo devoted himself to the military organization of the revolt, under Adolf's influence the camp had become a kind of picnic. All day the men dug up, transported and burned the bodies, but when the work was finished they sang, danced and played under the approving eye of the Germans. Because the heat of the day made work in the ditches impossible, the prisoners began at four in the morning and stopped at one. After lunch they were shut inside the barbed-wire fence that surrounded the Ghetto and were free to do as they liked.

In spite of the physical presence of the corpses, the process had been the same as in Camp Number One. When Adolf arrived, the Germans had already been trying to "cheer up" the Jews for some time. But the laughter had remained bitter, and the majority of the prisoners had quickly boycotted the festivities to the great dismay of Karol Petzinger, who was their moving force.

Adolf's arrival changed everything. But unlike Camp Number One, where except for Sunday the distractions were the privilege of a minority, at Camp Number Two everyone took part in them. Whereas Camp Number One contained eight hundred persons, Camp Number Two counted only two hundred—two hundred prisoners who, except for the women, all lived in the same barracks. Being less numerous, they were closer to each other. Furthermore, they could follow the progress of the cremation, or the camp's agony, from one day to the next. Every corpse that they carried or burned brought them closer to the end, and they knew it. If the distractions enabled them to confuse the Germans, they also served as an outlet for anxiety. Orchestrated by Adolf, the afternoons of Camp Number Two were simply an uninterrupted succession of parties.

Singing, dancing and games succeeded each other until evening. The women, affected by the madness around them, threw themselves into this frantic life, and soon their quarters lacked only a red light over the door. Eroticism was suddenly exacerbated, in spite of the presence of the bodies or because of it, in spite of the proximity of death or because of it, in spite of the anxiety that gripped them more every day or because of it.

Adolf and Djielo encouraged these excesses. Djielo, not content to encourage them, even participated in them. Her name was Masha; she had an awkward boy's body and a fiery expression; and she had arrived, at the end of April, with a convoy of rebels from Warsaw. The story she had told of the city in flames, dying sword in hand, had played a major role in the moral awakening of the prisoners. As a member of one of the Zionist youth organizations, she had personally taken part in the uprising. For these slaves who were the prisoners of Camp Number Two she had become the living symbol of revolt.

Djielo, who had felt isolated until then, found in her a precious ally. In his early days in Camp Number Two he had experienced that descent into the abyss which Adolf had helped him to avoid on his arrival at Treblinka. And in the face of the skepti-

375

cism of the other prisoners he had been feeling the futility of his sacrifice. Masha's arrival had changed everything.

The first time he spoke to her of the revolt, she rushed weeping into his arms. After that she became his warlike muse and, some time later, his mistress. Hesitantly, he mentioned her to Adolf one evening. Adolf encouraged him.

"First of all, because you love her, and it is an extraordinary thing to be able to love here, and next because it fits in with our plan."

But Djielo had a last officer's reflex: "What will the men say?"

"That you are lucky," Adolf replied, smiling.

And Djielo took the path to the women's house.

Summer succeeded spring. In this dream atmosphere the ditches emptied inexorably, to the fanfare of the orchestras. Treblinka had just had its first birthday, and everyone felt that its days were numbered. The anxiety of the prisoners reached a paroxysm. The Germans seemed about to win the race against time and death, the final phase of the extermination.

It was then that the cry that was to precipitate the action arose. On Friday, July 20, 1943, Camp Number Two delivered an ultimatum:

"We are starting the last ditch. In two weeks the camp will be liquidated. If you have not given us a final and irrevocable date within forty-eight hours, we will launch the revolt."

XXVI

WHILE THE FESTIVITIES continued at a faster and faster pace, the machinery of the revolt was set up in Camp Number Two.

As soon as they had recovered from their stupor, Djielo and Adolf had begun the work of organization. The first steps were difficult and disappointing. They encountered the same obstacles that Galewski had met when he started organizing the revolt in Camp Number One—the same egotism, and above all, the same skepticism. Dr. Zimmermann was dead, and Camp Number Two had no moral leader. Escape, individually or in groups, seemed to everyone to be the only chance. Djielo and Adolf were strangers; they had not known the camp from its beginnings, they had not suffered along with the others. They received some help in getting along, of course, but they remained strangers. They suffered enormously from their new living conditions and they had trouble getting used to the constant proximity of the corpses, which the others, through callousness or habit, seemed no longer to see. One thing especially shocked them: a certain "professional" language on the part of the prisoners. Every living man was regarded as a future corpse to be carried. When a prisoner ate too much his friends would tell him, "Hey, Moshe! Don't eat so

377

much, you'll gain weight. Think of us who'll have to carry you!" A good convoy was a convoy of poor people, because, not having eaten for a long time, they were thin and therefore light. Slackers were known as "child specialists." The arrival of the tanned and well-built Balkan Jews had been an event. In the barracks that night this comment could be heard: "How beautiful they were, but how heavy!"

Djielo and Adolf managed to rally a few men, but the majority did not follow. One of their first recruits was Shlomo Finkelstein, head of the commando in charge of sweeping the "road to heaven." This was how they were able to send their first message to the Committee.

Then there had been Herzlik and Wiernik the carpenter. But contact did not occur, and the two speleologists of hell were beginning to despair. The ditches were still being emptied. It was then that Masha arrived in one of the first convoys from the insurgent capital. Her account of the Warsaw revolt played the same role for the prisoners of Camp Number Two as Langner's plea for those of Camp Number One.

The catch was sprung. At night in the barracks everyone told the story of the great battle of the Jews. It was repeated endlessly, and a thousand apocryphal details were added. Djielo felt the atmosphere vibrate with hope and longing, and suddenly in the dark barracks he threw out, "And why not us?" This anonymous voice emerging from the obscurity struck the prisoners. God himself would not have spoken otherwise. Conversation ceased, but minds began to work.

After that, while Adolf was busy organizing the entertainments, Djielo began to prepare a plan. Since Camp Number Two did not have to play the leading part in the revolt, the strategy was simple. The important thing was that every man be ready to leap over the embankment as soon as the revolt was launched. Djielo, Adolf and a few specially selected men would have the job of destroying the weak garrison. Any Germans and Ukrainians who would be in the yard would present no problem. There were never more than a dozen of them and they would be taken care of quickly by making the most of the surprise effect and by carefully synchronizing the operation. The watchtowers were trickier. There was one in each of the four corners of the camp, and their machine guns covered the whole yard implacably, as the story of the raven who had come to raid the corpses one winter day proved.

"They will have to be eliminated at all costs," said Djielo. "or it will be a massacre. We won't be able to do anything as long as those birds are perched on their nests. The watchtowers must be our first objective."

The first plan had been to burn them, but Djielo pointed out that they covered each other and that anyone who came near one would immediately be within range of the other three. "Not to mention," he added, "that burning a watchtower isn't as easy as striking a match."

The problem seemed as insoluble as the riddle of the chicken and the egg, when Wiernik had an idea. His talent as a carpenter had earned him a certain esteem on the part of the Germans, and consequently a certain respect from the Ukrainians. This had enabled him to study them and in so doing he had discovered the extraordinary magnetic power that gold exercised over them. He had made experiments: the sight of the yellow metal put the Ukrainians literally into a trance.

"Their love of gold is as strong as their fear of the Germans," he explained.

The meeting was being held on his bunk in a far corner of the barracks in the purple obscurity of the night of Treblinka.

After pausing to let the others reflect, he had developed his idea. "I'm sure that a Ukrainian would come down from his watchtower to get a gold piece. He might hesitate at first, but he

379

could not resist the temptation. What we have to do is to get them used to coming down this way. We would do it a few times to create precedents. Then the day of the revolt we would make them all come down at once."

"The Fox and the Crow," Adolf had commented, but no one knew La Fontaine's fable. He explained. This literary precedent seemed convincing and they decided to try. The results were completely satisfactory.

The ditches were still being emptied.

It was May 15, and the countdown was approaching zero. Djielo demanded the go-ahead from the Committee.

At Camp Number One the situation was not promising. Rakowski was in power, and his activities hindered the Committee. Galewski replied that they must wait.

Some time later Rakowski was executed. Chatskel, who boasted that he would become the new Jewish commandant of the camp, filled the Committee with dread. Galewski made an effort to appear in good health. The shoemakers made him some special boots, a corset was found for him in the store so he could stand up straight, and he rouged his cheeks every morning to give himself color.

On his return from leave, Lalka fell into the trap and reappointed him Jewish commandant of the camp.

The "road to heaven" transmitted the message: "Be ready, will advise you of date in a few days."

The ditches were still being emptied and the revels were going full blast when a terrible mishap occurred in Camp Number Two. Because of the heat, work hours were rearranged and the work ceased at one o'clock. After this hour the prisoners were shut inside the fence that surrounded their barracks and could therefore do nothing. A solution would have to be found, but meanwhile they were stymied.

New message: 'Snag, cancel operation until further notice."

At Camp Number One the Germans were reinforcing their surveillance as a precautionary measure. The Committee forced itself to be cheerful to calm the impatience of the prisoners. It even made a few improvements on the original plan: Rudek would seize the armored car and Yatzek, his assistant at the garage, would blow up the gasoline supply.

At Camp Number Two, the solution was found after several days of reflection. The weddings had started, and Djielo and Adolf decided to organize a ceremony on the day of the revolt. This way all the Germans, who regularly attended the weddings, would be under their control. They looked for candidates; they were rare. Schlomek, who greased the motor that fed the gas chambers, agreed. He was a weak man whom the work had partially unhinged. Masha took charge of finding the fiancée. She was short and plump, her name was Esther. At first she refused, but Masha made her understand that it was important. Djielo advised Camp Number One that they were ready.

The Committee's answer: "The date is set for the last Monday in May."

Camp Number Two acknowledged the message and confirmed that everything was ready and that it was waiting impatiently.

The ditches were still being emptied.

Sunday passed in a whirl of merrymaking. Nobody slept that night. Monday morning the prisoners were leaving for work when the mournful whistle of the locomotive was heard. Galewski was on the platform when the deportees got off the train. Many were wounded, some were burned. The Germans and Ukrainians treated them with terrible brutality, killing off the wounded with the butts of their rifles and mutilating the able-bodied. These were the last rebels from the Warsaw ghetto. The Germans were so afraid of them that the train was accompanied by an armed guard of one hundred men. Galewski decided to postpone the revolt. The forces would be too unequal. The counter order was transmitted to Camp Number Two at once.

That day the savagery of the S.S. and the Ukrainians knew no limits. On the "road to heaven" Ivan, an enormous brute of twenty, slashed open the bellies of the women vertically with a huge sword. Other women were thrown onto the bonfires alive. First their children were thrown on, then they were told to join them. Some jumped on of their own free will, others hesitated. Those who hesitated were told that they lacked the maternal instinct, and were thrown on too. The tension mounted among prisoners of both camps, and the secret organization had trouble restraining them. Adolf was obliged to knock down a man who tried to attack Ivan. The latter, after collecting the disemboweled women at the exits of the gas chambers, forced the prisoners to mount them and simulate the act of love.

The next morning Djielo sent an urgent appeal: "Hurry, we can't control the men." The Committee replied that it had to let things calm down so the Germans would forget that the Jews could revolt and so the prisoners, who were at the final degree of hatred, would not ruin everything at the last moment.

Then Djielo realized that the alibi of the wedding was no longer good. They would have to find something else. The solution came after several days of reflection.

First, the group from the kitchen would ask permission to go and get water from the well outside the enclosure. On that day Adolf would leave with the group, which would be composed of reliable men. Second, they would have to see to it that all the corpses were not loaded in the morning, even at the price of the worst beatings. After lunch Djielo would volunteer to finish loading the fires with a group of determined men. This way the door would remain open to allow the mass of the prisoners to flee.

The ditches were still being emptied.

Life resumed, slowly at first, then more and more frantically. Pain and agony had abolished memory at Treblinka.

There was a new anguished message from Camp Number Two, and a new dilatory reply from the Committee: "Two weeks maximum."

The fever mounted. The agony increased. The ditches were still being emptied.

Time was running out when a disturbing incident occurred. For several days, in preparation for the last act, the final extermination, the S.S. had been supervising the installation of a dense network of antitank obstacles reinforced by an inextricable tangle of wire all around the camp, fifty yards outside the barbed-wire fence. The Committee watched the progress of the job with anguish. It felt an implacable vise closing around the camp. The incident occurred in the course of this work, which was performed by the camouflage commando. Only by a miracle did Kleinmann, leader of the fighting unit of this commando, manage to avoid disaster. To lay the antitank obstacles they had to clear a little wood. While they were doing this, one of the prisoners found a pistol at the foot of a tree. Just as he was slipping it into his pocket Kleinmann noticed the bluish glint of steel. He came over and asked the man to give him the pistol. The man refused at first, then gave in. Kleinmann took the weapon and before hiding it in his belt, he looked at it. It was almost new and the steel was not tarnished. This surprised him and he hesitated. Suddenly he understood: it was a trap, a test. He returned the pistol to the man who had found it and ordered him to put it back under the tree, wait a few moments, then pretend to find it, and take it to the S.S. officer. As the man handed him the weapon Kleinmann watched the German's face from a distance. Now he was sure it was a test.

The Committee met that night. Galewski told the story of the pistol. The conclusions were obvious: the Germans did not know

383

anything, but they were suspicious. If they had known, they would have exterminated Camp Number One, which they hardly needed any more; but they were suspicious, as this incident proved. The leaders of the Committee disagreed bitterly. Rudek wanted to stake everything, at once. Galewski proposed that they keep waiting to lull the Germans' suspicions.

Rudek was a strong and simple man. In his opinion all this subtle strategy was only a façade for fear, a way of covering up the helplessness of the Committee, which was made up of old Jews who would rather talk than act. He was the spokesman for the men in the combat units:

"You're preparing a revolt as if you were studying the Talmud. This isn't a resistance committee, it's a *yeshiva!*"

But Galewski's arguments were not without validity. First he reminded them of the previous attempt and the premonition he had had. Then he explained that the revolt would be difficult and that the only chance of success lay in the effect of total surprise.

"If the Germans are on their guard, we haven't a chance, not one man will get out of here alive. And we must not lose sight of the fact that our purpose is not to choose our own death, but to get some men out of Treblinka, and in sufficiently large number that at least one will survive and be able to tell the story. We are not desperate men! Our aim is not suicide! We have a mission to carry out. I'm not afraid to die. But I want one man to be able to tell the tragedy of our death."

"You are a broken man," Rudek flung at him. But he gave in. The Committee decided to wait.

The ditches were still being emptied. The revels were going full blast.

In this hypersensitive world in which tension had gone beyond paroxysm, everything seemed to proceed in an atmosphere of unreality and magic. Every day the Committee grazed the abyss, skirted some catastrophe which was only avoided by a hair. One day Kurland thought that this time it was all over.

The "natural selection" of the Lalka system continued to operate implacably. It generally took place in the evening at roll call. On this particular day Kiwe decided to liquidate a whole shop in which many weak men worked. This shop had been created by the workers themselves to find a less strenuous occupation for their exhausted comrades. The work was as easy as it was useless. It consisted of painting the handles of saucepans black. Why not? For a long time the Germans had closed their eyes. Then one day, probably so as to have less work when the time came to exterminate everyone, they took the prisoners of this commando outside and led them to the "hospital."

Among the condemned men was a former Warsaw journalist named Kronenberg. He was a middle-aged man, sick and near exhaustion. When he came to the edge of the ditch he was suddenly seized with a formidable will to live, a terrible fear of death. He knew that the revolt would soon take place, and he found the idea of dying so close to deliverance unbearable. To have lived through it all only to die now was impossible, it was too unfair. So much effort for nothing, so much suffering only to die anyway, and just when life was about to begin again.

He looked up pleadingly and begged the Ukrainian, who was already raising his gun, to spare him. The Ukrainian, who was not used to seeing Jews resist death, paused in the middle of his gesture. Kurland had heard the man shouting and weeping and had left his hut. There was a moment of hesitation as the three men looked at each other. Then the victim resumed his protest with a kind of fury in his voice. The Ukrainian's gun began to rise again toward the neck of the man, who was now almost stammering. Kurland sensed what was coming before it happened.

Suddenly lifting his head Kronenberg cried, "Spare me and I'll tell you a secret, let me live and I'll tell you about a plot."

385

Not listening to him, the Ukrainian was about to pull the trigger when, losing control, Kronenberg shouted, "There are some men who are preparing a revolt. They plan to destroy the camp."

The Ukrainian hesitated. Deathly pale, Kurland tried a desperate measure. He walked over and motioned to the Ukrainian, who turned to him. Then Kurland tapped his forehead with a knowing smile to show that Kronenberg was crazy. The Ukrainian returned his smile and pulled the trigger.

"Poor man," said Kurland, now at his side. "He wasn't all there. Death was a blessing for him."

The other condemned men had followed the scene. They bowed their heads, murmuring the *"Sh'ma Yisroel."* "Hear, O Israel, the Lord is our God, the Lord is One." The Ukrainian raised his gun a second time, then a third, then a fourth, and each time the murmur became weaker, until it ceased. The Ukrainian straightened up and smiled; he had finished his work.

Kurland was still trembling when he described the scene to the Committee.

The ditches were still being emptied. Panic slowly overtook the prisoners.

The camouflage commando tried to revolt. One day in the forest the men began to march slowly on their guards. Kleinmann had a hard time stopping them before it was too late, before the guards noticed them. The scene resembled a dumb show. Not a word was spoken; everything was done by expression. Kleinmann won out, but he knew that next time he would not be able to control his men. That evening he came to the Committee.

"The men are at the end of their rope. This thing may explode any day. We are no longer in control of the movement we have started."

The ditches were still being emptied. Treblinka had become a powder keg.

At Camp Number Two things were even worse. At night in the barracks the men talked only of the revolt. Adolf, who had kept control of the situation up to now, was losing it. He himself was profoundly shaken by the memory of the horrible scenes he had witnessed when the last rebels of Warsaw had arrived. To ward off the terrible impatience of the men he multiplied the distractions. Everything became permissible. Adolf had no choice but to encourage all this; but he knew that when the situation finally got out of his control he would not be able to answer for anything. The secret of the revolt would be at the mercy of a joke or an idle word. Every evening the Germans mingled with the prisoners, and every day Adolf was terrified that one of them would attack a German, that he would hear one of them say that the score would soon be settled. But he also knew that if he tried to stop the runaway machine he would blow it up. His only chance was to rush ahead.

The women were now strolling half naked in the yard while the prisoners joked. In the laundry where they worked they took off all their clothes. The spectacle drove the prisoners crazy. But Adolf did not care about morality. Anything was good that kept his men under control. Every night he begged Djielo to send an S.O.S. to Camp Number One. Every day Djielo requested the Committee more and more urgently to set a date.

Still the ditches were being emptied, and still the Committee wanted to wait. It seemed fascinated, as if overcome with vertigo in the face of all this force which it had unleashed and which it no longer controlled. In Galewski's opinion it would be madness to launch the revolt now. The surveillance was too strict and the atmosphere too tense. Tirelessly he replied that first it was necessary to calm the men, whose nervousness was increasing the Germans' suspicions

But the Jews could no longer be calmed. The unreality of the world, their impatience for the revolt, and the proximity of death combined in them and transformed them into firebrands.

After the mass of the prisoners it was the men of the shock troops who lost their self-control. Herzl Weinstein and a few others made an agreement with the man in charge of the tool store, whom everyone called the Monkey because of his ugliness, to dig a tunnel. The store adjoined the prisoners' barracks. They all met at the bunk that ran the length of the partition between the barracks and the store. They dug a tunnel under the wall and every night they took turns slipping into the store where the entrance of the tunnel was. The dirt dug up was ill-concealed; the most cursory search would bring it to light.

The ditches were still being emptied.

At Camp Number Two the ashes from the corpses, after being screened and reburned, were mixed with sand and the ditches were filled in with the mixture. On top, grass was planted and white gravel paths were laid out. Wooden benches were set up, as in a public park. Every trace of Treblinka's function was disappearing. The ditches were still being emptied.

A strange anxiety seized the prisoners at the sight of this peaceful Luna Park. It was no longer merely death that threatened them, but nothingness: the absence of human life, traces or memories. The fear of death is nothing beside the fear of nothingness. Death is natural; it is part of the course of history. But nothingness brings man to the edge of the abyss that was the world before the Creation. In the face of nothingness everything ceases to exist. The songs became screams and the dances barbaric rites.

It was in this atmosphere that the last ditch was opened. It contained ten thousand corpses. Ten thousand corpses meant two weeks. In two weeks, Treblinka would be liquidated.

It was Friday the thirtieth. Lalka had just gone on leave. Djielo delivered his ultimatum. The answer came the next day: *"Monday 2 August 1943. Will confirm that morning as planned. The rallying cry will be 'Revolution in Berlin!'"*

XXVII

THE SUN WAS lingering in the sky. The day had been fair and hot, the evening was soft and luminous. The last night was falling on Treblinka.

At Camp Number Two Shlomo had managed to spend a few moments with Malka in a quiet corner of the yard. Throats tight with emotion, they had not been able to speak. Theirs had been a mute dialogue consisting of handclasps, looks, and sighs. Would the end of Treblinka be the end of their love? Malka seemed exhausted, she leaned back limply against the barbed-wire fence, her eyes closed as if she wanted to die here and now. Embracing her violently, Shlomo said, "I'll come and get you tomorrow and we'll run away together."

"Yes, that's right, we'll run away together," she replied in a faraway voice.

Sholek Blumenthal, who had been Dr. Zimmermann's assistant, was lying on his bunk. A bone disease had locked his joints and he could not move his arms or legs. He got around only with great difficulty. It was a miracle that the Germans had not executed him. But this did not matter now. He knew that the next day he would not be able to escape and that he was going to die anyway. Silently he watched the reflection of the long flames of the bonfires play against the barracks wall. He was not sleepy. Tomorrow he would go to sleep for good.

Joseph Rapoport, crowded against his friend Passamonik, was trying to master his feelings. As soon as he closed his eyes he saw the camp ravaged by flames. But because he wanted to fix in himself every memory of the last moments of Treblinka, he would open his eyes at once. "I must forget nothing. I must remember everything," he repeated to himself over and over; but the scenes were mingled in his head in a Dantesque jumble. To curb the tumultuous tide of his memories, to assure himself that he remembered everything, he asked himself questions. His arrival? A blank—he no longer remembered the date. He reflected; oh yes! it was Rosh Hashana, or rather the day before, he remembered clearly; it was that evening that Berliner had killed Bielas. Bursting the bonds of his will, his memory turned into a nightmare, and he clutched Passamonik. Carried along by his memories, he next evoked his arrival at Camp Number Two, his shrinking at the sight of the piles of bodies, and Erwin, the sadistic S.S. officer who killed fifty prisoners a day for the fun of it. Standing on a little promontory of sand, he would call the elect, who would rush forward to get it over with faster, starting to take their clothes off as they went. When they reached his feet they were already naked—it was an order; those who were not naked were horribly beaten before they died, as were those who were too slow and those who did not bow their heads low enough. So the prisoners had submitted. With a single movement they would run up, take off their clothes, fall to their knees and bow their heads. The luckiest died instantly. The whole thing resembled some dreamlike ballet.

"Are you asleep?" murmured Passamonik.

"No. I'm having a nightmare. Do you remember the raven?"

"Yes."

"No one has ever suffered like us."

"No."

"Do you think we will succeed?"

"Yes."

"Will we see each other some day?"

"No."

"Tomorrow we'll sleep in the forest, on the moss, with big trees over our heads. The air will smell good. There won't be a sound, we'll sleep forever. I can already see myself lying and watching the sky, listening to the wind, smelling the air. Freedom is good, life is good."

"Yes."

"Don't you think so?"

"Yes, but things will be a bit warm first."

"But we'll beat them, won't we?"

"Yes."

"Are you sure?'

"Yes."

"I love you, Passamonik. You are my only friend."

Djielo and Adolf were lying side by side.

"Well, it's all over," said Djielo.

"For us, you mean. Not for the others. It's never over."

"What do you think of the plan?"

"It could be worse, but we have some chance of getting a few men out."

"Do you think the Germans suspect anything?"

"No. At least they don't know anything; but they're suspicious just the same. They don't trust us. Until now they have been able to convince us that there was a little hope, but now it's all over: no more hope, no more nothing. It's the end of the operation. They knew it was going to be tricky. I think they're planning to surround the camp with armored cars the day they choose to liquidate us."

"But we're ahead of them."

"By a split second."

"What do you think happened on the Committee?"

"They were looking for perfection and couldn't make up their minds. And then, they aren't men of action. There was the fear too, and the fatigue. Try to imagine what they have been through since the first day the Germans arrived: the yellow star, the ghetto, the hunger, the beatings, the fear, the hope subtly distilled, then Treblinka—the plunge into the other world, the horror, life in reverse."

"Yes, I think I understand now. I have come to understand many things since my arrival here."

All barracks humming, Treblinka saw its final night sky swing toward the setting sun. Overcome with fatigue and nervous tension, the prisoners dropped off toward morning.

At Camp Number One, Avraham Silber carefully prepared his meager baggage: a piece of soap, a sweater, and an extra pair of shoes. So no one could steal it from him he placed it under his head. He fell asleep much later, a sleep heavy with fear and hope. Suddenly a dream bursts into his head. The camp is one huge fire. He wants to shout his joy and triumph, but no sound comes out of his mouth.

Suddenly he opens his eyes. A blinding light dazzles him. He turns and looks up. Through one of the windows of the immense barracks the sun is shining in like a burning shaft, illuminating it completely. Silber realizes at the same time where he is and what is going to happen. The horror of the past and the joy of the future struggle for a moment within him. He trembles with emotion, ready to burst with joy or break into tears. Then he begins to pray, to praise the Lord, to thank Him. He does not know for what or why: for being, for creating this luminous sun and for permitting him to look upon it. He raises himself to one of the windows, and far beyond the triple enclosure of barbed wire he looks at the countryside damp with dew and the wood, over which a fine morning mist is scattering. He is going to live, he knows it. Life is too strong, nothing can resist it.

The barracks is coming slowly to life. Silber returns to his bunk and stretches out motionless, bathed in the light of this radiant day.

Six o'clock. Roll call is beginning. Herzl Weinstein cannot tear his eyes away from two old trees, black and still, between which the S.S. officers march. Mute witnesses of so many dramas, they lift their gnarled branches, indifferent and tranquil.

Galewski comes forward, holding himself erect by sheer force of will, walking firmly to keep from falling. He stops, gaunt and tired. His mouth opens, he speaks:

"A new day is beginning. It will not be the last. I hope that every man will try as always"—change of tone—"to do his job to the best of his ability." His face brightens and all the prisoners see him wink. "Our masters the Germans have kept their promises, and we who have been here a long time know what they have done for us. It is up to us to keep ours, to do our work well."

He turns to the Germans and salutes.

Nine o'clock. Heniek turns his cart into the path to the armory. Only the sun that gilds its separate stones is different. Same barracks, same sentries at both ends, same prisoners a few yards behind. Nothing has changed since the other time. Five months already. . . .

In the fresh clear air the wheels creak on the gravel, hesitate and stop. The first notes of the "Hatikvah" rise, melancholy. The window is already open. All three cases appear at once. With a single movement the prisoner sets them in the bottom of the cart. Heniek, watching first one sentry, then the other, feels the cart shudder three times. The Committee has decided to take guns too. Heniek sees the butts appear one by one. They rise, tip and disappear. A hand appears and signals blindly. The window closes again. The cart starts off. Everything has happened without a word.

According to the new plan the guns will be divided between two points of distribution: the potato cellar and the garage. As he comes opposite the garage Heniek slows down. A prisoner walks up to him. "Five guns," Heniek murmurs, without turning his head. The cart stops in front of a pile of rubbish. Three prisoners are waiting motionless. Suddenly they bend down, pick up as much of the rubbish as they can carry, and hurry away. Other prisoners have appeared and form a kind of chain to the door of the barracks.

The weapons pass through the chain like a shiver. It scatters as quickly as it had formed and the cart leaves again.

The main street is quiet. Turning into the Street of the Deportees, Heniek meets a German. The German looks at him and Heniek is afraid, but the S.S. man suddenly smiles at him.

The potato cellar. New chain, new shiver. It scatters, then nothing. Heniek sees Galewski walk over and disappear into the cellar. He thinks he saw a smile on the chief's face as he passed. Happiness thickens his blood and makes him suddenly numb.

Ten o'clock. At Camp Number Two work has started long since. Djielo has spread the word: work as slowly as possible even when you are beaten. The corpses are piling up higher and higher beside the fire. Djielo is playing his final comedy. He shouts and flourishes his whip, which falls at random on backs which move as if in slow motion. But neither blows nor insults succeed in speeding up the movement.

394

Adolf moves from group to group, now burning, now loading, now pouring bags of ashes into the screen; he checks everything, encourages the men, reminds them of their instructions. But gradually as the time passes he sees dawn and deepen in the eyes of the prisoners a single question, a single anguish: Is today at last the day? Is this to be the day of our death or of our victory?

Eleven o'clock. The commando in charge of sweeping the "road to heaven" has not gone to work today: contact with Camp Number One is broken.

Everything seems threatened. Only one man can still save the situation: Wiernik. Let us listen to his testimony:*

The leaders were worried, for we had no instructions about the time of the revolt. I could not stay in one place, and I had to watch myself every minute to keep from arousing suspicion. I tried to concentrate on my work, but I knew that if I did not find a way to establish contact with Camp Number One we were lost. The idea of a miserable death after so much suffering and so much effort was intolerable. I had to succeed—for myself, for the others, for the world, to save myself, to save them, to tell the story. From the big yard where my comrades were suffering their interminable death I felt the agony rise and grip me, and my heart turned over. I knew that this day would determine the justification or condemnation of our long agony, our terrible complicity. Under the blazing sun, agony and death gave off a horrible smell. . . .

Finally I thought of a way. My German boss, whose name I no longer remember, but whom we had nicknamed "Brown Shirt," respected me a little, for he admired my skill. I went to him and told him that I needed lumber (the wood was stored in Camp Number One). It was our last chance. When he answered that he would go there himself with a few men I felt a great hollow in the pit of my stomach and I collapsed in the back of the shop. I no longer remember how long they were gone nor what I did during their absence, but when I saw Brown Shirt appear in the doorway again, once again I

* Published secretly in 1944 in Warsaw by the Jewish Coordination Committee.

395

wanted to live and to go on with the struggle. My last trick came to me at that moment. I inspected the boards and took all their dimensions, then threw them aside with a disconsolate air, saying that they weren't right. Brown Shirt asked me if I wanted him to bring some more. I told him that we could lose a day going back and forth this way and that it would be better if I went myself. He must have been given orders, for he seemed upset. I added that after all it was all the same to me, and that if I didn't get the boards today I could wait. After a long silence fraught with hesitation, he finally ordered me to go myself.

I had not been to Camp Number One for a while, and I did not know how the signal would be given to me. I entered the camp, looking nervously around in the expectation of a sign, anxiously searching the faces of the prisoners I passed, which were smooth and closed. My question made no impression on them and their eyes seemed to have died of indifference. The man in charge of the lumber store was a Jew of about fifty who wore glasses. I knew him by sight, but knew nothing about him. When I reached the store I thought I had failed. The man looked at me without seeing me; and his face, when I scrutinized it, expressed nothing but boredom, nothing but the sadness of a protracted agony. I said to myself that the date must have been put off again. While my three aides struck up a conversation with the German in charge to distract his attention, I went to the back of the barracks to choose a few boards. It was dark and after the glaring light of the day I could hardly make out the objects that surrounded me. Suddenly I heard a voice murmur something. I trembled and slowly raised my head. The head of the store stood in front of me. Slowly, without a muscle of his face moving, he repeated, "Today at four o'clock." Then he added in a whisper, "The signal will be the explosion of a grenade." Feverishly I collected a few boards and told my companions to take them. When we emerged into the daylight again, the sun pierced my heart.

At Camp Number Two, the news spread like wildfire. A murmur rose, prayer and dirge, a rumble that swelled into savage cries: "Today the earth trembles and quakes. It is the Day of

Judgment." The whips flew, the clubs fell, the men ran faster and faster; and while the great ditch gaped and exhaled death, against a background of cloudless sky the sun continued its glorious climb toward the zenith.

Noon. At Camp Number One, the columns return to the Ghetto to receive their tins of mock soup and their hunks of petrified bread. Loud and false, they sing the hymn of Treblinka, " 'Til destiny winks its eye." "It was Galewski who winked at us this morning," thought Herzl Weinstein. Their stomachs knotted from waiting, the men do not even go to get their tins. The group leaders quietly make them line up in front of the kitchen windows. "Just as usual—everything must happen just as usual." The column forms listlessly. It straggles, motionless in the heat: as soon as they are served the men go and sit in the dust. No one eats. Under the white-hot sky the silence is absolute.

One o'clock. At Camp Number Two work is about to stop. The facts must be faced: all the bodies that have been dug up will not be burned today. Herbert Floss rages. Petzinger threatens. The odor has become stifling and the men, dazed by the heat and the smell from the ditches, sway in their tracks. Some fall. Then Djielo walks over to Petzinger. He volunteers to finish the work after lunch. He will take a group of able-bodied men. The S.S. officer thanks him and promises him a double ration.

Inside the barbed wire fence that surrounds the barracks the prisoners are prostrate under the implacable sun. The heat and the tension grip them.

Two o'clock. From long exhaustion the prisoners are beginning imperceptibly to lose control. Before resuming work with his commando of volunteers, Djielo orders Weinstein, the barracks guard, to shut them inside. He leaves to load the fires.

The Ukrainian guard closes the gate behind him.

397

Two-fifteen. The man in charge of the kitchens walks over to the Ukrainian. The water tank is empty and must be filled. The Ukrainian agrees to leave the door open and traffic begins to flow between the kitchen and the well, which is located some twenty yards outside the fence.

Two-thirty. At Camp Number One the heat has driven away Germans and Ukrainians, who have gone to take naps. Kurland is alone in the little shed of the "hospital." He puts his papers in order and slowly, as if reluctantly, leaves the shed to go and meet the Committee. Soon he will die, but first he must fight a little longer. Misery and exhaustion grip him. White with light, the camp is deserted and silent. Kurland walks slowly across it toward his final mission, his last battle.

Three o'clock. At Camp Number Two, inside the huge impassive barracks, the heat is stifling. The tension of the prisoners has reached the point of no return.

Around the fires Djielo's men work silently.

Sitting in the shadow of the well, three Ukrainians accept drinks from the Jews from the kitchen. They exchange a few remarks and seem friendly.

At the foot of the watchtowers other Jews seem to be engaging the sentries in a familiar dialogue. In the sunlight their hands occasionally cast a yellow glitter. And one by one the sentries come down.

Three-thirty. At Camp Number One, an S.S. officer strolls slowly through the zoological garden. Kapo Sudowich walks over and says a few words to him. They leave together. Avraham Silber, squatting in shirt sleeves on a lawn which he is pretending to decorate, watches them pass.

Hovering a few inches from the ground which vibrates with heat, the disinfection commando, a furtive and bizarre patrol, glides over the white surface of the vast esplanade.

Three-forty. In the tailor shop, where Galewski, Salzberg and Kurland have assembled, the silent wait continues. The door of the barracks has been left open, but the dead air does not offer the slightest breeze.

Facing the yard, his face bathed in light, Galewski wearily gathers the threads of his memory one by one. After reviewing the details of the revolt and reassuring himself once again that all is in order, he abandons himself to the painful remembrance of his long journey: his meeting with Choken and Berliner, their first battle, his appointment, the sense of his mission, friendship in hell, then Choken's departure, Berliner's death and solitude again, the long night of agony, Adolf, then Chorongitski, then Kurland, Salzberg, Moniek and finally Djielo; winter, the epidemic, the first revolt, its failure, the convoys arriving endlessly, endlessly, like a haunting leitmotiv to remind them that death is their business; spring, the celebrations, the new revolt, the victory of the dead, the escape from the grave. Today he is sure of success, he knows that in a few hours he can die at last, justified, avenged, appeased. One last effort and it will all be over. Already peace is filling him with a sweet numbness. A film of tears dissolves the world that surrounds him, his sight becomes cloudy and fails.

Suddenly there is a cry, dull and full of pain. The barracks freezes. Galewski trembles.

Like a bird of ill omen, Kiwe, the Angel of Death, walks into the Ghetto. With a foreboding of catastrophe the men in all the workshops follow his slow progress. With his clumsy walk he heads for the door of the large barracks-dormitory. Darkness engulfs him. Time stands still.

Thirty seconds. One minute. Two minutes. A scream. The dark rectangle of the door comes to life. Three figures appear in the light. First two men with their heads bowed, and behind them Kiwe.

The two prisoners had hidden in the barracks. They empty their pockets: gold pieces fall out.

Galewski watches Kiwe push them toward the gate of the Ghetto, toward the "hospital."

Kurland remembers the story of Kronenberg and murmurs, "They will talk. We must start the revolt at once."

"A volunteer to kill Kiwe!"

Suddenly the statues come to life. Everyone rushes forward. Galewski chooses Wolomanchik, an ex-thief from Warsaw whom Adolf had picked as one of his standbys.

The intervention group of the Committee has at its disposal five rifles, a revolver, and a grenade—the grenade which is to give the signal. Wolomanchik takes one of the rifles. He runs through the Ghetto and takes up a position at the corner of the large barracks. He kneels, shoulders the gun, and waits.

Kiwe is walking along the fence of the Ghetto. Thirty yards away Wolomanchik follows him through the peephole of his sight. He sees him, can distinguish every feature on his face. His index finger closes slowly on the trigger. Kiwe keeps walking. He will be dead in less than a millimeter. In the barracks the grenade is ready, unpinned. One of the men holds it, his arm flung back, motionless.

Kiwe reaches the extension of the barracks. Wolomanchik stiffens, holds his breath, and fires. The gun jumps, Kiwe falls. The silence is deafening. Then, calmly, Wolomanchik aims again and fires. The body of Kiwe gives a last jump and subsides for good.

Galewski yells to Wolomanchik to lie flat. The grenade appears, rolls on the ground, stops, and explodes.

The revolt has begun.

The premature outbreak petrifies the camp. Men in the combat units, prisoners, Germans, and Ukrainians stop in their tracks, surprised, confused, dumfounded. The echo of the explosion rolls interminably and dies.

The combat units are the first to recover. Half formed, they rush to their battle stations. It is the first rumble before the storm.

Suddenly the thunder breaks loose with a great roar. Dozens of grenades explode as if in a chain reaction. The air is shattered. Immediately the gunfire begins, ragged, sporadic, furious. The fire rises, glows and crackles. Then from all corners of the camp rings out a vast hurrah, the first cry of freedom. But the Germans are recovering too. The orders are transmitted, the Ukrainians run, the gunfire redoubles. The ragged fire of the rifles is now answered by the slow hammer of the machine guns.

The battle is joined.

The premature outbreak has disorganized the attacking force. The leaders understand that the outcome of the battle depends more than ever on their altruism. Galewski, surrounded by the Committee, musters the men of the reserve unit. Their mission: to transform the Ghetto into a stronghold, to try to fix the enemy so the prisoners can escape, to hold out down to the last cartridge, the last man.

Running, jumping, shooting wildly, Rudek and his combat unit cut through this fury of shouts and explosions. They rush through clouds of acrid smoke and swarms of bullets. All is disorder and confusion, but they plow on, blind to the sheets of flame that surround them, deaf to the entreaties of the wounded. They do not even slow down when one of their men crumples, picked off as he runs by the bullet of a Ukrainian lying in ambush. The fate of the revolt depends on their speed. They must neutralize the armored car positioned near the guard station. Everything has been planned, prepared, rehearsed. A crossfire was to have prevented the crew from reaching its vehicle. But the revolt has broken out too soon. Now, all plan forgotten, their only recourse is this mad race to reach the car before its German crew.

Rudek is the first to reach the big yard. He sees the armored car, a big black beetle inert in the sunlight. He sees the guard station on the far side of the vehicle. He sees the door of the guard station open and a gray silhouette materialize out of the shadows.

Rudek's bullet hits the S.S. man while he is still yards away from the armored car. The German clutches his stomach with both hands and takes a few more steps, very slowly. His astonished eyes look at Rudek and his men who, lying flat on their stomachs, open fire on the windows of the guard station. He turns in his tracks, crumpled at last, and dies facing his men.

The door of the guard station has been closed again, but shots are coming from all the windows. Rudek yells that they must save ammunition and retreats with one of his men, crawling behind the corner of a barracks. The others, their momentum cut short by the German fire, have fallen flat on their stomachs at the edge of the yard. They can neither advance nor retreat. They can only use up their ammunition and die. Rudek thinks that it will happen quickly. Within a quarter of an hour the rest of the crew will leave the station without danger. The armored car will then go into action and crush the revolt. It will run down the fighters in their absurd refuges. Nothing will resist the fire from its heavy machine gun. The man who is with Rudek feels the latter's hand fall on his shoulder. He looks at his chief. His face is so full of pain, he thinks that he has been wounded.

Rudek cannot tear his eyes away from the armored car. He grips the shoulder of his companion for a few seconds. The

man does not know what to say, or even if Rudek is waiting for
an answer. He seems unable to catch his breath. Carefully he
places his gun against the wall of the barracks and leans forward slightly. He probably does not know that he screams as he
dashes into the yard. But his men hear his cry and they see him
stagger after a few strides. Then he is shot at from all the windows. By the time his men open fire to cover him. Rudek has
already reached the car.

The fire ceases on both sides. What follows is unreal. The
sun-drenched yard is silent—a little island of attentive, almost
religious silence—as Rudek's men, the butts of their guns
propped against their cheeks, watch their leader scale the side
of the armored car. And Rudek's climb seems itself unreal, for
the precautions he takes make no sense. He is protected from
the German bullets by the whole thickness of the steel carapace.
He could reach the turret in a single bound. But Rudek ad-
vances slowly, clinging to the side as if he wants to become
part of it so that he will be indistinguishable from it at that
infinitely dangerous moment when he will have to open the
turret hatch and jump in.

When he reaches the summit, when he has only to hold out his
arms to touch the cupola, his men aim their guns at the windows of the station and the joints of their index fingers blanch
as they tighten on the triggers. Across the way they hear the
harsh order to fire. They open fire at the same time. They do
not see Rudek's hand touch the latch of the hatch, then draw
back in a flash as if the turret were white hot. But the German fire
slows, and Rudek's men see that his hand is red. After that
everything goes very quickly. The hatch opens and, with an in-
credibly swift and supple movement, under a hail of whining bullets that ricochet off the armored car, Rudek slips into the
turret.

Or has he fallen into it, fatally wounded?

Again, silence. A silence that is interminable. Then there is
a peculiar grinding as of rusty iron as the turret pivots. The
venomous shaft of its machine gun, which until then has been
pointed toward the camp, describes a very slow arc toward the
guard station. The Jews, prone on the ground, hear the cries of
fear that the Germans utter, and they see the volleys fired by
Rudek shatter the last whole windowpanes and slash the walls.
The guard station is neutralized. They stand up, give the armored car a last look, and leave for other tasks, other deaths.

Yatzek and his unit take the garage without firing a shot. They
tear down the shelves where the barrels of gasoline are stored.
Three or four working together, they overturn the enormous
supports, which collapse with a terrible din. They roll the fifty-
gallon casks to the paved area in front of the garage from which a
gentle slope leads to the German barracks. They unscrew the
caps. The gasoline forms first a puddle, then a little pool that
grows, that moves, that becomes a stream, then a brook, then a
river—a river that slowly runs down the gentle slope leading to
the German barracks. And Yatzek's men look at the German
barracks, the figures that can be seen moving behind the windows, and the little river of gasoline that is falling toward all
this. Then Yatzek orders them to scatter and they obey. They
disappear.

Yatzek is alone now. He picks up a steel rod and goes over to
the gasoline pump. His step is heavy—hesitant and determined,
firm and fearful at the same time. As if he were felling an oak,
Yatzek smashes the pump. A heavy smell of gasoline rises and
fills the air. Then he puts down his steel rod and pulls the pin
from a grenade. He backs off a few steps and turns around. He is
very much alone, very pale. He faces his death. When he has recognized and accepted it, he lifts his arm with a slow, controlled
movement and throws his grenade into the gas tank. And it is as

if an explosion rends the earth. A geyser of flame bursts from this wound and Yatzek disappears, caught in this eruption, and the little river which has reached the bottom of the gentle slope suddenly becomes a river of fire, fierce and destructive.

One by one the watchtowers flame like candles. . . .

At Camp Number Two Djielo is the first to understand what is happening. As soon as he hears the first shot he stops. When the grenade explodes, he rushes to the well, shouting at the top of his lungs, "Revolution in Berlin!" It is the signal. The Jews attack the guards who have come down from their towers.

Djielo reaches the well in time to see the last of the three Ukrainians disappear into the hole. In their haste the men have thrown two of the guards into the well along with their guns. Djilo takes the third gun and begins to fire on the Ukrainian barracks.

Wiener knows his mission: to destroy the motor that feeds the gas chambers. Carrying a can of gasoline, he heads for the building. In the half-light of the "machine room" the well-oiled motor gleams dully like a sleeping monster. Wiener empties the can and strikes a match. The explosion shakes the air; then through the ruined door a thick black smoke begins to escape. Disfigured, his clothing torn, Wiener suddenly appears, staggering. He takes a few steps, stops, sways, and crumples: dead with his hatred.

Adolf is running toward the gas chambers. He is going to set fire to them. Suddenly Ivan, the sadistic giant, appears in his path. The Ukrainian seems a little bewildered, surprised, but not frightened. His black eyes stare at Adolf, Adolf's hands, Adolf's belt, looking for a possible weapon. They do not see one. Ivan decides not to draw his revolver. His knees slightly flexed, his hands open, he waits for the little Jew who keeps running toward him. Ivan smiles. He is completely at ease in his skin, in this body

405

rich with blood, flesh and muscle. He blocks without flinching when Adolf tries to butt him in the stomach. Knotting both hands around Adolf's throat, he lifts him up and lays him on the ground. Lying on Adolf, crushing him with his full weight, he begins to strangle him. He dies in the act. One minute later, when Djielo reaches his friend's body, he will see first the wide back of the Ukrainian, and then the dagger planted in it with Adolf's hand still clutching the handle. Adolf's dead body is covered by Ivan's, but in his eyes is an expression not usually found on the faces of strangled men. It is as if, at the very moment he died, Adolf felt only the immense joy of knowing that he had finally managed to unsheathe the Ukrainian's dagger and had dealt him a mortal wound.

Karol Petzinger is running. He runs into Camp Number Two. His arms raised, his face contorted with surprise and fear, he is yelling something. "Don't shoot, it's your friend Karol!"

In the barracks at the other end of the big yard Weinstein turns toward the door. His face gleams with sweat, his eyes have a glint of savagery. He rushes at the door shouting, "Revolution in Berlin!" The cry bursts into the light-filled yard. Karol Petzinger stops.

Behind Weinstein the mass, a force too long pent up, rumbles and roars. Tide, river, lava, herd, the Jews—slaves, accomplices, sublime heroes or accursed people, broken, gassed, burned, killed a thousand times and a thousand times reborn—the Jews, one solid mass of humanity, unleashed, blinded, catapulted by hatred, hope and rage, explode and flow and roll and charge and erupt; in a wild gale, a torrent of hatred, hope and rage, they howl and run and leap, those who abandoned their own, those who pulled their teeth out, who gassed them, burned their bodies, and reduced their bones to powder, the Jews of abdication and of the miracle, the Jews of death and of life, of agony, of faith, and of desperate hope.

Petzinger raises his arms higher and yells louder, "Stop, it's your friend Karol!"

Like a mad machine, blind, out of control, like an enraged herd, like a torrent of hate, the mass runs into him, knocks him down, and tramples him, leaving in its wake only a black, red, and white heap, broken, smashed, dismembered.

Malka is lying on her bunk, her eyes wide open, motionless. "Malka!" yells Shlomo, breaking open the door. He sees her, runs to her. "Malka, Malka, come quick." She does not answer. She seems paralyzed. Something has snapped in her under the too-great pressure of the emotion. Without looking to see whether she is dead or alive, Shlomo bends down, picks her up, and rushes out.

The first prisoners have reached the antitank obstacles. They rush into the tangle of barbed wire and try desperately to extricate themselves. The other prisoners trample them. The panic is so great that nothing can stop them.

Scholek Blumenthal throws his stiffened legs in front of him. He is the last, he is going to die. His vision clouds, but grotesque and unsteady, he keeps going; one leg, then the other, one leg then the other. The gunfire starts up again behind him. Suddenly the miracle happens: his knees bend, he can run, he is saved. Weeping with joy, with emotion, with fear, with everything, he runs faster and faster toward the dark mass of the woods.

The camp is empty. Djielo gives his men the order to withdraw. Masha is with him. Running, head down, he rushes toward the wood which the first prisoners are already entering. Suddenly Masha, who is running beside him, gives a little cry, staggers and falls. Djielo sees the car just as he bends over Masha. He hears her murmur, "Run, Djielo! Please live, for them, for our love!" Full of S.S. men, bristling with rifles and machine guns, the car is heading for the prisoners, who are running unarmed. In a few

minutes it will be upon them. Djielo has understood. He knows
what he has to do, he knows that he will never reach the wood.
Still kneeling beside Masha, he picks up his gun which he had laid
on the ground, calmly shoulders it, aims, and fires: once, twice,
three times. In the middle of the plain the car swerves and stops.
It starts again slowly, describes a wide arc, and picking up speed,
bears down on him like a bird of prey, like a wounded bear. Deliberately Djielo shoulders his gun again and fires, fires, fires.

The last prisoners have reached the wood. The car gets bigger
and bigger, and all of a sudden Djielo stops shooting.

At Camp Number One the fire has divided the camp in two.
To the north, Sudowich is gathering his last men. He rushes after
the prisoners who have rejoined the fugitives from Camp Number
Two in the wood where they have taken refuge. They are close to
two hundred, confused, dazed. Sudowich realizes that this protection is absurd, that the prisoners must scatter. From now on, it
is every man for himself. His unit has been decimated during the
retreat. There is nothing more he can do. He yells to the prisoners
to scatter, but they seem in a trance. They hug each other, stammer, hesitate. So he takes his gun, fires into the air, and yells,
"The Germans!" The mad race resumes.

Rudek lies beside the armored car. He tries to start it, but he
does not succeed. The instrument of victory has become his tomb.
When the ammunition is gone, he tries to escape.

In the stronghold of the Ghetto the Committee is still holding
out.

The last prisoners are fleeing.

To the south, the losses have been even heavier than to the
north. Of the four unit leaders only Kleinmann is left. The remaining fighters have regrouped beyond the first enclosure. There

are a dozen of them. They hesitate, but there is no longer a single prisoner climbing the embankment which hides the camp from the railroad tracks at this point. They wait a little longer. Then, as if reluctantly, Kleinmann leads them toward the forest.

But the Germans and Ukrainians have recovered. They rush after the prisoners. The bullets begin to whistle around the rear-guard unit. Instinctively the men move faster. An old fear rises in them again, the fear of the Germans, those strong and invulnerable men. Under the bullets they become once again those Jews who have been taught for centuries, "If a goy hits you do nothing, and he will spare your life." This old fear assails them, magnified tenfold by the long and terrible subjection which they have just been through and from which they have almost died. So they run faster and faster. In front of them there is a big open space; they will be sitting ducks. Beyond this plain is the edge of the forest: the haven they must reach. They run. Then they begin to fall, struck down on the threshold of salvation. Suddenly Kleinmann realizes that no one is going to reach the forest.

"Lie down," he yells, and throwing himself to the ground, he turns and opens fire on the pursuers.

A second man lies down, then a third, then all of them. They have forgotten their fear. Facing the enemy, they open fire.

Now it is the Germans and Ukrainians who are in unprotected terrain, who are sitting ducks. In the open plain their bodies stand out against a background of flame. Running has scattered them. The first men fall. The second group, about a hundred yards behind, stops, seems to hesitate, then as if seized with panic, runs away.

The Jews have started running again when to their left they see the first detachment of reinforcements arrive. Fifty men strong, the group is heading for them. Kleinmann sizes up the situation. He hasn't a chance in open terrain. The miracle of a little while

409

ago will not repeat itself. They must reach the edge of the wood before their pursuers. Half a mile away, it appears dark and inviting. The last stragglers are just entering it.

"Faster!" he yells. "We must get to the forest before they do."

Summoning all their remaining energy, the men run faster. The S.S., who have understood Kleinmann's maneuver, try to cut him off, but they are too far away. The edge of the wood gets nearer, the trees get bigger. The Germans who are running cannot fire. Kleinmann can now see the embankment that borders the forest.

"Faster, faster," he repeats over and over, as much to encourage himself as to push the others.

He can no longer see the forest. Fascinated, he watches the embankment get bigger. Suddenly it is in front of him. All the men are scaling it at once.

"Take positions," murmurs Kleinmann, who cannot catch his breath.

The men have understood. They throw themselves against the embankment, facing the plain over which the Germans are advancing.

"Let them come closer," murmurs Kleinmann again. "Nobody fire until I do."

The Germans are approaching. Sure of themselves, they are running in a pack, they are going hunting and not to war. Kleinmann watches them get bigger in his gun sight. He thinks of something Adolf once told him: "Wait, wait; one always shoots too soon. When you feel as if the man is on top of you, count to three slowly and fire on three."

Kleinmann can see the face of the man who is bearing down on him. One, two, three. The eyes roll back, the man falls. Gunfire explodes on all sides. Eight Germans are lying peacefully in the short grass of the plain a few yards from the forest. The others keep running as if carried along by their momentum. Kleinmann orders his men to fire at will. And the miracle occurs a second time: the Germans retreat.

Kleinmann bows his head and begins to weep. Around him the men are wild with joy. They hug each other, weep, cry, roll on the ground. They are free, they have come out of hell.

At the other end of the plain, Treblinka is nothing but a blazing mass which has almost disappeared in the flames. Over the water tower the flag still floats, swimming over a sea of fire. Suddenly, its framework consumed by flames, the tower falls to pieces. The flag with the swastika on it drowns and disappears, caught by the flames. A few more shots are heard, then silence falls. Galewski and his companions lie, finally at peace.

The revolt is over.

Day wanes, darkness overtakes the forest. The sky, a glacial blue at the zenith grows purple in the west. The grass on the plain trembles imperceptibly under the gentle breeze that has arisen. The earth is soft and sweet-smelling. Dazed with exhaustion, the men lie motionless, clinging to this moment of happiness.

"Friends," Kleinmann calls gently. "Get up, we must leave. We have not finished our long journey."

AFTERWORD

ALL THE MEMBERS of the Committee and most of those who played a role in the uprising of the camp died in the revolt. Of the thousand prisoners who were in the camp at the time, about six hundred managed to get out and to reach the nearby forests without being recaptured.

Of these six hundred escapees there remained, on the arrival of the Red Army a year later, only forty survivors. The others had been killed in the course of that year by Polish peasants, partisans of the *Armia Krajowa*, Ukrainian fascist bands, deserters from the Wehrmacht, the Gestapo, and special units of the German army. These forty survivors are still alive today. They are scattered all over the world: twenty-two in Israel, five in the United States, three in France, three in Poland, two in Canada, and one each in England, Germany, Czechoslovakia, Australia and Argentina. They are all married or remarried and have at least one child.

Some time after the revolt the camp at Treblinka was razed and the land plowed. All the documents were destroyed. To reconstruct the history of Treblinka we have relied almost solely upon the testimony of the survivors. Indeed, the bibliography is almost as nonexistent as the official German documents. To our knowledge, only three books have been published on the subject: *On the Camps at Treblinka,* by Rachel Auerbach, who during the war collaborated with Emmanuel Ringelblum in Warsaw, was a member of the Court of Inquiry on Nazi Crimes in Poland after the liberation, and who today runs the department of testimony at the Yad Vashem Institute in Tel Aviv; *A Year in Treblinka,* by Yankel Wiernik, a testimony published secretly in Poland, then in the United States before the end of the war; and *The Hell of Treblinka,* by a war correspondent in the Soviet army who interviewed the first witnesses.

Before personally interviewing the witnesses, I studied all the testimony already gathered by the Polish Court of Inquiry in 1945 and later by the Yad Vashem Institute. The testimony of 1945 is briefer but more vivid, for time had not yet effaced any of the horror. Generally speaking, the testimony gathered by the Yad Vashem Institute is much more complete. With more time at its disposal, the Yad Vashem Institute insisted on asking for new and more exhaustive testimony from some of the survivors who had already testified before the Court of Inquiry in 1945. In this way fourteen pieces of testimony were gathered which form a very important text for study.

The sum total of this testimony already represented a substantial body of material. Nevertheless, I have preferred to interview a number of survivors, some of whom had already given their testimony in written form. The interviews with these witnesses were sometimes pathetic, and while I am anxious to thank them for all their help, I also want to ask their forgiveness for coming into their homes and breaking the spell of their new lives, plunging them once again into the hell which they are trying so desperately to forget. For the same reasons, I have changed their names in this narrative, whenever requested.

I would also like to thank all those who have helped and guided me in my research: Mr. Leon Czertok and Mrs. Olga Imbert, of the Center of Jewish Documentation in Paris; Mrs. Sophie Mareni; Misses Reine Silbert, Judith Rapoport and Diana Fisher; and Messrs. Dan Omer and Jean Henochsberg.

Finally, I would like to express my wholehearted gratitude to Constantin Melnik, who made it possible for me to write this book.